MOVING EXPERIENCES
Understanding Television's Influences and Effects

For Helen Thompson and Michael Mulkay,
although they deserve better books;
but especially for Robert Prior
because he'll be quite happy with this one.

MOVING EXPERIENCES
Understanding Television's Influences and Effects

David Gauntlett

John Libbey

LONDON • PARIS • ROME

British Library Cataloguing in Publication Data

Gauntlett, David
    Moving Experiences
    Understanding Television's Influences and Effects
    Acamedia Research Monograph: 13
    I. Title   II. Series
302.2345

ISBN: 0 86196 515 9
ISSN: 0956-9057

Series Editor: Manuel Alvarado

Published by

John Libbey & Company Ltd, 13 Smiths Yard, Summerley Street,
London SW18 4HR, England.
Telephone: +44 (0)181-947 2777: Fax +44 (0)181-947 2664
John Libbey Eurotext Ltd, 127 rue de la République, 92120 Montrouge, France.
John Libbey - C.I.C. s.r.l., via Lazzaro Spallanzani 11, 00161 Rome, Italy

Contents

Acknowledgements

This is my second book. The first, never seen by a publisher, was a love story. Sharp-eyed viewers may notice some differences.

The work developed almost accidentally in the early stages of my PhD, which is an altogether different project – on the role of television, and video production, in the formation of children's environmental consciousness – which is more varied, more constructive, and contains better jokes. However, the present text seeks to offer an introduction to research about the effects of television on its viewers, which aims to be reasonably accessible, thorough, and containing as many relevant examples from TV programmes as I could slip in without looking gratuitous.

I would like to thank Dr David Morrison, Research Director of the Institute of Communications Studies, University of Leeds, for all of his generous help and assistance in the preparation of this book, and, indeed, for suggesting that I write it in the first place.

Many thanks are also due to Helen Thompson, Robert Prior and Dr Brent MacGregor for their encouragement, assistance and useful comments on the manuscript, and to Christine Bailey, Dr Martin Barker, Dr Barrie Gunter, Professor James Halloran, Lynda Heyes of Granada Television, Rosanna Keefe, Martin Pickard, Professor Nicholas Pronay, Tricia Ritchie, and Pat Shute of University of Leeds Brotherton Library Inter-Library Loans, for their various bits of invaluable help in its preparation.

Past debts for guidance and inspiration are owed to Marsha Jones of Beauchamp Community College, Leicester (1987–89), whose artful teaching and infectious enthusiasm locked sociology into my life; Professor Michael Mulkay and Dr Elizabeth Chaplin at the Department of Sociology, University of York (1989–92), who showed by example that sociology could be based in social experience and yet flow like liquid gold; their colleagues, Arthur Brittan and Dr Colin Campbell, who were equally eloquent guides through the subject; Dr Beverley Skeggs, Director of Women's Studies at the University of Lancaster (1992–93), who demonstrated that colourful cultural debate could be fostered even in that grey city; and my parents, Susan and Clive Gauntlett, who continued to give kindness and support even when it became clear that I wasn't about to become a computer whiz, brewer, or merchant banker. Vicky Stott, whose finely developed understanding of the sociology–art–life interface has been a continual source of delight and envy, deserves special thanks, and love.

I am also pleased to acknowledge the financial support of the ESRC (1992–93) and the University of Leeds (1993–), which has made my work possible. Finally, I am grateful to the publisher, John Libbey, and my editor, Manuel Alvarado for their enjoyably staggering combination of leisurely charm and breakneck production.

All responsibility for the quirks, foibles and other contents of this volume is, of course, my own.

1 Introduction: The end of effects research

Research into the 'effects' of television has been conducted for several decades, producing a vast quantity of results. Popular concerns about possible effects – a term which is 'traditionally and still commonly used to refer to the supposed direct consequences and impact of media messages on individuals' (O'Sullivan, 1994, p. 100) – have led to a research industry which has attracted considerable quantities of both funding and publicity. Despite such a massive exertion of research energy, however, confusion still reigns over what the findings show, with opinions ranging from the claim that television has been found to have a dangerously detrimental effect on young minds, to the view that the research has failed to show anything specific at all. The time has come for firm conclusions to be drawn from this unprecedentedly voluminous body of work.

It is not new for commentators on this field to voice strong doubts about the usefulness of traditional effects research, or its capacity to produce findings which are uncluttered with other variables and possible explanations (for example, Klapper, 1960; Halloran, 1978). However, the work goes on, both in more traditional approaches, and in 'new' forms which are either still closely tied to that paradigm, or have strayed so far from the questions about the effects of television which are most commonly asked that they constitute a different form of communications research altogether.

The central position of this monograph is that the work of effects researchers is done. The effects paradigm should be laid to rest, of interest only as part of the natural history of mass communications research. We should note, however, that this is not to say that television does not have an *influence* on the thoughts and perceptions of its viewers, and their attitudes to life, and relationships, and their expectations about the world. It is important to make this distinction, or else this argument can quickly become a case of having one's cake and eating it, and the analogy of literature (another form of mass communication) is a useful one: there can be little doubt that novels can have an impact on the thinking of their readers, and few would argue that literature does not have influence on how readers see the world, learn from its examples, form opinions and knowledge, and behave in the light of this worldview. However, there is no apparent public concern about 'the effects of the novel'. The very idea sounds humourous, almost nonsensical, and historical accounts of the moral panics blaming 'penny dreadful' comics and 'dime novels' for rising crime and amorality in late-nineteenth century Britain and America (Pearson, 1983, 1984; Barker, 1993) raise only a wry smile today.

To return to television, we can similarly have little doubt that the medium has some *influence* on viewers' thoughts, but the notion of direct television *effects* on behaviour, rather than seeming absurd, is commonly recognized as entirely viable, and a cause for concern. It is likely that this is a result of the ever-recurrent moral panics in the press and other media, and the sheer persistence with which the question has been investigated by the academic community. So often is the possibility – or rather, supposed *likelihood* – of television having direct effects pushed into the public eye that it can seem naïve, even perverse, to argue against the contention. Some academics are even willing to make public statements in strong support of the simple view that TV or video violence has direct effects, despite the paucity of convincing evidence, and occasioned not by the release of new research but simply at the call of the press and politicians. A typical example of this occurred in April 1994, when 25 senior psychologists in Britain publicly declared support for a seven-page 'report' which announced that video violence has serious effects on children (Newson, 1994) – written, it transpired, not on the basis of new evidence, but at the request of David Alton MP, whose amendment to the Criminal Justice Bill outlawing 'unsuitable' videos was due to go before Parliament that month.[*] Similarly, in the autumn of 1993, the four US television networks introduced parental advisory warnings about violent content, shown before the start of selected shows and available for publication in TV guides, in a bid to fend off the congressional threat of legislation imposing a ratings system on programmes, which had received support from anxious psychologists as well as 'concerned' pressure groups. It is for such reasons that the available research, however poorly designed or politically motivated, cannot be dismissed out of hand but has to be evaluated as carefully and rigorously as possible.

By far the largest proportion of 'effects' studies have been into aggression – specifically, the hypothesis that the viewing of acts of aggression or violence on the television screen causes people (or young people) to act in similar ways – and this review, of necessity, follows that concentration to some degree. The fact that this particular potential effect has been so much more heavily studied than any other (and many possibilities spring readily to mind: political attitudes, language use, awareness of current affairs, and so on) is an indication that the direction of research over many decades has been influenced by the political desire to blame television for social problems, and by fears about the prominence of the 'new' medium. Whilst political, the issue of TV violence is determinedly not party-political, and is almost uniquely capable of arousing the public horror of left and

---

[*]   See reports in the *Daily Mirror* (1 April 1994, p. 1 & p. 11), *The Daily Telegraph* (1 April 1994, p. 1, p. 4 & p. 22, and 2 April 1994, p. 1 & 3, & p. 17), *The Times* (1 April 1994, p. 3), *The Sunday Times* (3 April 1994, p.14), *The Independent* (2 April 1994, p. 1, p. 2 & p. 19), *The Guardian* (1 April 1994, pp. 1 & 26, & p. 2; 2 April 1994, p. 3 and 7 April 1994, p. 23 & section 2, p. 5); and coverage in all British media around 12 and 13 April 1994, when the Home Secretary announced that legislation to further limit the availability of films on video judged to be 'unsuitable' for home viewing would be added to the Criminal Justice Bill.

right-wing critics alike. Whilst their fears about the dysfunctions supposedly produced by television may slightly differ, campaigners across the political spectrum are united in a belief that television is a powerful force which can seduce children away from their 'better nature', and which constitutes an attack on more 'authentic' or 'essentially human' behaviour (Buckingham, 1993, p. 8).

The subject of TV violence clearly appeals to popular concerns, and is never far from the headlines. Serious news reports become entwined with more speculative accusations about the influence of television or video, such as reports throughout the British news media about the alleged influence of a horror video on the murder of two year old James Bulger (November 1993),[*] the concern in the USA about the possible influence of the fire-obsessed MTV cartoon characters *Beavis and Butt-Head* on instances of arson and fire-starting (October-November 1993),[†] the tenuous linking of the movie *Natural Born Killers* to a number of murders (October-November 1994), and the spontaneous revival of the 'video nasties' panic in the British press (April 1994) which was reported in other media as if it was itself news.

Whilst not all press and media coverage of these issues has supported the case for greater censorship,[‡] it is clearly the arguments against violence on television and video which tend to dominate the mass media coverage. However, there is some evidence that the tone of this recurrent 'public outcry' tends to exaggerate the concerns of the majority of the public. A survey conducted by the BBFC (1993), which polled 1,000 people representing the UK population of videocassette renters, found that:

> Nobody in fact professed to prefer watching films on television where 'they cut out anything which is distasteful'. People accept the need on occasions for controversial or even offensive material to be shown. What they want is adequate information about how to decide for themselves (and for their children) what to watch and with whom (p. 18).

David Docherty (1990) found, in another survey of over 1,000 people in Britain, that a majority of people (90 per cent) said that they enjoyed at least one type of film which the

---

[*] See, for example, *The Sun* (25 November 1993, pp. 1–5, p. 9), the *Daily Mirror* (25 November 1993, p. 1, pp. 4–5), *The Guardian* (25 November 1993, p. 4), *The Guardian* (26 November 1993, pp. 2–3), *News at Ten* (ITN, 25 November 1993, 2200–2206 hours), and Frances Rafferty (1993).

[†] This story was itself the second item of news on the ITN *News At Ten* on 25 November 1993 (ITV, 2206–2208 hours). The popularity of the allegations seems to outweigh their validity, however: a fire in which a two year old girl died was the focus of the US media storm, despite the facts that the girl had apparently always had a fascination with flames, and that her house didn't even have cable, to receive MTV, in any case (*Newsnight*, BBC2, 26 October 1993, 2330–2341 hours).

[‡] Indeed, in the midst of this moral panic, some reports (such as in the *Guardian* (18 February 1994, p. 1 & p. 3), *The Independent* (2 April 1994, p. 2) and on the Children's BBC consumer programme *Short Change* (20 February 1994)), drew attention to arguments that the film and video classifications made by the British Board of Film Classification (BBFC) are overly stringent and are out of line with the rest of Europe, whilst adults have complained on *Right to Reply* (9 April 1994) that broadcasters' editing of films and late-night scheduling of certain programmes (such as *Beavis and Butt-Head* at 11.35 pm) is patronising and an insult to the intelligence of the audience.

study categorized as violent. It is clear that some public feeling that a programme is violent, or even upsetting, cannot be equated with the opinion that such programmes should not be shown at all. A study by Schlesinger, Dobash, Dobash & Weaver (1992) involved showing groups of women particular television programmes from videotape, and discussing with them their experiences of watching the scenes of violence in these programmes, and on television more generally. The women who had experience of domestic violence (52 of the 91 women involved) generally indicated that they found an episode of the BBC soap opera *EastEnders*, which included scenes of domestic violence, to be 'violent' and 'disturbing' (p. 87); however, they also felt very strongly that it gave a fair picture, and generally felt that it was important that the programme should have been shown, to raise awareness about the existence and nature of such assaults (pp. 102–103).

Whilst 'clean up TV' campaigners sometimes claim, somewhat contradictorily, that most viewers do not want to see violence, which is only put in to increase the ratings, a study by Diener & DeFour (1978) found that there was not a relationship between the amount of violence in action-adventure programmes and their audience size. The same researchers also conducted an experiment in which college students were shown one of two different versions of an action-adventure drama, *Police Woman*, one of which was unedited and contained several scenes of violence, whilst the other had almost all of these scenes removed. The subjects reported very similar levels of liking, whichever version they were shown. Such evidence suggests that violence on television is neither as loved nor loathed by the general audience as the more vocal minorities may claim. Nevertheless, it is not to be denied that there is a degree of public *concern* about violence on television. A recent survey of a representative sample of 1,296 adults in Britain found that 66 per cent responded that there was 'too much' violence on television, whilst 32 per cent said it was 'about right' (Hargrave, 1993). In addition, when asked whether their concern was greatest about violence, bad language, sex, or none of these, 56 per cent selected violence. Whilst it can be argued that such survey questions influence the responses (since it is less socially acceptable to say that violence, even if only on screen, is 'about right', or that one is not concerned about any of the three issues mentioned), the size of these findings shows there is clearly some level of public concern. The questions of *taste* in this area are, of course, quite separate from the question of whether television violence is a cause of real-life violence. However, the persistent controversies and public anxiety surrounding television violence make it all the more important that the available research is evaluated with the greatest of care and caution.

One further piece of research should be considered at this point. Whilst unable to provide results about effects as such, a study of the viewing habits and preferences of frequent young offenders in Britain by Hagell & Newburn (1994) sheds important light upon this issue. The research, commissioned by the British Board of Film Classification in association with the BBC, the Broadcasting Standards Council and the Independent Television Commission, involved interviews with 78 juvenile offenders aged between 12 and 18, and a survey of a representative sample of 538 school students in the same age range. The offenders had all been arrested at least three times within one year, and had or were alleged to have committed an average of ten offences in 1992. Most of them (83 per cent) were living at home, and for the minority in custody the questioning was directed at their previous experiences outside; the findings therefore do reflect self-selected habits, rather than those produced in detention. It was found that the offenders and the schoolchildren had similar tastes, with the top five programmes for both groups being uniformly 'family' shows, both sets including *Home and Away*, *The Bill*, *Neighbours* and *EastEnders* (pp. 26–27). However, 16 per cent of male offenders were unable to name a favourite programme. The two groups watched the same amounts of television between 9pm and 11pm, when most of the programmes containing the kind of violence which is complained about are screened, although the offenders were more likely than the schoolchildren to watch after 11pm, when of course rather than necessarily becoming more 'adult' or 'violent', television programming tends to fall back on cheap imports and music shows, plus the old Australian soap *Prisoner Cell Block H* which was the male offenders' fifth favourite programme. The offenders tended to report slightly more television viewing overall, but this was balanced by the larger proportion of offenders who reported watching none at all (such as 14 per cent of offenders at the weekend). Furthermore, the offenders had noticeably less access to television, with over a third having only one television set in the house, compared to just three per cent of the schoolchildren, and less than half having a set in their bedroom, compared to 78 per cent of schoolchildren (pp. 21–22). Therefore the repeated complaint that 'you just don't know what children have been watching' on bedroom TV sets would appear to be less rather than more applicable to the offenders. We should also note that the habits and preferences of those who had been convicted of *violent* offences were no different from those of the group as a whole.

Furthermore, the study found that whilst most of the schoolchildren were able to nominate television characters whom they identified with, the offenders were not:

> Thus, for example, they were asked 'If you had the chance to be someone who appears on television, who would you choose to be?'. In the main the offenders either did not or felt they could not answer this question. The offenders felt particularly uncomfortable with this question and appeared to have difficulty in understanding why one might want to be such a person ... In several interviews, the offenders had already stated that they watched little television, could not remember their favourite programmes and, consequently, could not think of anyone to be. In these cases, their obvious failure to identify with any television characters seemed to be part of a general lack of engagement with television (p. 30).

One third of the offenders hardly ever or never hired films on video, and over half rarely or never went to the cinema (pp. 32–33). Of the most common films viewed most recently, the schoolboys' selections were if anything more violent, including *Lethal Weapon 3* and the 18-rated *Universal Soldier*, whilst the top five for male offenders included romances such as *Groundhog Day* and *The Bodyguard* (p. 34). The 'new brutalism' films which had caused alarm in the press were clearly irrelevant to the offenders' lives, with *Reservoir Dogs* and *Henry: Portrait of a Serial Killer* seen by only one offender each, and *Silence of the Lambs*, *Man Bites Dog* and *Bad Lieutenant* not mentioned at all. This research, then, provides background information which is simply assumed in many other studies, and its findings are just the opposite of what is usually anticipated. Rather than corrupting themselves with non-stop horror videos and the most violent TV, young offenders had viewing preferences just the same as (and no more violent than) any other young people, but had less access to television sets, video recorders and satellite television, and they rented videos and went to the movies less often. Profiles of the most frequent offenders reflect lives of deprivation rather than depravation, and problems with causes far more complex than television, and indeed nothing to do with it.

* * *

Any review of this massive field is necessarily somewhat selective. It is hoped that as many as possible of the most interesting, sophisticated and varied studies and criticisms are included here. There is a deliberate bias towards studies from the past two decades, since such studies are either more sophisticated, or have little excuse not to be, and discussion of them is less likely to be as over-rehearsed and repetitive as that of older studies. The methodologies and assumptions utilized by the various studies are discussed in some depth, whilst detailed descriptions of certain studies are omitted where the flaws of their method – most notably in laboratory experiments – are such that their findings cannot be considered genuinely relevant to the question, at the heart of this review, of whether effects occur in the real world.

It should be noted that the focus of this book is primarily the possible effects of material which is transmitted on readily accessible British and North American television. Therefore pornography, for example, is not covered by the arguments made here. Feminist and other researchers have shown that in some cases men use such material as part of their abuse of women (see, for example, Everywoman, (eds), 1988; Zillmann, Bryant & Huston, (eds), 1994). Whilst it can be argued that the pornography is an accessory in situations where the men would be violent anyway, the extremely harmful *uses* of such material by a certain type of men are not to be denied. Much pornography, produced by men for men, can also be seen to have a broad, negative *cultural* impact on women's status and how they are regarded (Dworkin, 1981; Brittan, 1989). However, the uses of such pornography, and its place in sexist culture, are complex areas which are clearly quite separate and distinct from the much more straightforward examination of the possible effects of television, and even legal mainstream video material, on individual viewers.

Chapters 2 to 4 of this book concern the traditional effects research and its focus on the alleged undesirable consequences of television viewing. In chapter 2, some general problems and criticisms affecting the whole sphere of this kind of effects research will be discussed. In chapter 3, the research into television and aggression will be considered, taking each of the main methodological approaches in turn – laboratory experiments, field experiments, 'natural' experiments, correlation studies, and longitudinal panel studies – whilst chapter 4 discusses arguments about other negative effects. In chapters 5 to 7, the monograph moves on to consider the possible benefits and positive influences of television. Chapter 5 is concerned with research into 'pro-social' (positive, educational or altruistic) effects on viewers, from basic experiments with specially prepared materials to more sophisticated consideration of the overall influences of everyday viewing, and its place in socialization and moral development. In chapter 6 the particular case of campaign-type material which is specifically *intended* to have an effect is discussed, covering a wide range of public information campaigns, and advertising. With the complaints against traditional effects research firmly established, chapter 7 moves on to consider newer approaches to television's effect or influence, which have been developed in the light of criticism of earlier research, and suggests ways in which research may usefully proceed in the future. The penultimate chapter returns us to the recurrent attacks on television for its supposed negative effects, but seeks to place the research discussed in previous chapters into the all-important contexts which these studies are produced in, and address. Therefore the research is considered in the wider historical and social context of the recurrent moral panic about television and its possible effects, the associated fears and assumptions about social class, and through some comparison of actual popular television content with researchers' implied and explicit approaches to it. The conclusion summarizes the research review, clearly demonstrating that the television effects tradition has reached the end of what was always a hotly-contested, circuitous, and theoretically undernourished line of enquiry.

2 The question of effects, and the effect of wrong questions

The state of effects research

In Joseph Klapper's seminal *The Effects of Mass Communication* (1960), the author made a number of criticisms of previous effects research, and some prescriptions for the future. He noted the shortsightedness of the view of the mass media as a 'necessary and sufficient cause' of audience effects, and recommended that researchers should regard the media more 'as influences, working amid other influences, in a total situation' (p. 5). He also criticized studies which count up instances of portrayals of violence on television, noting that they almost all enumerate instances in television fiction, whilst ignoring portrayals of real violence in news or documentary programmes, without any apparent basis for this distinction. It was observed that these studies imply that more frequent depictions of violence will intensify their effects, without any basis for this assumption (p. 163). Unfortunately, the reader will find that Klapper's prudent reproaches apply just as well to many studies produced *since* his 1960 publication. Klapper hoped that researchers would move on from simply counting up instances of violence (or other kinds of depiction) and making assumptions about effects from the offending material alone, and would develop much more sophisticated approaches. However, in the time since Klapper's work appeared, well over 30 years ago, significantly improved studies have only occasionally been produced, and as we shall see, some researchers, in common with the popular press and politicians, are still quite happy to 'read off' effects from all kinds of televised fiction. Klapper, then, was over-optimistic about possible research progress, and his dismay at the wealth of inconclusive, contradictory studies providing 'evidence in partial support of every hue of every view' (1960, p. 2), would be just as warranted today.

The great majority of effects research is based on methods and assumptions which are inherited from the natural sciences, and are therefore of questionable applicability to the study of such complex systems as human psychology, behaviour and social life. Whilst natural scientists can generally hope to observe stable and verifiable effects of one object on another, similarly straightforward predictions about social action obviously cannot be made, although the quest for such simple forecasts seems to underlie many of the studies, even where a more sophisticated view is protested. It can also be argued that the approach of most studies to television programmes and films takes a correspondingly inappropriate 'scientific' view of what is basically art and/or entertainment material, intended for consumption by conscious audiences rather than content-counting analysts.

The fact that the viewers are reflexive individuals rather than inert receivers means that the status of researchers' claims about those people is further complicated. As Michael Mulkay (1985) argues, natural scientists are supposed to have privileged and reliable knowledge about particular phenomena, the *objects* of study, which the lay person is not usually in a position to question; however, when transplanted to the realm of social action, 'the object of study, that is, meaningful action/discourse, is not only available to but is actually provided by those social actors to whom the sociologist may try to give practical advice' (p. 14). The lay person in these cases is already aware of their own meanings and responses, and as such can talk back to the researcher with considerable justification. However, whilst effects researchers have relied upon their subjects to be accurate reporters of their own behaviour, they have rarely sought to ask these individuals about their own interpretations and meanings derived from the screen, let alone its relationship to their actions. As will be demonstrated at a number of points below, researchers have often implicitly insulted and patronized the audience, who appear in their texts as passive, ignorant and undiscerning sponges, absorbing the televisual spectacle with little thought or understanding, and even less a critical or ironic eye. When viewers do get the opportunity to give the familiar cry of 'it hasn't done *me* any harm', or to offer alternative suggestions about television's effects and the causes of behaviour, researchers are faced with the problem of how to explain why these viewers, or indeed the researchers themselves, have been apparently unaffected by the television 'stimulus' – a problem which has generally been side-stepped or ignored altogether. The old *Spitting Image* joke that TV morality campaigner Mary Whitehouse should turn out to be the most violent woman ever, having dedicated her life to watching the programmes most likely to offend her, reflects the important flaw in the argument of critics who implicitly excuse *themselves* from their claims about the effects of television content: effects are always something which happen to 'other people', or children. Whilst young people are almost always used as subjects in the search for effects, the assumptions that childhood equals dependency (Barker, 1993) and greater susceptibility to televisual influence are rarely reflected upon or accounted for. Further, there is a developmental theory implicit in the assumption that children will differ from adults in their responses to television, which is almost never examined (Hodge & Tripp, 1986, p. 73). Researchers therefore often seek to confer their work with 'scientific' status on the one hand, but ignore highly confusing inconsistencies, which we might expect would undermine such claims, on the other.

The integration and connection of television with the rest of social life presents another serious problem for effects research: does the medium present viewers with new attitudes and behaviours, or merely reflect these as they already occur? The world portrayed in television programmes is obviously not entirely separate from the social world inhabited by the audience, and so the desire to measure the influence of television on a particular social problem is almost bound to be frustrated by the embeddedness of the problem within social culture, where it will be fed by many other contributory factors. The search for direct or immediate effects has continued largely by ignoring this problem, and brings with it its own flaws, leading to neglect of other areas such as the less obvious impact of mass media on general consciousness and culture over long periods of time (Philo, 1990).

Guy Cumberbatch (1989) describes further important flaws in the dominant approach to 'effects'. First, there is the general assumption that individuals will respond in similar ways when they see the same media, and Cumberbatch emphasizes that this criticism draws our attention not simply to the fact that individuals differ in their responses to the media, 'but that the starting point for almost all effects research rests on a set of assumptions [that all people's responses to television will be identical] which are not supported by the facts' (1989a, p. 9; see also Dorr & Kovaric, 1981). Second, researchers frequently state a statistic for the amount of time children apparently spend watching television, to illustrate the sheer quantity of children's viewing and with the implication that this is at the expense of other, more interactive or otherwise 'wholesome' activities. However, the notion of children 'glued to the box' has come under attack in recent years, and we find that half of the time the television is on, the audience is doing something else (1989a, p. 9). Third, Cumberbatch asks *why* it is thought that children (or any viewers) will imitate criminal or violent acts simply because they have seen them on the screen. The viewer may learn how to commit certain acts from television (although most people should be able to devise techniques without such help) but lack the desire to enact them; the barrier which stops most of us from committing such acts is more motivational than knowledge-based (1989b, p. 36). One could add that since television most frequently shows police and crime-fighting action as positive and worthy of reward, if the imitation hypothesis had any substance then children would be significantly more likely to imitate that pro-social behaviour than other genuinely antisocial acts, which are rarely rewarded on screen.

Further to this, Cumberbatch notes that effects research has failed to look at psychological processes in any kind of sophisticated way. Effects are crudely assumed to be likely to occur, without any consideration of why or how they might do so (1989b, p. 49). It is arguable that a theory is not always necessary to explain why findings might appear; however, the particular hypothesis that simply watching television will have consequent or predictable effects on behaviour is sufficiently abstract and without obvious reason, that we can justifiably demand that some explanation should be proposed as to what the particular mechanisms held to cause imitation or other effects might be. The effects studies consistently fail to address this important question. Finally, Cumberbatch draws our attention to the way in which results are filtered and selected before we get a chance to see them: psychologists and other researchers have a tendency to only regard studies with 'significant' findings as worthy of consideration, and journals (particularly in the field of psychology) will only publish studies with 'positive' findings (1989b, p. 48). The consequence for effects research is that we cannot know how many studies have found that effects do not exist, let alone the details of such studies. It is therefore possible that a

11

number of studies of good quality have failed to find effects, but as a consequence have not been published, despite being just as valid as studies which do claim to have found significant results. Obviously, it will also follow that researchers will attempt to avoid 'wasting time' by producing studies which do not show effects – a contingency which may help to explain some of the rather desperate measures used to produce 'positive' results, which will be discussed in chapter three.

Misconceptions about 'effects', 'violence' and television

'Effects' researchers all too often fail to define, examine and reflect upon precisely what it is that they are concerned about. The question 'what is the effect on viewers of all the violence on television?', for example, is asked as if it were just as clear-cut as any other scientific problem about the response of a liquid to heat, or the role of a component in an electrical circuit. And yet throughout this review we will be dogged by the unavoidable demands of exactitude and authenticity: What effects? Which viewers? Whose violence?

Hodge & Tripp (1986, p. 2) note that the very term 'effects' is problematic because these 'effects' of television, if they exist at all, are 'self-evidently not effects of the same kind as that of a bat hitting a ball'. Any effect which may occur could only do so very indirectly, as television merely sends out information which is perceived and interpreted by individuals who are responsible for their actions; television can suggest meanings and values, but the influence of these has to be far removed from the usual definitions of 'cause and effect'.

The terms 'violence' and 'aggression' have been misused and abused in a similar way, but with even greater variety, in many of the studies. Most obvious are the varying definitions of 'aggression' in television content, which may include or omit the depiction of heated conversations or the aggressive treatment of inanimate objects, along with the more widely accepted elements for inclusion such as person-on-person assault, in their analysis. Measures of the behaviour of human subjects vary even more widely, as will be discussed below, at times treating questionnaire responses, or actions against dolls and toys, as analogous and identical to physical assault against another person. More subtly pernicious is the way in which many researchers write about 'violence' as if its portrayal in a programme defines that entire programme, regardless of context (Hodge & Tripp, 1986). Many reports classify programmes as 'violent programmes' or 'aggressive programmes',[*] a quite ridiculous label to apply to entire shows which (presumably) contain some scenes where acts of violence are depicted in a particular context, most usually as 'bad' acts committed by the villains, or as justifiable acts perpetrated by the heroes in their attempt to bring the 'baddies' to justice. Singer & Singer (1983, p. 211), for example, mention the 'violent programs' which are the focus of their research, and are typical of those considered by others: *The Rockford Files*, the listless detective show; *Quincy*, the series about an overconscientious but hardly violent Chief Coroner; and *Wonder Woman*,

---

[*]   For particularly heavy-handed examples of this, see Friedrich & Stein (1975, p. 28); Coates, Pusser & Goodman (1976, p. 138); Johnston & Ettema (1986, p. 144); Rushton (1982); Huesmann, Lagerspetz & Eron (1984, p. 753); and most other studies mentioned in this review treat programmes in this way to some extent.

Starsky and Hutch and *The Incredible Hulk*, all rather 'comic-book' in their outbreaks of violence. All of these are transparently fantasy programmes, most involving humour and a generally moral message. To dissolve such programmes to the tag of 'violent programme' is not only unreasonable, it also distorts that which is being reported, and implicitly castigates those children who prefer to watch such shows. The 1970s *Batman* and *Superman* animations, to take another example, are carelessly categorized as 'aggressive cartoons' by Friedrich & Stein (1972, 1975), yet show highly moral heroes strongly opposed to crime and mindless violence, and include some of the most explicit messages to be found on TV that the law is right and should be respected. To imply that those who enjoy these cartoons, then, are mere violence addicts with dubious moral integrity, and that the content of the cartoons is quite the opposite of anything 'good' or pro-social – especially in the terms of the authoritarian critics – seems bizarre. Research has shown that viewers' perception of a programme as violent is not dependent on the actual number of violent incidents portrayed, and cartoons in particular, whilst scoring very high on researchers' content analyses for violence, are not regarded as particularly violent by the audience (Gunter, 1987, p. 50). In addition, a careful and detailed three-year study of over 350 children in the Netherlands, which recorded viewing of both violent and pro-social television content, found a very high correlation between the two – in other words, children who saw a great amount of violence also saw a great amount of pro-social behaviour (Wiegman, Kuttschreuter & Baarda, 1992). There were no children who only watched predominantly violent television, which would have been difficult in any case since a content analysis (of all drama serials being transmitted in the country over the three years) showed that programmes rarely contained violent acts without pro-social ones, and *vice versa* (pp. 152, 159). Most other studies, in contrast, have tended to assume that 'violent programmes' are both distinct and common on television, and this recurrent flaw in the analysis and categorization of programme content is one with serious repercussions for almost all studies of the effect of 'violent' or 'pro-social' content, but one which is ignored by most reviewers of this area. The common treatment of television entertainment programmes displays not merely a lack of sympathy for the programmes, but a fundamental lack of understanding. Only such a misunderstanding could lead, for example, to programmes being divided separately into those with 'pro-social' and those with 'antisocial' content. More surprisingly, even reviewers of the literature have failed to criticize this specious categorization of programmes (see, for example, Sprafkin & Rubinstein, 1979, and Gunter & McAleer, 1990, pp. 100–101). I would argue that programmes which could reasonably be called an 'antisocial programme' are very rarely shown on television. As mentioned above, some parts of scenes may include the portrayal of antisocial actions, but the context of the programme will very rarely celebrate such actions; the exceptions to this will generally be where the (abstractly) 'antisocial' acts are a means to a 'good', pro-social end, where their portrayal cannot be seen as promoting 'antisocial' goals or actions in any case. Of course, there are odd exceptions. Edward Woodward's *The Equalizer* (1985–89), for example, generally levelled the odds for victimized individuals by setting disturbingly violent traps for their tormentors; although a few episodes briefly pointed to the consequent similarity between the hero and his opponents, it was only ever the bad guys who were surprised by his aggressive approach, whilst the clients were uniformly pleased. It is generally true that this type of TV programme was a phenomenon of the 1980s (see chapter eight), although perhaps less has changed in feature films; Arnold Schwarzenegger's character in *True Lies* (1994), for example, kills so many of the villain's hired hands that his justification – verbalized within the movie to his wife: 'but they were all *bad* ' – is weak and not verifiable. However, such indiscriminate behaviour would disgrace the average TV hero of any era, and is uncommon.

The idea that programmes can be sorted into 'antisocial' and 'pro-social' categories fails to recognize that such acts do not feature in distinct and separate types of programme, and such an idea is likely to be produced by a way of thinking which sees television programmes as almost always 'bad' and only occasionally 'good' for children. (This polarization of programmes occurs most explicitly in the studies of 'pro-social' television, and is further discussed in chapter five.) In fact, it is often those dramatic programmes with more 'antisocial' content – for example, with a murderer on the loose – which will also contain the stronger moral condemnation of such acts, and an emphasis on law and order. 'Antisocial' acts with no point, no moral justification, are almost *never* portrayed as good, or their perpetrators left unpunished. This is clearly shown by Belson (1978), whose study involved a sample of 139 television series from 1970–1971 being assessed and categorized by 74 independent judges, who were all school teachers. Only *one* of the 139 titles was found to fall into the category, 'A fictional programme in which the violence tends to go unpunished' (p. 108). We can note in addition that this series, *Callan* (1967–72), was also categorized as, 'A programme intended for adults'. There is no evidence to suggest that audiences in general would favour portrayals of unjustified and unpunished violence, and critics who infer that broadcasters transmit a diet of amorality which the audience is happy to consume, insult both parties and display a supremely pessimistic view of humanity, which is not supported by research.[*]

---

[*]   Some researchers seem motivated by a subjective fear or prejudice towards television, and stretch their academic credibility to breaking point in their enthusiasm to accept anti-TV arguments or 'findings', however unconvincing. An article by two leading American researchers in this field, Lefkowitz & Huesmann (1981), whose own original research is reviewed in the next chapter, provides a not untypical example. They report an experiment by Greenberg & Wotring in which high school students were shown a 'violent' television programme, a non-violent programme, or none at all, and then were observed in a simulation of car driving. The driving behaviour was not affected by the previous television viewing; nevertheless, Lefkowitz & Huesmann write:

> However, the violent show did not contain scenes of aggressive driving. Furthermore, adolescents rather than young children were studied. The authors suggest that perhaps a significant effect would have occurred if the violence viewing had consisted of aggressive car chase scenes like those presented in many television police dramas (p. 165).

The study, then, found no effects, but the authors speculate on what the results might have been if the study had been different; in effect, they proffer alternative results which are entirely made up and have no foundation in the actual study. The suggestion that the driving behaviour of young children should be studied is obviously just as bizarre, since young children are hardly frequent car drivers. In addition, Lefkowitz & Huesmann enthusiastically embrace the findings of experimental studies where the experimenter's apparent approval of violent films is highly likely to influence the outcome

One more case illustrates what off-target arguments can be produced by the combination of a lack of researcher knowledge of television programmes and a reductive content analysis. Palmer, Smith & Strawser (1993) attempt to assess the effect of television on children's perception of sex roles. They do this by presuming that effects can be 'read off' from their content analysis of sex role stereotypes in prime-time American television programming, which consists of a record of the occupations held by the principal characters in some examples of fictional TV entertainment. The study therefore suffers from a major and obvious flaw, since such an effect cannot be presumed, but must be tested with reference to the audience; as Durkin (1985) has noted, content analysts all too often 'assume that having exposed the nature of the beast we know only too well what it does to its victims' (p. 54). The reductive simplicity of the content analysis deployed here means that quite useless and inaccurate results are produced. The American series *Roseanne*, for example, comes out of this filter as an ultra-stereotypical sit-com with wife as waitress, husband as workman, period. The capacity of the programme to work around and challenge such stereotypes, which will be familiar to viewers of the popular show, is entirely ignored and overlooked by the short-sighted analysis, which, worse than telling us nothing, distorts reality by applying its own stereotypes (by reducing characters to their job title), and so would only misinform any academics willing to take such 'research' on trust. This view also insults and underestimates the large audience who enjoy the programme, suggesting that they are uncritical enthusiasts for a traditional, sexist comedy. Of course, the irony is that it is only the unsophisticated and outdated interpretation of the programme made by these researchers which produces such a view.

'Violence', then, like any other content category from 'swearing' to 'stereotyping', is not one clear-cut thing which is either present or not present in particular television programmes (Morrison, 1993); there is not simply 'violence' on television, but rather ways of showing violent encounters (Barker, 1993), which can cover an enormous range of possible acts and their associated meanings, intentions and motives. The view of many researchers that violence on television is something which can be simply counted up – an assumption shared by the popular press – has been of little help to the progress of meaningful research. As David Buckingham (1993, p. 12) comments, 'By isolating "violence" from other aspects of television, and "aggression" from other aspects of social life, researchers have effectively failed to explain either phenomenon'.

(p. 168, 175), a study which 'reveals' that when children are asked to act like an aggressive actor, then they do so (p. 173), and the view that violence on television is a 'national scandal' which has reached 'epidemic proportions' (p. 177). These examples, from two of the most prolific researchers in the field, give some indication of the surprising lack of rigour which these and other academics have on this emotive issue.

3 Television and violence

In this chapter the many and varied studies which seek to find whether depictions of violence on screen lead to greater real-life aggressivity in viewers will be considered. The studies are grouped by their type of method used, from the least naturalistic, laboratory experiments, through ones of varyingly greater sophistication, to those which are most grounded in unmanipulated everyday experience: longitudinal panel studies.

Laboratory experiments

In the laboratory experiment, subjects are randomly divided into two comparable groups, and in a specially prepared setting, one (experimental) group is exposed to a particular treatment, whilst the other (control) group receives a similar but different treatment, or no treatment at all, and then observations of the subjects' subsequent actions or behaviour are made. Differences in these responses are presumed to be attributable to the effects of the treatment given to one group and not the other.

Hundreds of laboratory experiments have been conducted in this area, and on their own terms have often produced positive results (see, for example, Bandura, Ross & Ross, 1963; Bandura, 1965; Berkowitz, 1962, 1965; Donnerstein & Berkowitz, 1981). However, many commentators, and researchers who have used more naturalistic methods, have cast serious doubt on the status of such results. The details of the experiments themselves are reviewed elsewhere (for example, Andison, 1977; Freedman, 1986), and do tend to show that violent films shown in the laboratory increase aggressive responses in the laboratory, although there can be necessary preconditions, such as that the subjects should be first angered or frustrated (as in studies by Berkowitz, Geen and colleagues, 1966–73). The problems with these non-naturalistic studies, however, are sufficient for us to consider the findings of such research irrelevant to the question of whether effects occur in natural settings, as a consequence of people watching television in their homes (or, say, films at the cinema). The main flaws are as follows.

First, aggression is generally measured through observation of actions which are only surrogates for genuine violence. For example, in a number of studies by Bandura and colleagues, children were watched hitting an inflatable plastic 'Bobo' doll (an large inflatable toy with a weighted base, which wobbles but remains standing when struck), which the children had seen being hit by a man in a film shown to them immediately beforehand. Such behaviour is quite removed from the sort of violence which the public and broadcasters are generally concerned about (Milavsky, Kessler, Stipp & Rubens, 1982a, p. 2), and actions directed at toy-like inanimate objects can hardly be equated with social behaviour; indeed, research tends to support the opposite view, that children will express to inanimate objects feelings which they would never display to people (Hartley, 1964, cited in Cumberbatch, 1989b, pp. 35–36). It has also been found that children who have not been shown any film stimulus will nevertheless hit a Bobo doll over the head with a mallet, if the mallet and doll are provided (Patterson, Littman & Bricker, 1967, cited in Cumberbatch, 1989b, p. 37). This is unsurprising, since this is by far the most obvious thing to do when left in a room with such unusual, and therefore intriguing, equipment.

This brings us to the second major problem, that of experimenter expectation or demand. If a researcher shows the experimental group of children a film of someone attacking a Bobo doll, without critical comment, and then leads them to the room just shown in the film, containing an identical Bobo doll, the expectation of what the children should do next could not be clearer. The sequence of events could seem to suggest that aggressive responses are acceptable, or even desirable (Freedman, 1986, p. 373). As Noble (1975) memorably comments:

> ... the very young child is usually anxious to please the experimenter and does what he [or she] expects the experimenter wants him [or her] to do – one four-year-old girl was heard to say on her *first* visit to a Bandura-like laboratory, 'look, Mummy there's the doll we have to hit'. (pp. 133–134).

Subjects who are treated to the quite bizarre and unusual experiences common to laboratory experiments are likely to realize that *something* is 'going on', and although the researchers should be well aware of the possible effect of experimenter demand, their methods show a surprising ignorance or indifference to it (as discussed by Howitt, 1989). A study by Borden (1975) found that subjects significantly increased their displays of aggression in the laboratory when being observed by a man, or by someone of either sex who appeared to be a karate enthusiast; when the observer left, the aggression declined in both instances. The presence of a female observer, or an observer of either sex who appeared to be a member of a pacifist organization, led to much lower levels of aggression being displayed, which did not change when the subject was left alone. These results suggest that the subject's behaviour was directly influenced by their assumptions or knowledge about the kind of responses which the observer would want or expect to see. This has important implications for all of the laboratory experiments into television violence effects, since a researcher who exposes children to films showing violence or aggression, without criticism or comment, would be likely to appear in favour of such aggression, thereby making the children feel less inhibited and more disposed to aggressive acts; and this factor alone could account for the differences between control and experimental groups in the studies. On the basis of such arguments, Freedman (1986, p. 373) suggests that a major reason why laboratory experiments find larger effects than field studies is simply the relative absence of experimenter demand in the field studies.

Third, for many of the studies there is the artificiality of the specially-made films shown to subjects, and their direct connection to the situations which the children are placed in afterwards. The screened material is often not regular TV or even cinema fare (Milavsky, Kessler, Stipp & Rubens, 1982a, p. 2), but unique scenes filmed by the experimenters, with no context or narrative, and often in the setting in which the children themselves will soon be placed. Although Friedrich-Cofer & Huston (1986, p. 364), in their defence of the laboratory experimental method, draw our attention to some studies where real television programmes or films were used, even these are generally edited, or simply violent excerpts, and so the effect may not be the same as that of viewing full programmes. This point is demonstrated in a study by Zillmann, Johnson & Hanrahan (1973, reported in Comstock, 1981, p. 131), which found that mildly provoked college-age experimental subjects were less aggressive to a tormentor after seeing a violent portrayal with a happy ending, than after seeing the same portrayal without such a resolution.

All of the factors described here make the experimental situation highly unusual, and quite separate from viewing as it occurs in natural settings. Such studies only measure very short-term effects, and direct imitation, providing little evidence that the results can be generalized across different situations and over time (Friedrich & Stein, 1975, p. 28). Furthermore, Jonathan Freedman (1986), from a detailed examination of the results of many laboratory experiments, observes that their findings have been less consistently positive than is often assumed, and not only because those studies which have not achieved such results are less likely to be published. Some experiments have found that children only produce aggressive responses in cases where they have been previously angered or frustrated (for example, where the children were briefly allowed to play with attractive toys, but then the toys were taken away). Experimenters have tended to ignore or gloss over the confusing and inexplicable inconsistency between these studies, and those which found aggression could be produced without prior anger or frustration. As Freedman observes:

> Ordinarily to be confident of a phenomenon we require either that we obtain consistent results, or that we can explain the lack of consistency on methodological or theoretical grounds (p. 373).

Other experiments which have included measures to detect possible effects other than just imitated aggression, confuse the issue even more. A carefully designed study by Mueller, Donnerstein & Hallam (1983), for example, looked at the effect of violent films on both aggression and pro-social behaviour. Subjects were treated either nicely or neutrally, and then shown a violent film, a neutral film, or no film. No effects were found for aggression, but subjects who were treated nicely and then shown the violent film acted in a more pro-social manner (by giving more rewards) than subjects in any other condition. Whilst we cannot take this result to prove that television violence promotes pro-social actions, it does demonstrate the complexity of its relationship to behaviour (Freedman, 1986, pp. 372–373). The result suggests an arousal effect, and implies that almost any response can be engineered in the laboratory as an 'effect' of screened violence, a possibility which would negate the experimental findings of a link between televised violence and aggressive behaviour. Further support for this hypothesis is provided by Tannenbaum's studies (1971, 1975, cited in Cumberbatch, 1989b, p. 38), which suggest that all kinds of results can be found when a study looks for them: humorous films produced more subsequent aggression than did control films, whilst violent films increased humorous responses to humorous material shown to subjects afterwards, and non-aggressive erotic films increased subsequent rewarding behaviour. This assortment of findings suggests that the arousal produced by watching television may be a more salient 'effect' than any of the more specific 'effects' which are 'found' by tests which, by their design, are incapable of revealing any potential effect other than the one which they seek to measure. As Freedman (1988) argues, any evidence that effects are due to arousal represents a significant alternative to the usual account of the apparent laboratory effects of violent programmes, which are couched in terms of social learning or imitation – that the viewer learns or copies aggressive actions. The possibility that the recorded short-term laboratory effects may be due to arousal is important, since it suggests than *any* exciting programme would have the same effect (Freedman, 1988, p. 147), and the differences in experimental results may derive simply from the difference in arousal of those children who have just watched exciting scenes, compared to those who have watched the bland control film. Whilst this line of argument suggests that television can have a direct effect on viewers in the laboratory, the potential effect would be produced by *any* programme containing material which excited or interested the viewer. If it was assumed that the laboratory reflects the real world, it could be concluded that all programmes with any capacity to interest the viewer are in some way dangerous and should not be shown, and therefore that the only acceptable programmes are those of absolutely no interest to anyone; however, this extreme and impractical view is not supported by the vast quantity of other evidence.

Cook, Kendzierski & Thomas (1983) make some important observations on the very nature of experiments. They note that whilst aggression in real life is a relatively rare event, laboratory experiments have to produce it to discriminate between the outcomes of different treatments. Therefore experiments are designed:

> (a) to minimize internal inhibitions against aggression, (b) to minimize external cues [censuring] aggression, and (c) to maximize the clarity and intensity of short-term experimental treatments that have been deliberately chosen because they are likely to foster aggression (p. 180).

Although arguably necessary to produce measurable results, such a situation is quite the opposite of that found in the natural setting of home television viewing, where children are generally likely to feel more inhibited, and are more liable to be chastised for aggressive outbursts. In addition, the maliciously aggressive characters seen on television at home, unlike those in the specially prepared laboratory films, would most usually be shown to be punished by 'hero' characters with pro-social qualities which would themselves presumably be worthy of emulation, although few commentators seem to recognize this. In 'controlling out' all of the conflicting factors which may influence or discourage the aggressive response in natural settings, laboratory experiments effectively destroy their own claim to tell us anything about the relationship between television and behaviour in those normal settings. Friedrich-Cofer and Huston (1986), in an attempt to defend the method, state that the laboratory setting may enhance or decrease the effect of television violence, implying that the reported effects are probably about right. However, as Freedman (1986, p. 373) notes:

> This view is contradicted by the research on many issues other than television violence, which shows that effects are typically greatly magnified in the laboratory. For example, decades of research showed that although it was easy to produce attitude change in the laboratory, it was exceedingly difficult to produce an equivalent change in natural settings ... In addition, as difficult as it is to affect attitudes outside the laboratory, it is generally acknowledged that it is far more difficult to affect behavior.

The laboratory setting, then, is unlikely to produce convincing results which are generalizable to the world outside of the laboratory, and the method is crippled by its flaws and assumptions.[*] The removal of as many external variables as possible creates a rarefied situation which is as clearly distinct from 'real life' for the subjects taking part as it is for readers of the studies produced, and which cannot therefore be relied upon to inform us about effects as they may occur in the real world.

Field experiments

Field experiments have the virtue of not removing their subjects to unfamiliar locations, although the settings used in some cases are not representative of most natural viewing situations, and the implementation of an experimental method immediately makes the study non-naturalistic. These experiments (reviewed in greater detail by Cook, Kendzierski & Thomas, 1983, and Freedman, 1984), often conducted by means of controlling the viewing diet of different experimental and control groups in residential schools, cannot boast the internally consistent 'positive' results found by many laboratory studies. An early study by Feshbach & Singer (1971), which randomly assigned 625 boys living in seven residential schools to watch either 'violent' or non-violent television programmes for six weeks, was originally believed to suggest a 'catharsis' finding, since some of the boys who watched non-violent programmes were observed to be more aggressive in social relations with their peers, whilst the behaviour of those watching violent programmes was unaffected. However, whilst some commentators have found this finding plausible (Noble, 1975), it has been strongly argued more recently that the result was due to the fact that many boys in the groups confined to 'non-violent' programmes were thereby denied access to their favourite programmes, and that it was the frustration caused by this which led to the increase in aggression (Milavsky, Kessler, Stipp & Rubens, 1982a, p. 4;

---

[*] We can also note Dennis Howitt's (1989) points regarding the apparent underlying beliefs of experimental researchers themselves. If the experimenters truly believe their own findings that the materials which they show to subjects have effects which make them behave in violent or antisocial ways, he asks, how could they ethically conduct the research? Howitt suggests that experimenters do not appear to seriously believe their own claims, the sole defence that subjects are 'debriefed' being irrelevant if such behaviour is beyond full cognitive control, as the studies would suggest.

Freedman, 1984, p. 230); followers of *Batman*, for example, were particularly annoyed, to the extent that the experimenters were eventually forced to allow them to watch it. The same general result was found in a replication of the study by Wells (1973, cited in Milavsky *et al*, 1982a), and in a similar but smaller study by Sawin (1990). Sawin suggests that in his study, boredom with the programmes which were not categorized as 'violent' induced the aggressive activity, although we cannot, of course, presume that it was the lack of violence *per se* that made those programmes less interesting. Whilst we cannot assume that the behaviour of the experimental and control groups in these studies was a direct product of their television viewing within the experimental period, then, Feshbach's reasonably large-scale study nevertheless clearly showed that the groups shown a diet of violent programmes over six weeks were not affected. It also demonstrated that the interference and deprivation of regular habits which any field experiment must involve, produces 'side effects' which distort and invalidate the results.

Subsequent studies have only provided results which are inconsistent, weak or questionable. Experiments by Leyens, Parke, Camino & Berkowitz (1975), and Parke, Berkowitz, Leyens, West & Sebastian (1977), although seriously flawed in their analyses since they treat boys living together in residential buildings as independent subjects (Freedman, 1984, p. 230), and unrepresentative of the general population in their sampling since they use delinquent boys in reform school (Dorr, 1986, p. 74), found some increases in aggression for some instances of the boys watching 'violent' programmes, but not others. Friedrich & Stein (1973) used all of the children in a summer nursery school as their subjects, who were divided into three groups shown 'aggressive', 'pro-social' or neutral television programmes over twelve days (one film per day). No effects on any of the four measures of aggressive behaviour were found. The authors of this study seek to emphasize some weak effects of violent films on initially more aggressive children whose aggression declined less after viewing, than those in the other conditions, although this 'finding' only appeared when *verbal* 'aggression' was combined with the measures of physical violence (Freedman, 1984, p. 232), and in any case does not suggest any increase in aggression following the viewing of violent films. Furthermore, a reanalysis of the data by Armor (cited in Kaplan & Singer, 1976, p. 59) found a greater post-treatment increase in aggression amongst those who had seen the *pro-social* programmes, a result which itself is small and of little consequence due to its contrived experimental origins, but which certainly emphasizes the point that the original conclusions drawn from the data are partial and problematic.

A study by Loye, Gorney & Steele (1977) used wives as observers of their husband's mood changes over a week in which they watched a set diet of programmes, one of which was high in violent content. The method of asking people to observe their spouses as they watch television is clearly unreliable, since as untrained observers they are likely to have differing standards for judging emotions, are emotionally involved with their subjects, and the situation (particularly with the contrived viewing diet and the husband's awareness of being studied) is far from natural. In any case, no significant mood changes were found as a result of either viewing diet.

Such field experiments are obviously subject to criticisms similar to those made of laboratory experiments. The situations are unnatural, even if the settings are normal for the subjects involved, who themselves may not represent the general population in the case of the studies conducted in institutional schools or children's homes. The experimental conditions are clearly different from normal experience, and may lead to frustration as well as the inevitable knowledge of being studied and the consequent possibility of experimenter demand effects. In any case, whilst getting a little closer to the real world, not one field experiment has found a clear, consistent significant effect (Freedman, 1986, p. 375), and the weak, inconsistent or null findings provided by the studies do not therefore provide convincing evidence for the causal effects hypothesis (Kaplan & Singer, 1976; Cook, Kendzierski & Thomas, 1983; Freedman, 1984).

Natural or 'found' experiments

Unlike the other types of experiment, these studies have an excellent methodological basis, since the method involves looking retrospectively at circumstances which have in some way created their own natural experimental and control groups – specifically, in these cases, where people in comparable areas or times have for some reason had markedly different access to television, or violent television. This method is the only one where the 'subjects' are in wholly natural circumstances at all times, since the retrospective 'experiment', by using only historical data collected originally for other purposes, does not interfere with or touch their lives in any way (see Phillips, 1986).

The outstanding study of this type is by Hennigan, Del Rosario, Heath, Cook, Wharton & Calder (1982). The authors took advantage of the fact that there was a 'freeze' on new broadcasting licences in the United States between late 1949 and mid-1952. Some communities had television before the freeze ('pre-freeze'), whilst others had to wait until it was lifted ('post-freeze'). The study was based on the hypothesis that if the introduction of television caused an increase in crime, the level of crime in the pre-freeze communities should have increased in comparison to the post-freeze communities shortly after they began to receive TV, and then a few years later the post-freeze communities should have shown a relative increase in crime compared to the communities already receiving TV, when the freeze was lifted (Hennigan *et al*, p. 464). Years in which at least 50 per cent of households in a sample of communities had TV sets were selected for comparison (1951 for pre-freeze cities and states, 1955 for post-freeze cities and 1956 for post-freeze states), as well as one year on from each, when approximately 65 per cent or more of households had TV sets. Although not strictly randomly assigned, the authors made efforts to ensure that the cities and states were otherwise comparable; and content analyses of television from the time show that crime and violence were frequently portrayed. We should note, of course, that television at this time was in its infancy, and that there was a dominant cinema culture in cities with and without television; nevertheless, the introduction of varied television programming available at home each evening would have constituted a significant disjuncture with the cinema experience, and this research meets the concerns expressed about the impact of a TV diet.

The study found no consistent evidence of an increase in violent crime due to the introduction of television in the years tested. There was no effect on murder, aggravated assault, burglary or auto theft. The only effect found was an increase in larceny following the introduction of television.[*] The authors note that whilst violent crime appeared commonly on television dramas, larceny and other instrumental crimes are shown very rarely, and so an imitation effect is highly unlikely. Rather, the increase in petty theft is attributed to relative deprivation felt by viewers who envied the wealthy characters portrayed in television programmes and advertising. To support this claim, the authors cite research by Head (1954) whose analysis of television network dramas shown in 1952 showed that 85 per cent of the characters were from the middle and upper socio-economic classes, whilst the lower classes (who were the heaviest viewers) were rarely portrayed in a positive light (Hennigan *et al*, 1982, p. 474). However, even this assertion of a less serious effect due to relative deprivation is speculative, and is not a conclusion which can be drawn directly from the data.

This important and rigorous study, then, examined the effects of a whole diet of television programmes, as voluntarily watched in natural settings by whole cities and states of viewers in all their variety, and found no effect on aggressive crimes as recorded in official FBI figures. There is absolutely no reason to suspect that these figures would not have reflected even a mild increase in violent crime, but such an increase in the type of crime most frequently depicted on television did not occur.

Milavsky (1988) conducted a very simple, but basically similar study, by examining United States violent crime rates in comparison to the rise in availability and popularity of videotape rental. He notes that the massive expansion of home video in the early 1980s, and consequent wide availability of horror and action films on videotape with content far more explicitly violent than average TV fare, should have led to a rise in violent crimes if these videos have the effects which critics have claimed. The finding, however, is that whilst crime rates were still high, they actually decreased since 1980, when the new media had not been widely available. Milavsky cites figures which show significant declines in homicide and aggravated assault from 1980 to 1985, and notes that rates for rape have fluctuated, but show a clear downward trend (p. 167). The use of official statistics, of course, has many problems, such as whether, why and how crimes are reported, how they find their way into the statistics, and the effect of changes in crime categorization. Nevertheless, if the availability of more graphic and violent videos had the effect on behaviour which critics claim, we would certainly expect to see some increase in these figures, which is not there.

A study by Steven Messner (1986) made use of the fact that the television programme ratings produced by the American company Nielsen are aggregated on the basis of

---

[*]   Larceny theft is property theft which is not forcible or violent. It excludes burglary (breaking and entering), and includes theft of bicycles, car accessories, shoplifting and pickpocketing.

'Designated Market Areas' (DMAs), geographical units comprised of the counties served by local television stations. To judge how much 'violent' television was watched in each area, the audience sizes for the five most 'violent' regular, prime-time series, as judged by the content analyses of the National Coalition on Television Violence, were used as a measure. These levels of 'violent' television viewing were compared with the levels of violent crime in smaller areas within the DMAs, known as 'Standard Metropolitan Statistical Areas' (SMSAs), measured by the FBI rates of such crimes reported to the police. Statistical analysis of this data showed, to Messner's evident surprise, that the amount of viewing of the more violent television programmes was significantly related to violent crime rates in an *inverse* direction: the areas with the larger audiences for these 'violent' series were those with the lower violent crime rates. At the same time, other factors such as the level of economic inequality, and the population size in each area, were positively and significantly related to the violent crime rate. More sophisticated analyses, and an analysis which looked for an effect only amongst the supposedly 'high risk' group of males aged 18 to 34, found the same results.

It is not so difficult to account for these findings when we note that whilst the NCTV figures for violent content of prime-time series appear to be reliable, the violence viewing scale is based on ratings for programmes which are nevertheless popular entertainment shows, aimed at family and child audiences: *The Dukes of Hazzard*, *The Incredible Hulk*, *Enos*, *Fantasy Island* and *Hart to Hart*. For example, in the early 1980s, *The Dukes of Hazzard* and *The Incredible Hulk* were shown in Saturday teatime slots, and *Hart To Hart* in the early evening, on British terrestrial television. In one way, therefore, this study is disappointing since its sample of 'violent' programmes is actually a group of programmes which adults, especially the males aged 18 to 34, might be likely to find rather tame and childish. Looked at from this perspective, it is a shame that the study did not focus, for example, on the effects of the more genuinely violent content of feature films shown later in the evening. However, it is important to note that American prime-time action-adventure or drama programmes of this kind, with relatively higher levels of violent content, are often the target of criticism for their supposed effect on viewers. In addition, Messner reports a strong correlation between his viewing of violent programmes measure and exposure to television more generally (1986, p. 228), increasing the likelihood of such viewers having seen other potentially more violent programmes and feature films. Messner's study consequently demonstrates that whilst other sociological factors do appear to contribute to the levels of reported violent crime, the viewing of these television programmes does not.

These 'found' experiments, which are of sound design, all provide results which are in some way surprising, but which uniformly refute the hypothesis that watching depictions of violence on television increases aggression. Whilst this aggression is measured in the three studies by official crime statistics, which represent the tip of the iceberg since aggression only occasionally develops into reported criminal offences, we would nevertheless expect any potential increases in violence due to the television conditions to be reflected in the figures in at least a small way. However, the results have shown absolutely no increases due to the presence of television or televised violence. Some even indicate an opposite effect, which is unlikely to be genuine, but which certainly emphasizes the lack of a demonstrable effect of screen violence on aggressive behaviour.

Correlation studies

Simple correlation studies are relatively straightforward to conduct, and researchers have not had much difficulty in producing findings which show that children who enjoy 'violent' television programmes are often more aggressive than children who do not. The major problem with such findings is well-known: a correlation cannot demonstrate causality, but can only show where two variables occur together. Thus, the finding of a correlation between a certain level of aggression and an amount of viewing of television programmes containing depictions of violence, does not show that the viewing causes the aggression, or that the aggression causes the viewing, but simply that the factors occur together with a greater regularity than we would expect by chance. We might similarly happen, for example, to find a correlation between home ownership and the frequent viewing of television news, but would be unwise to deduce that ownership of a house *causes* people to watch the news, or that TV news causes people to buy houses.

Freedman (1984) reviewed several correlation studies,[*] and found that the correlations between viewing television violence and aggressiveness are weak (mostly falling between 0.10 and 0.20, where a perfect correlation would be 1.00), and provide minimal evidence for a causal link. Most of the results are not statistically significant, and would not normally be acceptable as evidence in support of a hypothesis; in addition, almost all of the studies rely on the self-reports of subjects not only for their viewing habits and preferences, but also for their aggressivity, and such responses are of questionable reliability. Aside from the usual problems associated with getting individuals to review and measure their own behaviour, there is the additional flaw in these cases that those respondents whose social activity includes watching violent television programmes – which boys often see as a test of masculinity (Barker, 1984, pp. 18–19; Wood, 1993) – are likely to be those who may also exaggerate their aggressive prowess. Cumberbatch (1989b, p. 42) observes in addition that many of the studies focus on programme preference, rather than the mere exposure to violent programmes which experimental research has concentrated upon, thereby increasing the likelihood of positive findings.[†] He also notes that the findings of the better-known and reasonably large-scale simple correlation studies, McLeod, Atkin & Chaffee (1972) and McIntyre & Teevan (1972), become statistically insignificant when

---

[*]   For example, McLeod, Atkin & Chaffee (1972); Friedman & Johnson (1972); McCarthy, Langner, Gerstein, Eisenberg & Orzeck (1975); Greenberg (1975); Hartnagel, Teevan & McIntyre (1975).

[†]   Cumberbatch actually claims that this 'contradicts' the experimental research, which is not strictly true: the idea that preference of violent programmes may lead to aggression does not contradict the wider claim that mere exposure will lead to aggression, although the former claim should be easier to prove if either hypothesis is true.

the samples are subdivided by age and sex, so that like is compared with like (1989b, pp. 42–43).

The findings of positive correlations between watching television violence and aggressive behaviour are easily accounted for by the likelihood that those with more aggressive personalities will also enjoy television programmes with violent content. This view is strongly supported by the sophisticated and large-scale study by Milavsky, Kessler, Stipp & Rubens (1982a, 1982b), discussed in full in the next section, which shows that correlations between violence viewing and aggression are stable over time, with viewing not causing increases in aggressive behaviour. Only if correlations increased with age would it be possible to argue that a cumulative effect of viewing on aggression exists, although such increases could just as possibly be a result of increasing physical strength and aggressive courage, and the greater opportunities to view more violent programmes as an individual gets older. In any case, a review of the many studies shows no such consistent effect (Freedman, 1984). Furthermore, a study of over 2,000 young people aged between 11 and 16 by Lynn, Hampson & Agahi (1989), discussed in greater detail below, found that correlations between television violence viewing and aggression had an *inverse* relationship to the age of their subjects. As Barwise & Ehrenberg (1988, p. 141) suggest, a correlation finding between respondents who are aggressive and who watch violent television could have one of several meanings, or no meaning at all: it may indicate that they are aggressive anyway, but work off some of this violent feeling by watching depictions of violence on television (no causality, and maybe the opposite), or that they like violence generally, whether on screen or in real life (no causality), or just that they have guessed what the study is about.

Correlation studies can also be problematic in ways which cannot be blamed upon the method itself, but rather the way in which it is used and subsequently reported. In a review of television effects, for example, Judith Van Evra (1990) earnestly describes a number of rather ridiculous correlation studies which 'find' certain variables which unsurprisingly co-exist, and then imply that one causes the other. For example we are told that children who enjoy violent television programmes are also the kind of children less likely to sit quietly for a few minutes when asked (p. 90), which is far more likely a consequence of a particular personality type than any causal effect; and that children whose parents were less concerned about the effects of television violence, were more likely to prefer watching it (p. 91), which is merely a self-fulfilling statement since children whose parents will not let them watch violent programmes are not in a position to express such a preference. Other correlations are clearly the product of a third factor, such as family background, which the simplistic correlations render invisible. A correlation between television violence viewing and lower educational achievement might be found, for example, but this might simply be because those parents who place a greater emphasis on encouraging their children to succeed in school, may also be more likely to censor and control their children's viewing. Thus, the variables might occur together, but one is most likely not the cause of the other, and the failure of these simple correlation studies to check for potential third factors renders their results pointless. The secondary reporting of correlation studies tends to exaggerate study findings by reporting correlations without describing their strength (usually weak), and by use of terms like 'relationship' between variables, which can seem to suggest that the variables interact and possibly cause one another, where this is entirely unproven (see, for example, Van Evra, 1990, pp. 81–93).

However, there are two larger-scale correlation studies which are notable for their more careful design and method: Belson (1978) and Lynn, Hampson & Agahi (1989). Belson interviewed 1,565 boys aged 12–17 in London. The boys were divided into two groups, higher and lower viewers of television violence, and then the means for the groups on measures of aggression were calculated. This found that the boys who watched more violence on television tended to commit more violent acts, particularly more serious acts, than the other group. As a test to see if the violence was a consequence of the viewing, or the viewing a product of aggressive tendencies, the calculation was also performed the other way around, with the boys divided into those higher and lower in aggression, and then their violence viewing averages revealed. Although the logic of this is questionable since other factors may affect the comparability of such a reversal (such as differences in the numbers of boys in each group due to the distribution of measures (Freedman, 1984, p. 237)), the finding in any case was that for three of the four measures of aggression used, the effect of aggression on television viewing (the reverse hypothesis) was *more* significant than the opposite effect, suggesting that viewing violence has no effect on aggression, and providing support for the view that correlations are found between the two factors because more aggressive personalities may seek to watch more violent material, without the television viewing being a cause of their violent behaviour. For the fourth measure, of more serious violent acts, the effect of violent television viewing on aggression was more significant than the reverse, and Belson treats this as evidence that television violence has an effect on serious acts of real-life aggression.

However, the data cannot be so simply interpreted, and critics who have looked more closely at the findings have noted a number of anomalies. The effect of non-violent viewing in the study is actually just as significant as violent viewing, and the effect of total television viewing is more significant than violent viewing alone (Freedman, 1984, p. 238). Viewers of very low amounts of television violence turn out to be more aggressive than viewers who saw a moderate amount, whilst very high viewers of violence were 50 per cent less aggressive than the moderate to high exposure group (Cumberbatch, 1989b, p. 44). Belson's method of analysis also produced findings such as an effect of newspaper readership on violent behaviour which is significant and, according to Belson's mode of interpretation, causal (Belson, 1978, p. 410). Such an effect seems extremely unlikely – no other study has suggested such an effect, and a public fear of newspaper readers has not been widely expressed – and this result therefore casts considerable doubt on Belson's other claimed findings of causal effects. It is also likely that the teenagers may have given inaccurate, and therefore invalid, indications of their viewing habits, since they were required to recall the frequency with which they had watched programmes which had been broadcast when they were only a few years old (Murdock & McCron, 1979). This is particularly significant, as Cumberbatch (1989b, p. 44) notes, since it has been found that subjects who make invalid claims about their viewing (by claiming to watch non-existent programme titles made up by researchers) are those whose responses dramatically increase correlations between television viewing and aggressive behaviour (Milavsky, Kessler, Stipp & Rubens, 1982a). Belson's own report also lists many other findings from the intensive interviews with the 1,565 boys which seem to contradict any conclusion that viewing violence has antisocial effects: the study found no evidence at all that exposure to television violence made boys more willing or inclined to commit acts of violence, or led to preoccupation with such acts, or made boys more callous towards real-life violence, or accept violence as a way to solve their problems (Belson, 1978, p. 16). The mixed findings of Belson's study, then, even when taken on their own terms, cannot be regarded as any kind of strong or consistent evidence for the causal hypothesis.

Lynn, Hampson & Agahi (1989) surveyed 2,039 children, aged 11–16, in three secondary schools in Northern Ireland. The study sought to compare the plausibility of the traditional effects hypothesis with a more sophisticated model, which took into consideration personality and family variables, as well as the viewing of violent television, in the attempt to account for aggressive behaviour. Questionnaires were used to measure the subjects' aggression, their viewing of 43 named popular television programmes, their enjoyment of TV violence, and their responses to Eysenck's personality measures of extraversion, neuroticism and psychoticism. The subjects themselves were asked to evaluate the amount of violence in the 43 programmes, and the mean of the older children's responses was used as the measure of screen violence. Information was also collected about each respondent's brothers and sisters, and 386 sibling pairs were extracted from the total sample.

The findings firmly contradict the traditional effects hypothesis that the amount of viewing of television violence has an effect on aggression. Children who scored high on the psychoticism scale (described as 'a broad sociopathic personality trait' (p. 149)) tended to express greater enjoyment of television violence, and also were more aggressive. The reported levels of enjoyment of TV violence within sibling pairs were unrelated, even though their levels of both total viewing and violence viewing were very similar (pp. 155–156). It was also found that whilst there was a weak correlation between siblings for aggression, which the authors attribute to genetic similarity, the higher aggression sibling did not have a tendency to watch more television violence (p. 159). These findings suggest that aggression and enjoyment of TV violence are due to personality differences, and are not an effect of television exposure. The authors firmly reject the hypothesis of a causal relationship between the amount of TV violence viewing and aggression, and argue that their results can be explained by genotype-environment correlation and interaction: that is, that parents transmit their characteristics to their children through both their genes and the environment in which the children are brought up, and that children react differently to the same environments in accordance with their genetic predispositions (pp. 145–146). This theory could be used to suggest that the viewing of television violence may have an effect on the aggression of certain children who are genetically predisposed towards high psychoticism. In this model, the *amount* of violence viewing would be of little importance,

29

since it would be the enjoyment of specific instances of depicted violence which may have an influence on aggression (p. 162). However, whilst the authors note that this model is tenable in relation to their data, whereas the traditional effects hypothesis is not, they appear ambivalent about whether they believe this model to be an accurate explanation. In any case, the correlational method means that causation cannot be demonstrated by this study. The findings do however provide strong support for the view that particular personality traits – whether produced by nature or nurture – are responsible for higher levels of both aggression and the enjoyment of television violence.

Longitudinal panel studies

Of the studies considered so far in this review, the strongest suggestions of a causal link between television violence viewing and aggression have come from studies 'in the wrong setting (the laboratory) with the right population (normal children), and in the right setting (outside of the laboratory) with the wrong population (abnormal [children])' (Cook, Kendzierski & Thomas, 1983, p. 192). The correlation studies, meanwhile, tend to take the right setting and population, but apply the wrong tests: those which cannot tell us about causation. There are however a number of longitudinal panel studies which use both natural settings and representative children, and apply more sophisticated methods: Milavsky, Kessler, Stipp & Rubens (1982a, 1982b), Lefkowitz, Eron, Walder & Huesmann (1972, 1977), Huesmann, Lagerspetz & Eron (1984), Sheehan (1986), Bachrach (1986), Fraczek (1986), and Wiegman, Kuttschreuter & Baarda (1992). By following cohorts of the same children over a period of time, the chances of being able to more precisely identify the effect of watching television violence on the child's later behaviour are much greater.

Covering a period of three and a half years (1970–1973), the study by Milavsky, Kessler, Stipp & Rubens involved approximately 2,400 elementary school boys and girls aged between 7 and 12 at the start of the study, and a further 800 boys aged initially between 12 and 16. The elementary school group were surveyed up to six times, the older group up to five times. It should be noted, however, that because of subjects leaving school, moving away or being absent, only 178 appear in all six waves of the elementary school sample, with 200 to 500 respondents available for analyses of intervals up to two years. In the sample of older boys, 302 subjects took part in all five waves. Respondents completed questionnaires and interviews, which were supplemented by data from samples of parents and teachers. Aggressive behaviour of the younger group was measured on a peer nomination system, in which several questions were asked of each subject which would provide data on the others, such as 'who tries to hurt others by hitting and punching?' and 'who tries to hurt others by saying mean things?'. For the teenage group, self-reports were used, since prior research had found these to be more accurate with subjects of this age. The study was conducted in two cities in the midwest United States, Minneapolis and Fort Worth, which are both in the Central Time Zone and so receive their programmes an hour earlier than in the east or west, allowing children the greatest possible opportunity for exposure to programmes with more violent content, aimed at an older audience. Both cities received an array of programming from both network and independent stations, and schools were chosen for the survey which would draw in children of diverse ethnic and socio-economic backgrounds. These conditions were chosen to maximize the possibility of any effects showing up, if they existed.

The panel survey design obviously does not aim to randomly assign subjects to particular conditions, as in experimental methods, but instead uses each individual in the study as their own control, by comparing their later behaviour with that recorded at an earlier point in time. Thus, prior aggression and the initial correlation between viewing and aggression can be controlled, which performs the same function as randomization, but does not interfere with the situation as it naturally occurs. This means that the effect of television viewing on behaviour can be separated from confounding variables such as the pre-existing correlation of viewing and aggression.

As Milavsky (1988) explains, the study took so long to complete – nine years from survey completion in 1973 to publication in 1982 – because the results were weak and inconsistent, and the data showed only tiny effect sizes. More sophisticated analyses and greater control of other variables only served to reduce these effects.

Milavsky *et al* (1982a, 1982b) concluded therefore that on the basis of the extensive analyses carried out, there was no evidence that television exposure had a consistent significant effect on subsequent aggressive behaviour. This was true both for the total sample and for the part of the sample identified as valid reporters of their viewing. Tests for curvilinearity (a less obvious relationship), effects of respondents leaving and joining the samples, and for measurement error, did not affect this conclusion. The use of alternative conceptualizations of 'violent' television exposure made no difference either, and complex analyses revealed no evidence that television had an effect on boys who could be considered *predisposed* towards aggressive behaviour.

Correlations between exposure to television violence and aggression at single points in time were found (as in previous correlation studies) but were not considered to reflect a causal link, since the much more sophisticated analysis over time did not provide evidence for any such connection (1982a, p. 482).

The study of elementary school children did identify factors which were more strongly correlated with aggression. Some of these factors – such as boys in low socio-economic circumstances, and families and schools where aggression is commonplace – proved to be predictors of increases in aggression over time. This not only suggests where the causes of aggression are more likely to be found, but also demonstrates that the analysis model used was capable of identifying meaningful effects (1982a, p. 487).

This study made particular efforts to draw out any potential effects of viewing on aggression from the mass of data, which itself was collected in areas where effects were most likely to be detected, and there can be little doubt that its sophisticated design and multiple analyses would have produced a positive result if there was one to be found. The

31

conclusion of no effects is therefore of considerable importance, and is certainly far more significant and relevant to the world as we find it than any number of contrived and unnatural experimental studies.

Lefkowitz, Eron, Walder & Huesmann (1972, 1977) surveyed 875 children in the United States third grade (aged eight to nine years), 427 of whom were successfully contacted again ten years later. The participants named three or four favourite programmes (which were used as the measure for television violence exposure), and aggression was measured on a peer nomination system. A cross-lagged panel correlational analysis was used; with this approach, the result required to suggest effects is the combination of positive, significant correlations between viewing and aggression at single points in time, as well as a correlation between early viewing and aggression ten years later which is higher than the correlation between early aggression and later violence viewing, which should be near zero.

The findings were mixed. No relationship between violence viewing and aggression was found for girls at all, whether at the same point in time, or over ten years. For boys, there was a small correlation at the same point in time at the earlier age, but not ten years later. However, the causal lagged effect described above was found for boys, although the correlations were not strong, and a more sophisticated analysis of the data by Kenny (1972) reduced them to a 'marginal' level. The study has been criticized for a number of reasons, and the United States Surgeon General, who commissioned the study, deemed its findings 'not conclusive'; the methodology is even politely but firmly taken apart in the introduction to the volume in which the study first appeared (Chaffee, 1972). The problems include the measure of exposure to television violence, which is based on a violence rating of only specific favourite programmes, and was different at the two survey stages (three programmes named by a parent at age 8–9, four programmes named by the subject at age 18–19); the measure of aggression, which also was different at the two survey stages, and required the older sample to recall behaviour of schoolmates from at least a year before; and the use of the cross-lagged correlational analysis, which places restrictions on the quality of the data which this study most likely did not meet (Dorr, 1986, p. 78), and is not the best technique available (Milavsky *et al*, 1982a, p. 6; 1982b, p. 145). The changes in the measures used are a particular problem for the cross-lagged correlations, which cannot work unless the measures are identical and equally reliable, which they clearly were not (Kenny, 1972). These multiple flaws mean that Lefkowitz *et al*'s results, which were weak in the first place, cannot be taken as evidence of an effect.

In a later article, Huesmann, Eron, Lefkowitz & Walder (1984) followed up the same sample at age 30, some 22 years after the initial survey. Almost all of those who had been reinterviewed at age 18 were located once more (409 subjects). Although not seeking to identify possible causes in this instance, the study found that aggressivity was reasonably stable over time, so that those who had been more aggressive at the earlier stages were likely to still be at the upper end of the range at the later age. Whilst the authors rather defensively state that the findings are 'not inconsistent' (p. 1133) with their former arguments about aggressivity being learned (from television, although here it is not mentioned), a variety of other factors are forced into the open which at least suggest that the causes must be more complex than they had previously argued. For example, their finding that 'aggressiveness is transmitted across generations within families' (p. 1131) is inconsistent with the argument that it is learned from television, unless TV viewing habits are also 'transmitted' intact in this way. The authors also discuss a 'propensity' for aggression which is evident from an early age and continues to characterize later behaviour – which again does not fit with their previous model of quantities of television violence generating aggressiveness over time, although it does fit with the counter-argument that a taste for violence leads to particular types of TV viewing. Other details, such as the finding of a connection between the current weight and aggression of women at age 30, and that the most aggressive men were born when their mothers were over 35, may demonstrate the authors' appetite for spurious and unlikely 'causes', or even a genuine result, but certainly have nothing to do with television. Indeed, in their conclusion Huesmann *et al* refer to the influence of genetic, hormonal and neurological factors in equal measure to vaguely-defined environmental and learning contributors, and on the whole inadvertently provide quite strong evidence against their own previous case.

Perhaps realizing that their 'television is bad' arguments were losing ground to the more sophisticated research being produced by others and now, ironically, themselves, Huesmann (1986b) re-entered the old debate with renewed vigour and a new unlikely theory. The argument here is that television (as well as other social experience) provides 'aggressive scripts for behaviour', whilst aggression in turn stimulates the desire to watch screen violence. Later depictions of violence can then 'cue' previously acquired aggressive scripts. Firstly we should accord some appreciation to this rare effort to produce some reasoning to support the all too often unexplained and unexplored assertions that the viewing of television violence should lead to violent behaviour. Secondly, however, we must note that whilst the theory suggests a way in which violent behaviour might be acquired, it still fails to suggest any reason or motivation for why such actions should be performed; it posits that television may suggest aggressive techniques or 'scripts' – new and interesting ways to be violent, perhaps – but not why anyone would want to copy them in the first place. Those who have supported and expanded this theory – such as Geen (1994), who at least applies a sophisticated psychological gloss to Huesmann's rather skeletal outline – have also entirely failed to answer this critical problem. The theory also, of course, overlooks the fact that human beings are generally quite imaginative and can readily invent their own novelty violence and aggression should they feel the need to. In addition, the theory is not supported by any further or stronger evidence than that which is used to support any of the usual 'viewing causes violence' arguments. Ultimately the routine, bald assertion that viewers simply copy TV violence is no different to the new, bald assertion that viewers learn and enact 'aggressive scripts', and so unfortunately Huesmann has not advanced knowledge or understanding any further with this contribution.

Returning to more straightforward research, the study by Huesmann, Lagerspetz & Eron (1984) is quite similar to the Milavsky *et al* study, although on a smaller scale. 505 children aged five to ten years old from the United States, and 178 from Finland, were surveyed each year for three years. Subjects indicated their favourite television programmes, which were rated for violence, and aggression was again measured by peer nomination. The findings are so inexplicably mixed that severe doubt is cast on the claimed finding of some small effects. For example, a significant effect of violent television viewing on later aggression was found for girls in the United States, but only a non-significant 'marginal' effect was found for boys in the United States (Huesmann *et al*, 1984, p. 757). A similarly non-significant result was found for boys in Finland, and Finnish girls showed no effect at all. Such results are difficult to account for, particularly in comparison with previous studies, and the single significant finding of effects is for American girls, a group who have not shown major tendencies toward violent crime compared to boys, and do not usually cause critics of television violence much alarm. In addition, this result contradicts the finding of the same researchers in the Lefkowitz, Eron, Walder & Huesmann (1977) study, where they found no effect at all for girls. The willingness of the researchers to overlook such glaring inconsistencies does not inspire confidence in their work. In an attempt to account for their finding and maintain their argument that effects exist, Huesmann *et al* suggest that 'Finnish society might be placing less emphasis on training girls to be aggressive than is American society' (1984, p. 772), which is wholly unfounded speculation – America's still-popular image of the 'apple-pie Mom' is hardly an aggressive one – and in any case, the study is supposed to be claiming that the aggression is a product of exposure to television violence, not anything else, and Huesmann *et al*'s temporary withdrawal from this hypothesis is an inexplicable and tremendous flaw in their work.

The results of this study were similar to those of Milavsky *et al* in direction, magnitude, and the low frequency of statistical significance, but Huesmann *et al* chose to interpret the data as evidence of an effect (Cook, Kendzierski & Thomas, 1983, p. 191).[*] Perhaps as another response to the weakness of their argument when taken in this form, Huesmann *et al* propose that there is a 'bidirectional' causal effect, with aggression increasing violence viewing, as well as vice versa. Their report does not provide clear justification for this assertion (see 1984, p. 747, pp. 770–773), and does not defend it from the obvious criticism that it is a confusingly circular, chicken-and-egg argument. The implication that viewers are motivated to watch programmes with violent content because the viewers themselves are violent is clearly not generally the case, with the popularity of many programmes which include scenes of violence clearly extending far beyond the small number of already-violent viewers. The lack of either any substantial evidence or coherent argument in favour of this 'bidirectional' model means that there is little reason to accept the contention. Even if we only consider the study in terms of what it shows about the influence of viewing on aggression, given the weakness of the findings, their inexplicable inconsistencies and contradictions, and the stubbornly ideological position displayed in the authors' special pleadings (displayed also by one of these researchers in the Lefkowitz

---

[*] Cook *et al* (1983) are able to comment on Huesmann *et al*'s 1984 article since they refer to an earlier, unpublished version.

& Huesmann (1981) article discussed in chapter two), we can conclude that their claimed 'finding' of a causal effect is highly questionable, and does not have a firm basis in the evidence.

The above study represents the American and Finnish components of a project established by Huesmann & Eron (1986), which also involved replications of the same method in Australia, Israel and Poland. In Australia, Sheehan (1986) studied two cohorts, one of children aged six to seven at the start of the study, the other of children aged initially between eight and nine, so that by the end of the three years all ages from six to twelve had been covered. Samples of 106 younger and 120 older children participated for the full period. The violence ratings for programmes classed the BBC's drama series *Grange Hill* (1978–), which had just won a BAFTA award for best children's programme, in the most violent 25 per cent, giving some indication of the hamfisted approach to 'violence'. In any case, multiple regression analyses found that later aggression was *not* significantly related to any of the three measures of earlier TV habits: television violence viewing, regularity of television viewing, or identification with television characters. Instead, the best prediction of later aggression was simply the child's earlier aggression. Sheehan states that 'None of the regressions provided results that would by themselves allow one to conclude that TV violence viewing causes aggression among Australian children' (p. 186).

The parallel study in Israel, conducted by Bachrach (1986), involved 73 children drawn from two kibbutzim, and 85 who lived in a town close to Tel-Aviv. Again spanning three years, the study found no effect of television on aggression for kibbutz children, but did identify an apparent relationship between earlier viewing of TV violence and later aggression for the city-dwelling children. The correlation was greatest for city girls, although their levels of aggression were low, and for either sex was not strong. Bachrach himself seems rather doubtful that the statistical relationship reflects a causal link from television to aggression, noting that 'it is surprising to this author that such results should occur in a country in which only a few violent programs are broadcast late at night each week and in which the environment contains regular examples of real salience to which the child is exposed' (p. 234). He takes the lack of a relationship between television and aggression in the kibbutz to be 'the most important finding', developing an argument that television violence should be of little concern if the wider society has clear values and norms of behaviour, emphasizes accountability to society, and is seen to condemn real-life violence.

The third replication of the study, by Fraczek (1986) in Warsaw, matched the Australian study in using two cohorts over the three years, one group of 108 children aged seven at the beginning, and another 129 initially aged nine. Early viewing of television violence was found to be a significant but weak predictor of later aggression. Initial aggression was found to be a far better predictor of later aggression, as is usual, and Fraczek notes that 'the [TV violence] effects are not large and must be treated cautiously'. As in Israel, the researcher seems reluctant to make much of the weak link between screen and real aggression, although the sponsors of the study, Huesmann and Eron, were clearly keen for the idea to be entertained. The author's own description of Polish television at the time of the study (1979–81) suggests that, aside from the organized 'violence' of certain sports, individual acts of screen violence were infrequent: instances in children's programmes were rare and negatively valued, and the occurrences in the popular war films involved larger groups, with emphasis placed on 'a character who defends important social values or acts for important social reasons' (p. 127). Thus all of the reasons that one feels uncomfortable with the TV effects hypothesis for western Europe, America or Australia, seem to be magnified for the Polish case, and the author's preference for explanations relating more to society and parental behaviour (p. 152) seems well founded.

These three replications give us little reason to accept the hypothesis that screen violence causes real-life aggression. Half of the studies rejected it outright (in Australia and in the kibbutz group), whilst the weak links suggested by the others (in Poland and in the Israeli town) failed even to convince the authors, who both pointed to more salient non-TV factors, and the unlikelihood of the limited amount of screen violence in those countries having a notable impact.

The longitudinal study by Wiegman, Kuttschreuter & Baarda (1992) also began life as part of this cross-national project set up by Huesmann & Eron, but the connection was severed (see Huesmann, 1986a) when the Dutch researchers decided to develop different and more appropriate measures, and ended up with data which could not be used to suggest a television effect. The study investigated the effect of televised aggression on 354 children in the Netherlands over three years. In each year, each child's aggression was measured by peer nomination, and subjects indicated their amount of viewing for every drama serial available on television at the time (a superior measure to that of only favourite pro-grammes, as used by Lefkowitz et al and Huesmann et al). The amount of violence in each serial was assessed by independent raters. Sophisticated analysis of the data showed that the results gave 'no support for the hypothesis that television violence will, in the long term, contribute to a higher level of aggression in children' (p. 155). The reverse hypothesis, that pre-existing aggression leads to greater violence viewing, received partial support. Although based on a smaller sample, the data used in this study was of a higher quality than that used by the Lefkowitz et al and Huesmann et al studies, and so its findings are arguably more reliable. This well-designed longitudinal study certainly adds further weight to the case that the viewing of television violence does not have an effect on aggression.

It should be noted that almost all of these longitudinal studies used measures of aggression which would include acts of boisterousness or incivility, in addition to the more clearly antisocial acts of physical aggression or violence which we would expect, and so levels of actual violence are likely to appear greater than they really were (Cook, Kendzierski & Thomas, 1983, p. 193). It should also be remembered that even where 'significant' results are found, these effects of television (if we trust the studies) still only account for about five per cent of the variability in aggressive behaviour over time – leaving the other 95 per cent arising from influences other than television, and which are unaccounted for (Dorr, 1986, p. 84).

Clearly, none of these more elaborate and methodologically sound studies suggests effects of any remarkable size. Indications of potential effects tend to be positive but are rarely large enough to be significant, and flaws in the studies are likely to exaggerate them. Summarizing his discussion of the most thoughtfully designed study of them all, Milavsky (1988, p. 165) frankly admits:

> Our conclusion was that any effect of watching television violence on children's aggression either did not really exist or was very small. The data did not permit a firm choice between these two interpretations, but based on what happened when controls were introduced, our judgment was that it was somewhat more likely that the effect was zero rather than that it was small.

Mass compilations of existing studies

Three studies have used slightly different methods to draw together the existing masses of data on this subject, integrating study findings to produce conglomerate effect sizes. Andison (1977) used the data cumulation method to bring together the 67 available studies from between 1956 and 1976 which hypothesized a relationship between television violence viewing and aggression. Hearold (1986) used the meta-analysis technique to integrate the findings of 230 empirical studies from the late 1920s to 1977 that measured effects of a television or film treatment on an antisocial or pro-social behaviour or attitude. Paik & Comstock (1994) updated this meta-analysis with improved statistical treatment, a more refined focus on antisocial behaviour, and by including more recent studies, using a total of 217 studies dating from 1957 to 1990. Whilst computer technology makes these compilations relatively simple to produce, it is less clear why they are desirable; the results are only worthwhile if the original studies which they are compiled from are entirely trustworthy and without flaws, which as this review has shown has often not been the case. Otherwise, all that is produced is an unhelpful average of poor findings based on weak methodologies.

Both Andison's cumulation and Hearold's meta-analysis found what is best described as 'at least a weak positive correlation' (Andison, 1977, p. 323) between viewing television violence and aggression.[*] However, Andison admits that the problem that positive results are published more often than negative ones may have led to an over-representation of positive results in the data (p. 316), whilst Hearold just as unsatisfactorily includes unpublished studies (26 per cent of the studies used). More importantly, 72½ per cent of studies cumulated by Andison, and 77½ per cent of results integrated by Hearold, used an experimental method (Andison had 42½ per cent laboratory, 30 per cent field experiments; Hearold had 60 per cent laboratory, 17 per cent field experiments). The fact that the stronger positive findings come from these experimental studies (Andison, p. 323;

---

[*] Hearold also found that the pro-social effects of pro-social television were twice as powerful as the antisocial effects of 'violent' television. This result is probably not as interesting as it may at first appear, since the smaller number of studies of pro-social effects, and the even higher percentage of laboratory experiments amongst them, with all their associated flaws discussed both above and below, means that this finding is questionable to say the least.

Hearold, p. 97), with their many methodological problems as described above, casts severe doubt on the validity of these undiscriminating compilations.

Paik & Comstock (1994) were more careful in their analysis and presentation of results, keeping different categories and methods of study more separate. The results again indicated significant but generally small positive correlations between screen and real-life aggression, although of course the meta-analysis is flawed by the same inability to discriminate or cope with flaws in the original studies. The findings are more interesting for the questions which they produce, rather than those which they directly seek to answer; the statistical compilation of results from various studies, when broken down by various details of method and treatment, reveals more contradictions and paradoxes than it does solutions. For example, when effect sizes are tabulated by programme type (p. 530), we find that action-adventure, crime and western dramas – the focus of much concern – are at the weakest end of the scale, on a par with news and public affairs programmes, which have traditionally been considered benign. Sports shows, rarely the target of social unease, are higher up the scale, alongside non-violent (and also violent) erotica. The apparent effect of non-violent erotic images on aggression cannot be explained by the hypothesis that people imitate screen violence, suggesting that flaws lurk in the theory or the method of such studies. At the highest end of the scale are cartoons, although their apparent effect seems to be focused on the youngest children in the short-term, and would appear to decline with age. Furthermore, actual real-life 'demonstration' of violence would seem to have double the effect of screen depictions. The argument made earlier in this review that supposed effects are strongly determined simply by the *measure* of 'antisocial behaviour' used by studies is given firm support here, with Paik & Comstock admitting that 'the effect size decreases as the aggression measure becomes more realistic' (p. 531). This meta-analysis is therefore perhaps more valuable for the empirical support it provides for the suspicions we might have about the flaws and inconsistencies in the body of studies surveyed, than for its uncritical assembly of manifest findings.

Clearly, large proportions of these three compilation studies serve only to elevate low-quality studies to an unwarranted level of importance, with an effect akin to framing a large amount of unsifted mud only because it contains a few grains of gold. It surely makes more sense to concentrate our attention on specific good quality studies, with an awareness of their methodological strengths and flaws, than to blindly add any old studies together in the hope that quantity of data alone will give the findings substance.

4   Other feared effects of television

There are three further types of claimed effect which deserve some consideration, although the hypothesised consequences relate more to the attitudes and cognition of viewers, rather than behaviour. Two of the contended effects, the desensitization hypothesis, and a kind of criticism here categorized as the 'zombie' hypothesis, are not supported by any convincing evidence, and contemporary concern along these lines appears more often in the popular press than in serious academic work. These alleged effects are therefore dealt with here relatively briefly. The third hypothesised effect, based on the method of cultivation analysis developed by George Gerbner, is that 'heavy' viewers of television come to believe that the world is like that shown on television, and in particular develop an exaggerated fear of crime.

The desensitization hypothesis

The common argument that exposure to television portrayals of violence may 'desensitize' viewers to the unpleasantness of real-life violence, is not supported by any methodologically sound research. Van Evra (1990, pp. 96–97), for example, reports a number of studies which suggest that viewers find television portrayals of fictional violence less shocking if they are used to seeing such scenes; however, this is entirely different from the question of how television may affect the way in which people react to real-life violence when they see it. Lack of shock when an actor hits another actor in television fiction – which we *know* is not real – does not mean that one would not be sickened by seeing genuine violence in real life.

Fortunately, Belson's (1978) study of over 1,500 teenage boys, described in chapter three, provides a wealth of valuable data on the desensitization question. Hypotheses that high exposure to television violence would render boys more callous in relation to either directly experienced violence, or distant violence presented by the news media, received no support whatsoever in the study; for distant violence the index of effect was 'virtually zero' (p. 475), whilst for directly experienced violence it was slightly *negative* (p. 471), suggesting that exposure to television violence makes boys less callous and more concerned about real-life violence – although to a degree which was not statistically significant. Other hypotheses, that exposure to television violence would increase the degree to which boys would like, or be willing, to commit the forms of violence shown on television, or that high exposure to television violence would reduce boys' consideration for other people or respect for authority, were all absolutely refuted by the extensive evidence (pp. 461–464, pp. 511–516). The reasons why Belson's results discussed in chapter two were rejected – primarily because the correlations found did not suggest a convincing and consistent causal link between violence viewing and violent behaviour – do not apply here, since the study did not even find the basic correlations which would need to appear before the question of causation was considered. This large-scale and detailed study, then, provides a firm refutation of all aspects of the desensitization hypothesis.

Only a small number of other studies have sought to examine whether exposure to screen violence affects individuals' responses to real-life violence, and these have almost always been laboratory or field experiments. These studies have presented conditions which are likely to have appeared plainly contrived to the subjects involved, and may have even given the impression that the experimenters were seeing how long subjects could restrain themselves from intervening in a situation (see the studies cited by Van Evra, 1990, pp. 97–98). Such studies have also only examined the short-term effects of a particular selected screening, rather than the cumulative effect of quantities of television violence viewing over the longer term, as is usually hypothesised. If subjects in these experiments believed that they were seeing genuine violence, and that it was not part of an experiment, the most relevant aspect of their reaction if a desensitization effect exists would not be whether they had seen a violent film within the last hour, but rather their sum exposure to violent television during, say, the past five years, and studies have failed to examine this. In addition, the study by Hagell & Newburn (1994) of juvenile frequent offenders showed that their actions were unlikely to be due to the television 'desensitizing' them to the seriousness of their acts of crime and violence, since they watched if anything less television, and no more screen violence, than their non-offending counterparts. There is therefore no evidence of an effect of viewing televised violence on reactions to real-life violence.

The 'zombie' hypothesis

Tabloid newspapers and critics of television have built up a picture of another alleged effect: that television turns children into mindless 'zombies', who uncritically lap up anything broadcast, and are unable to discern the difference between television and the real world. This hypothesis is little more than a campaigners' cliché, and is not supported by the evidence. Indeed, the newer research which regards children as distinctly 'active' rather than passive viewers – described by Hawkins & Pingree (1986, p. 233) as a new paradigm in effects research, although its emergence has been far from total – provides any number of findings to refute the 'zombie' argument.

Hodge & Tripp (1986), for example, rally evidence to argue that in watching television, children 'are learning important and complex structures of meaning, and developing capacities for thinking and judgment that are a necessary part of the process of socializa-tion' (p. 10). Neumann's (1991) review of relevant studies found absolutely no evidence to support the claims of critics that television reduces children's attention spans, impairs their ability to think clearly, causes television 'addiction', leads to illiteracy or reduces cognitive abilities in any other way. Furthermore, research has suggested that children's early initiation into narrative formats and genres, via television and video, means that they are quicker to develop literate and sophisticated understandings of books when they come to read them (Marshall, 1994).

Durkin (1985) and Buckingham (1993) have shown that children, rather than being confused about the differences between television and the real world, are able to talk easily about them. Durkin, for example, found that children as young as six years old were able to distinguish between television sex role portrayals and real world conventions (p. 78), whilst Buckingham found in interviews with children aged eight, ten and twelve that they were not only aware of the nature of television adverts, but were often cynical about advertisers' methods and motives (1993, pp. 247–248). The children often saw 'other people' as being influenced by advertising, but rarely described themselves in this way; in other cases the children rejected the idea that many people would be influenced by adverts. Eight year olds assumed that advertisers try to deceive viewers by making products look better than they really are, and by telling viewers that they need them when they don't. The substantial amount of other research on advertising, reviewed in chapter six, has similarly demonstrated that children are not taken in by its appealing promises. Indeed, when Buckingham, Fraser & Mayman (1990) sought to initiate children into viewing television critically, they found that their initial assumptions about children as relatively passive TV consumers had led them to give the children exercises which, rather than being challenging and new, were routine and 'actually rather easy for them'. The researchers observe that, 'These 12-year-olds have already mastered the skills we were attempting to teach. Short of taking them through Barthes in the original French, it is difficult to see what one might do next' (p. 41). Such evidence suggests that the moral panic image of the undiscerning television 'zombie' has little foundation in reality, and with no evidence in its favour there is no reason to give this fictional stereotype any credence whatsoever.

Cultivation effects

George Gerbner's argument that heavy viewers of television take on a distorted view of the world, which corresponds to that portrayed on the screen, has become well known in the television effects field. Content analyses in the United States have shown that violence occurs much more often on television than in real life, that men outnumber women three to one, and that minorities, blue-collar workers, young children, and the elderly are underrepresented (Gerbner, Gross, Morgan & Signorielli, 1980, 1986). Gerbner and his colleagues argue that heavy viewers of this distorted television world become more fearful of crime, anomic, sexist, and ageist. However, whilst the underrepresentation of women and minorities can be considered unfair and potentially offensive, the argument that the unrealistic television world has consequent direct effects has not been demonstrated. The possibility that television cultivates sexism, racism, or other prejudice is extremely difficult to study, since such prejudices are so deeply rooted in our culture that the contribution of television to them would be virtually impossible to discern; however, Durkin's (1985) comprehensive review of studies which have tested the hypothesis that children who watch greater amounts of television will have more strongly stereotyped beliefs and attitudes about sex roles, found that 'none of them has demonstrated a strong or convincing relationship between the two variables' (p. 68).

The research emphasis, therefore, has been on the effect of television's portrayals of violence and crime on viewer's paranoia and fear of crime in the real world (for example, Gerbner & Gross, 1976; Gerbner, Gross, Morgan & Signorielli, 1980, 1986; Signorielli, 1990); these studies all rely on correlations between amount of television viewing and fear of crime or other anxieties, and assume that when both are high, the fear is a consequence of the television viewing. Such studies have been widely criticized. The correlations found between amount of viewing and fear of crime tend to be very small (Wober, 1978), and when multiple controls for other contributory factors are applied, the effects are substantially reduced or disappear altogether (Cook *et al*, 1983; Gunter, 1987; Cumberbatch, 1989a). Other researchers have exposed anomalies which make Gerbner *et al*'s claims much less clear-cut. Hirsch (1980), for example, re-analysed data used by Gerbner and his colleagues, and found that people who did not watch any television at all were more fearful and alienated than viewers of any amount of television, whilst 'extreme' viewers who watched over eight hours per day were generally *less* likely than Gerbner's 'heavy' viewers to have these fears. We can also note that Gerbner *et al*'s own data shows that whilst white viewers' fear of victimization increases with their amount of viewing, non-white viewers' fear, whilst greater than that of whites overall, actually *decreases* with amount of viewing, even though (as Gerbner *et al* frequently state) such minorities are more often portrayed as victims of crime (see Gerbner *et al*, 1986, pp. 31–34).

The correlations between television viewing and anxiety can be explained by a crucial third factor in all cases. The relationship between heavy viewing and a greater fear of crime is easily explained by the fact that light viewers tend to be middle class and live in areas with lower crime rates than heavy viewers. In addition, middle class viewers watch less crime drama (Wober & Gunter, 1988). Therefore, the greater fear of crime can be explained in terms which have nothing to do with the effect of watching television: in fact, the heavy viewers' greater fear of crime can be accounted for entirely by their knowledge of their neighbourhood as it exists in real life. Gerbner and colleagues have been forced to admit that it is viewers who live in such areas with high crime rates who are most fearful of crime, but they claim that television here produces a *resonance* effect, reinforcing viewers' fears of their neighbourhood (Gerbner, Gross, Morgan & Signorielli, 1980, 1986). Whilst this is a possible reading of the data, it is only speculative, and not the most obvious interpretation. The fact that an individual watches large amounts of television is obviously not a characteristic randomly distributed in a population, as Gerbner *et al* seem to assume, but is likely to itself be at least partly a consequence of other factors, such as the viewers' anxieties about the outside world, social attitudes and worldview; it is these variables which may influence opinions about the world just as much as, or more than, television – but would also lead an individual to stay indoors watching it. Other researchers have found that viewers do not confuse television representations of crime with real life, and that in any case attempts to replicate Gerbner's findings outside the United States have frequently failed (Gunter, 1987). A study by Wober (1978) polled a representative sample of over 1,100 UK residents and found no evidence of this paranoid effect of television on feelings about the trustworthiness of other people or the likelihood of being a victim of robbery. A further, more sophisticated survey by Wober & Gunter (1982) found correlations between social attitudes and level of television viewing which suggested that people who feel less in control of their lives and have a generally fateful outlook tend to stay in watching television more, and express the fearful attitudes tested for by Gerbner *et al* in their studies. This result reinforces the case that it is not television which has a causal effect on the fears expressed by heavier viewers, but rather those anxieties which cause people to *be* heavy viewers in the first place.

The complaint of Gerbner *et al* that the demographies and crime rates of television entertainment do not match those of the real world is also notably obtuse. The argument that women and minorities should be fully and positively represented on screen is readily justifiable, of course, but to stipulate that television should be as uneventful as real life seems rather to miss the point of its very existence and popularity. Whilst the 'TV world' may have greater levels of crimes, accidents and arguments than 'real life' – and lower levels of sleeping, housework and TV-watching – it seems highly unlikely that most viewers would want television programming adjusted to match the content of an averaged picture of everyday human experience.

The theory that television has a direct effect on viewers' perceptions, at least for the more verifiable effect of television on fear of crime, is not supported by the evidence, then, and this simplistic conception can be discounted. However, more sophisticated applications of cultivation analysis have suggested that the method may be of some use in the study of television's *influences* on viewers' thoughts and perceptions, and these more complex approaches will be considered in chapter seven.

5   Pro-social effects of television

Comments on 'pro-social' effects research

The 'pro-social effects' of television considered in this literature generally refer to such 'positive' influences on behaviour as increases in altruism, helpfulness, generosity, and other social skills. This conception is obviously based on a value judgement, although these traits are likely to be considered desirable by most people. The body of research into the potential positive impact of television is less extensive than that into aggression effects, and the area lacks the support of major longitudinal, non-experimental studies – although some interesting work involving a more sophisticated conception of possible pro-social influences has been developed. Like the violence research, the area has its share of rather poorly-designed experimental studies, often based upon ill-informed assumptions about television entertainment. It could be said, for example, that the television violence researchers often appear to believe that most television fare is largely antisocial, offering a host of unjustifiably violent 'role models'. Rather than taking a different view, many of the pro-social effects researchers generally share this perspective; indeed, they often seem to take it further, implicitly suggesting that the only decent programmes with anything positive to communicate to young people are *Sesame Street, Mister Rogers' Neighborhood* and *Lassie.**

Barbara Lee (1988, p. 238) notes that the term 'pro-social' originally came into use in the 1960s to distinguish between types of aggression, 'pro-social aggression' being that kind of aggression which may be necessary or desirable for some wider purpose or reason. However, this meaning seems to have been largely lost, since most studies (from the 1970s onwards) treat 'pro-social' and 'aggressive' as mutually exclusive terms. The heroes of most fictional television are rarely considered 'pro-social', despite the fact that they – particularly on children's and 'family' shows – almost always have a clear sense of right and wrong, and are on the side of 'good', often shown in clear contrast to 'bad', mean, nasty people and criminals. Indeed, these television portrayals often tend to polarize 'good'

---

*   These programmes are all American, and appear frequently in these studies. *Sesame Street* is a well-known, long-running and highly popular programme, largely for the under fives, which features its own distinct cast of Jim Henson's Muppet-type characters, with regular human actors and guest celebrities. It teaches about numbers, letters, and being nice to each other. *Mister Rogers' Neighborhood* is similar but less well-known, and without the Muppets. *Lassie* is a well-known film and television drama series for children about a heroic dog and her owners.

and 'bad' characters to an extent which is not realistic, ignoring the complexity of human characters for the sake of providing the audience with traditional, perfect 'heroes' to empathize with. However, as mentioned in chapter one, the highly moral and pro-law content of programmes such as *Batman* and *Superman* (in their cartoon or live-action forms) seem to be considered by many of these researchers as representing just the *opposite* of 'pro-social' television (for examples of this, see Friedrich & Stein, 1975, p. 28; Coates, Pusser & Goodman, 1976, p. 138; Rushton, 1982; Johnston & Ettema, 1986, p. 144).[*]

Once again, the context of actions is ignored, so that 'bad' actions are any which involve aggression, regardless of the reason and motivation, whilst the 'good' acts are usually only ones where a character is explicitly and observably *nice* to another one in some way. This rigid, content-analysis type view means that the TV hero who risks everything but ultimately manages to knock out a villain who was about to kill 200 people, would only be counted as 'antisocial' (since they hit someone) but not at all 'pro-social' (since they didn't hug anyone or give them a present). The content analysis approach and method is severely flawed by its inability to recognize the content or meaning of acts (see Morrison, 1993), and because of this is liable to give an exaggerated impression of levels of screen violence, which is easy to count but not always antisocial, whilst under-counting pro-social acts, which may be more subtle. Even despite such factors, a content analysis of American television by Greenberg (1980, cited in Cumberbatch, 1989a, p. 23) recorded an average of 20 acts of altruism per hour over a three year period (1975–1978), which compares favourably with an average American rate of five to eight acts of violence per hour (Cumberbatch, 1989a, p. 23), or less than half this violence rate on British terrestrial television (Gunter & McAleer, 1990, pp. 77–78).

As with the violence studies, the apparent failure of some researchers to understand television entertainment tends to place their studies on shaky foundations from the start. Judith Van Evra is not untypical as she asserts that television portrayals of antisocial acts may have more of an effect because of 'the fact that antisocial content is meant to entertain whereas pro-social content is only meant to instruct' (1990, p. 101). This view is far from unequivocal. Antisocial characters and acts shown in television fiction are almost always punished or put right by a pro-social lead character. Programmes with antisocial actions left entirely unpunished and unregretted are rarely shown (Belson, 1978), particularly when the aim is to entertain (although we could add that they sometimes intend to instruct – the opposite of Van Evra's claim – by showing the horror of violence); and pro-social characters are far from being exclusive to purely 'instructional' programmes: indeed, it is difficult to think of an entertainment programme which does not feature at least one generally pro-social character. This is important, since the apparent consensus opinion about popular television held by many of these researchers seems surprisingly misinformed.

---

[*] We can note also that the movies *Superman III* (1983) and *Batman Returns* (1992) both feature sections where the hero appears to other characters to have turned antisocial, and this is clearly perceived as horrifying, and a total contrast to the hero's normal behaviour and 'true' character.

Experimental studies into pro-social effects

As with the review of research into aggression effects, we again begin with some rather poor laboratory experiments. Several of these could be happily ignored, but have some significance thrust upon them by others who report their claims uncritically: for example, the 'findings' of the disastrously flawed studies by Stein & Bryan (1972) and Wolf & Cheyne (1972), described below, are related by Rushton (1982), and Gunter & McAleer (1990), with a surprising lack of critical comment.

In the study by Stein & Bryan (1972), the experimenter told each child subject how to play a game, and then showed them a video of another child playing the game. The film shown to subjects in the experimental group showed the child cheating a little, and explaining why she felt the cheating to be justified. The group who had seen this film were then found to be a little more likely to cheat when they played the game. However, since the experimenter themselves had shown the subjects this film without critical comment and apparently as a demonstration of how best to play the game (why else would they show it?) this is far from surprising, and if anything only shows that all of the children basically tried to do what they had been told. The fact that the cheating model was shown on a television screen seems entirely irrelevant, since its function in the experiment (as far as the children would have been concerned) was simply as a tool to demonstrate how to play the game, and any conclusion that television can encourage or discourage children to obey rules, in this context, is redundant.

Wolf & Cheyne (1972) conducted a similarly flawed experiment, in which children were taken individually to a room containing two 'attractive' toys, and were told not to play with one particular toy. They were then shown a video of 'another child playing' in the same setting (without comment from the experimenter), and were left alone. In cases where the video had shown a child playing with the forbidden toy, the subject was then observed to be more likely to play with that toy. Again, this is extremely unsurprising, since the experimenter is seen to voluntarily show a film depicting the forbidden act, which would almost certainly suggest to the child that the 'rule', spoken once, could not be terribly important, or that it had simply been misheard. As in the previous example, the child subject is placed in a very confusing situation with contradictory suggestions of how to behave which both basically come from the same authority figure; conclusions about whether television can discourage or encourage 'deviant behaviour' can hardly be drawn from such a study.

Whilst these two examples are amongst the worst designed of the studies, there are several other experiments which nonetheless suffer from the same serious flaws of the method as affected the experiments on aggression. A study by Sprafkin, Liebert & Poulos (1975, cited in Feshbach, 1988, p. 264, and Rushton, 1982, p. 249) indicated that an episode of *Lassie* in which Lassie's owner risked his life to rescue Lassie's pup, would increase children's willingness to help puppies in distress at some cost to themselves. However, this result is deduced from the subjects' behaviour in a game, in the course of which they were able to help (fictional) 'puppies in distress' although this would interfere with earning

47

points towards a prize. The analogy is not bad, but is hardly the same as risking one's life; however, it can be accepted that the *Lassie* episode did increase the children's empathy for some fictional puppies in the short term. We do not know how enduring this effect would have been, however, and there is the possibility of experimenter demand: the connection between the puppies in distress in the film and in the subsequent game could well have been obvious to the children.

Coates, Pusser & Goodman (1976) conducted a small field experiment with 26 children in a university nursery. The children's behaviour was observed before, during and after a period of four days in which the children were shown 15 minutes of either *Sesame Street* or *Mister Rogers' Neighborhood*, both of which are self-consciously 'pro-social' children's programmes. *Sesame Street* was found to encourage the giving of positive reinforcement and punishment to, and social contact with, other children and adults in the nursery for those children who previously had scored low on measures of such behaviour, although children whose scores were already high for these traits were unaffected.* *Mister Rogers' Neighborhood* significantly increased the giving of positive reinforcement to, and social contacts with, other children and adults in the nursery, for all of the subjects in that group. However, the sample was small (only 13 children in each group), and an experimenter demand effect is not unlikely since the children could easily have guessed the implication of their being shown models of virtuous behaviour and the coincident observation of their performance.

A more complex field experimental study was conducted by Friedrich & Stein (1975), again looking for possible pro-social effects of *Mister Rogers' Neighborhood*. For one week, 73 nursery school children were divided into five groups, one of which was shown 'neutral' television and given training in an irrelevant subject, whilst the others were shown *Mister Rogers* and given one of two types of training, or both types, or the irrelevant training. When interviewed two or three days after the viewing, the children were found on the whole to have learnt from the content of the pro-social programmes, in that they could *describe* more pro-social behaviours, and generalize them to situations different from those shown on the screen; however, their actual behaviour was not affected. For the groups given additional training, the only significant effect on behaviour was that boys who had received role-play training (where the desired 'effects' were physically demonstrated to, and acted out by, the children) were more likely to help their friends. However,

---

* As mentioned, researchers into 'pro-social' television have typically taken *Sesame Street* as a model of such programming (see Watkins, Huston-Stein & Wright, 1981; Rushton, 1982; Gunter & McAleer, 1990; Graves, 1993). However, as Neumann (1991, pp. 20–21) reports, some have found cause to condemn even *Sesame Street* as bad for children. One critic alleges that the lively programme causes children to 'compulsively recite numbers and letters like restless, wound-up robots', whilst others accuse it of creating restlessness and a need for instant gratification. In this view, the programme is *too* pacey, arousing or just plain interesting, and so causes children to be less interested in other attempts to educate them; in short, the programme is too good at its job, and this is made worse by its popularity. Complaints such as these make the distance between television researchers and broadcasters, as noted by Stipp (1993), far from surprising. Other experimental and field studies of viewers have not shown these complaints to be justified (Watkins, Huston-Stein & Wright, 1981, p. 55).

the surprising lack of another experimental group to receive the training without being shown the programme, means that we cannot rule out the strong possibility that the programme (which on its own did not significantly affect behaviour) was irrelevant to this process, and that the behavioural effects were a result of the interactive training. The whole point of testing for the effects of television programming with additional training is eliminated if there is not a separate and comparable test for the effects of the training alone. Friedrich & Stein suggest that if children watched the programmes over much longer periods of time than the single week of the experiment, the generalizable learning (which was found to take place) might influence behaviour. This is possible, but entirely speculative.

Other experimental studies (see summaries in Watkins, Huston-Stein & Wright, 1981; Rushton, 1982; Feshbach, 1988; Gunter & McAleer, 1990) have generally found that programmes which have intentionally 'pro-social' content do have some effect on increasing children's observed displays of kindness and consideration, generosity, or altruism. However, the nature of such experiments means that we can only know about short-term effects, which are potentially influenced by experimental demand, particularly since the 'required' behaviours are socially approved actions which can only reflect well on those who produce them for the research. In addition, we can note that these studies all cover behaviours which are both socially valued and not controversial, and so arguably not difficult to influence to a small but significant degree for a limited period of time. A study by Gantz & Greenberg (1990) found that two television programmes on AIDS, a less comfortable and more personal subject, provided their high school and college student viewers with information on the subject, but did not stimulate greater interest in the topic, make it a more acceptable subject of conversation, or affect behaviour. Other studies of campaigns (see chapter six) have similarly found that behavioural changes of a less simplistic and immediate nature than those looked for in these experiments are much more difficult to obtain.

Other field studies into pro-social effects

A relatively small number of more sophisticated studies have been conducted, with results more clearly applicable to natural situations and longer-term influences. Johnston & Ettema (1982) studied 7,000 children in seven cities to examine the effects of *Freestyle*, a 13-part television drama series aimed at changing the sex-role stereotypes of nine to twelve year old viewers. The series was developed by the National Institute for Education in the United States, and broadcast like any other programme by television stations. The study sought to evaluate the impact of the series for children who watched the programme at home with minimal encouragement (a weekly reminder from teachers), for those who were shown the programme in school, but with no subsequent discussion, and for those whose viewing in school was supplemented by teacher-led discussion and support activities. Questionnaires were used to measure effects, with questions relating to *beliefs* about boys' and girls' competence in non-traditional activities (such as girls in sport and boys in child care), *attitudes* about boys and girls engaging in such activities, and the subject's own *interest* in such activities.

For those who watched the programmes at home, the only effect was on the subject of females performing mechanical tasks. Girls who had watched at least seven of the programmes, and boys who had watched at least ten, expressed significantly more positive beliefs and attitudes on this topic, and the girls' personal interest in the area was increased.

The viewing of all 13 programmes in the school setting produced larger changes on certain measures. Girls again were apparently the most affected, with significant changes on 50 per cent of the belief and attitude measures, and an increased personal interest in mechanics. Boys changed on only 25 per cent of the belief and attitude measures, and showed no increase in non-traditional personal interests. The supplementation of the programmes with discussion and support activities significantly boosted the changes in attitudes and beliefs, typically doubling them. The programme's ability to increase personal interests in non-traditional activities remained limited, however, again reflecting the fact that beyond television, there is a world full of many more complex, social influences on children. Johnston & Ettema state:

> 'Specifically, class discussion probably has two effects. In attitude change, confronting the problem ... is more powerful than simply viewing confrontation on the screen, and adult-mediated discussion can make up for deficiencies in dramatic production ... To achieve similar effect sizes at home probably requires more programming and more efforts to encourage viewing.' (1986, p. 145).

However, they also note later that even this assumption that adult involvement will enhance effects is not certain; Sprafkin & Rubinstein found one situation where the effects of 'pro-social' television were reduced by adult mediation (Johnston & Ettema, 1986, p. 158).

Also of interest is the study's finding that viewers recalled best the most dramatic scenes of the programme. When the 'message' was embedded in such scenes, it was much more likely to be remembered and understood than if it was merely verbalised in a scene with no associated action (Johnston & Ettema, 1986, p. 152). This might suggest that the good work of heroes such as 'Batman' and 'Superman', far from having negative effects as some researchers presume, is likely to have pro-social results due to the strong integration of exciting action with a moral stance. It certainly suggests that the messages of deliberately pro-social *and* exciting fictional programmes are more likely to be conveyed, such as those which form a fundamental part of the plots in the environmental action-adventure cartoon series *Captain Planet and the Planeteers* (1991–92), for example.

This purposefully designed pro-social programme, *Freestyle*, does seem to have had an effect on certain attitudes and beliefs, and a lesser effect on particular personal interests, in its relatively modest 13-week run. The study also demonstrated that discussion and activity about such a programme can increase its intended effects, and that viewers were able to generalize belief and attitude changes beyond those shown in the programme.

Again, however, there is some possibility of a researcher demand effect, even in the more naturalistic home viewing setting, since the children were reminded to watch the programme by teachers, and were aware that they would be questioned about it. Unfortunately for the research, it is also likely that those children who made the effort to watch a high number of episodes at home would be those already more disposed to the anti-sexist ideas in any case.

Longitudinal studies of *Sesame Street* have found more positive results gained by viewing without additional support activities. Studies by Bogatz & Ball of the first two years of the programme's impact (1970–1972, reported by Lesser, 1974, and Watkins, Huston-Stein & Wright, 1981)[*] showed that viewers who watched the programme more frequently, whether in home or classroom settings, showed significant increases in their scores on assessment tests which were designed to measure learning from the actual content of the programmes (such as the letters, numbers, and relational terms covered, rather than general cognitive functioning or 'IQ'). These findings appear to demonstrate that the programme was effective in its aim of teaching information and intellectual skills. In addition, it was found that viewers of the programme were influenced by its demonstrations of friendship, social harmony and other pro-social behaviour. The respect and appreciation of racial differences shown on *Sesame Street* was also found to have made an impression on regular viewers, who showed more positive attitudes towards children of other races in the large-scale evaluational studies which were conducted as an integral part of the programme's development (Lesser, 1974, p. 225). School teachers who were asked to rank children in their classes on various measures, and who did not know the children's *Sesame Street* viewing levels, rated those who had been regular viewers as having better relationships with their peers, and being better prepared generally for school life (Lesser, 1974, p. 224). It is possible that the self-selected viewers may have been those more inclined towards greater ability and these behaviours and attitudes already; however, the extensive *Sesame Street* research also compared children who could and could not receive the programme, but were otherwise matched on age, intelligence and background, and again found significant positive results for the programme's viewers (Lesser, 1974, p. 222). This research does suggest that regular viewing of the programme at home had some tangible, positive effects.

A large-scale study by Ball-Rokeach, Rokeach & Grube (1986) made use of an ingenious method to avoid researcher demand effects or other interference which occurs when people know that they are being studied. A programme intended to change attitudes and actions towards issues of equality and the environment was broadcast on normal TV channels, and the adult respondents were only contacted afterwards, so that the viewing situation was entirely voluntary and natural. In addition, the tests for subsequent changes in attitudes and behaviour were designed so that subjects were not aware of being studied, again removing the possibility of researcher demand effects.

---

[*] See also Cook & Curtin's (1986) detailed consideration of the evaluational research on *Sesame Street* and other educational programmes. Note that the Bogatz & Ball studies are sometimes referred to elsewhere as the ETS (Educational Testing Service) studies or evaluations.

The researchers prepared the single 30-minute programme, entitled *The Great American Values Test*, to a professional standard, using well-known presenters. The second half of the programme included 'needling' messages from the presenters, intended to make viewers examine their commitment to three target values – 'freedom', 'equality', and 'a world of beauty'. The show was advertised in newspapers, *TV Guide* and on radio and television, with the particular intention of attracting viewers who were strongly dependent on television for their social and self-understanding. All three commercial television channels in the experimental area (the Tri-Cities area of eastern Washington) broadcast the programme simultaneously, whilst in the control city (80 miles away, with a similar population), the programme was blacked out. A random sample of residents of both cities were pre-selected, and after the broadcast the 1,699 respondents in the experimental city were contacted for the first time by telephone. Interviewers who claimed to be calling from a television station (to separate the call from the research enterprise) established whether the respondents had watched the programme, their level of attention, and whether the viewing had been uninterrupted, as well as basic demographic information.

To detect possible changes in basic values and related social attitudes, a questionnaire was used, which required respondents to rank 18 values (including the three target values) in order of importance. This part of the questionnaire was based on one used in a national survey of values, which had been discussed in the television programme. The survey also sought to measure related attitudes towards sexism, racism and environmental conservation, and the extent to which the respondent depended on television for their understandings of self and society. This questionnaire was sent to half of the samples from the two cities seven weeks before the programme was broadcast, and to the other half four weeks after the broadcast. The large size of the samples meant that the results should have been able to indicate significant changes in average overall attitudes, even though individual viewers were not questioned both before and after the programme.

To detect changes in actual behaviour, all of the participants in both cities were sent solicitations for money eight, ten and thirteen weeks after the programme. These requests were sent directly from relevant genuine charities or organizations in different Washington cities: one from an organization providing opportunities for black children in cultural activities, one from a university women's athletics programme, and one from an anti-pollution campaign group.

The researchers estimate that only 26 per cent of the preselected respondents watched the programme, and that only half of those watched without interruption, even though the programme achieved excellent general ratings. Nevertheless, the findings are impressive. Respondents from the experimental city sent significantly more donations in response to the solicitations than those in the control city, and the appeals also received significantly fewer abusive, negative responses from the experimental city.

The 'needling' messages in the second half of the programme would appear to have had an effect, since uninterrupted viewers significantly increased their rankings of 'freedom' and 'equality', and (to a lesser degree) 'a world of beauty'. The associated social attitudes towards the environment and towards black people also increased significantly, and attitudes towards women increased but to a lesser extent. Non-viewers, and those who were interrupted (and so had comparable initial motivations to watch, although they were prevented from doing so), were unaffected. More importantly, uninterrupted viewers donated four to six times as much money as non-viewers in both cities, and (surprisingly) about nine times as much as the interrupted viewers. The authors also claim that viewers who were highly dependent on television for understanding themselves and society were more likely to watch the programme, to watch with high levels of attention and involvement, and to be more affected by it in both their attitudes (as expressed in the survey) and behaviour (as demonstrated by their donations to associated causes). However, the authors do not make clear quite how this television dependency, established from the questionnaire responses, was defined or measured, and so it is difficult to assess the authenticity of this finding.

The study has some further flaws. Concern for the environment is measured by a ranking of the value 'a world of beauty', which is an ambiguous term not exactly synonymous with, say, 'a safe and unpolluted planet'. The national sample of Americans rated 'a world of beauty' 15th out of 18, a fact mentioned in the television programme as part of one of the 'needling' points (Ball-Rokeach *et al*, 1986, pp. 284–285). However, a closer look at this study shows that the national sample placed the not dissimilar value 'a world at peace' an impressive second, after 'family security'. It could be argued that those who saw the television programme and were informed that the phrase 'a world of beauty' was equated by researchers with environmental concern (rather than, say, a love of beautiful objects and home furnishings) thereafter placed it higher. More importantly, it could be argued that the kind of people who would watch such a programme as the one prepared would be the kind of people who would donate money to the causes involved in this study in any case. However, this would not explain the difference between the overall donations sent from the experimental and control cities, or the large difference between the donations of interrupted and uninterrupted viewers. The apparent changes in attitudes and beliefs are also evidence against this case, although the deliberate pitching of the programme at those more likely to be influenced by television may account for some of these changes.

Nevertheless, the apparent changes in some values and attitudes, and particularly related behaviour (which is usually much more difficult to affect), made on adults by one 30-minute programme seem quite striking. The findings appear to illustrate and indeed magnify the argument made by Mendelsohn (1973), that the close collaboration of social scientists and broadcasters can produce public information campaigns which are able to achieve specifically targeted goals. However, the much more substantial experience of campaign researchers discussed in the next chapter would suggest that these results, even if valid, are rather unique.

Pro-social effects from everyday programmes

Of the programmes discussed in the section above, *Freestyle* was a drama series, and *Sesame Street* is also based around fictional, dramatic interactions, although it lacks the narrative drive and more complex plots which we might normally associate with television drama. However, these are programmes made by educational organizations with quite explicit learning goals – which is not, of course, to their discredit, but does make the programmes distinct from most TV output, and viewing them may at least in part be motivated by 'self-improvement' impulses (whether originating from the child themselves, or a parent or teacher) which are different from those which motivate more day-to-day TV viewing. The *Freestyle* study has already shown us that pro-social messages are more likely to be remembered and understood when they are embedded in dramatic action; this suggests both that pro-social arguments can be made more clearly when dramatised in a particular context, and that they are most readily accepted when the viewer does not feel that they are simply being 'preached' to.

This view is supported by the findings of Mielke & Chen (1983), who conducted formative research for a Children's Television Workshop series designed to promote interest in and give information about science and technology, *3–2–1 Contact*. Although formative research is used in the development of programmes, testing the potential of various ideas and pilot items rather than the 'final product' series itself, this research was by no means small-scale, involving more than 50 field studies with over 10,000 children aged eight to twelve. Various imaginative comprehension tests were used, to see what children understood and misunderstood in video material. Such tests included showing a child a section of programme, and then playing it again with the sound turned off and asking the child to provide the narration; and discussion of perceived meanings at certain points where the video was frozen. The research team also developed a 'Program Evaluation Analysis Computer' system, which had 40 individual hand-held units connected up to a computer, so that groups of children could record their basic responses ('interesting or fun to watch' versus 'boring or not fun to watch') by pressing buttons as they watched the television material, allowing the researchers instant data on which formats and items were most appealing to target-age children. Becoming even more ambitious, the researchers also tested items on the QUBE Interactive Cable System in Columbus, Ohio, where 737 children (randomly selected from QUBE subscriber data) participated in a one-hour survey in which they responded to pilot material narrowcast to their homes, using buttons on their home cable console to rate segment and character appeal on a four point scale from 'very interesting' to 'very boring'. The findings from these and other parts of the research, both qualitative and quantitative, provide a number of insights into the television interests and preferences of children aged eight to twelve. Despite being relatively young, they enjoyed a broad range of programming (predictably stemming well beyond that intended specifically for children) and held 'high standards for production values, often stating the need for "action" and "good acting" and criticizing material that is "corny" or "silly"' (p. 52). Plotted drama was clearly and consistently preferred over the segmented magazine or documentary format, although documentary segments which followed a storyline from development to resolution were also able to be appealing. Active visuals, unifying themes, and appropriate humour (not 'silly' or 'babyish' attempts) were also found to enhance appeal. This information was then used to make *3–2–1 Contact* as successful as possible; here, however, our interest is in what the findings tell us more generally about the potential for the pro-social influence of television on children: it would seem that the non-didactic format of regular drama-entertainment programming is at least as likely to carry positive learning messages as the 'educational' format of non-fiction magazine programmes such as *Blue Peter* in Britain or its PBS equivalents in America.

This hypothesis (in its crudest form) was tested by Wiegman, Kuttschreuter & Baarda (1992) in their three-year longitudinal panel study on 354 children in the Netherlands, described above in the section on longitudinal studies into aggression, which also looked for possible pro-social effects of a natural TV diet. As with aggression, in each year every child's pro-social behaviour was measured by a peer-nomination system, and subjects' indications of their amount of viewing of each drama serial on television at the time was multiplied by ratings of the amount of pro-social behaviour shown in each programme, to produce an exposure score. No significant relationship was found between viewing pro-social behaviour on television and real-life pro-social behaviour, reflecting the similarly null findings for viewing violence and real-life aggression. The authors incidentally note that exposure to depictions of pro-social behaviour was strongly correlated with exposure to depictions of violence; viewers who saw more of one saw more of the other – they were simply heavier television viewers (p. 156). This study, then, returns us to the point that there is no simple or predictable relationship between viewing and behaviour. However, it is perhaps rather simplistic to limit the enquiry to observable behavioural changes connected to the viewing of programmes containing pro-social behaviour. Whilst this type of approach was appropriate in the violence studies, since the public concerns about effect were directly related to behavioural consequences, it here restricts our opportunities to see if, at least, certain prime-time programmes have influenced *attitudes* or *values* in pro-social directions.

The distinction being drawn here between 'educational' and 'general viewing' programmes may seem a spurious one, but as we have seen it is one generally closely drawn by broadcasters themselves. In the United States in particular, it is left to the Children's Television Workshop and the National Institute for Education to produce shows like *Sesame Street* and *Freestyle*, and their placement in 'children's' slots, whilst not inappropriate, marginalizes them still further. In Britain, BBC Education is a distinct department within the corporation, and identifiably more 'educational' programmes are likely to show up in 'children's' slots or on the more specialist channels of BBC2 and Channel Four. On the other hand, British soap operas such as *EastEnders* (1985–) and *Brookside* (1982–) have sought to challenge attitudes to homosexuality and racism, for example, through dramatic confrontation; and such issues have also been tackled in US series such as *thirtysomething* (1987–91), *Roseanne* (1988–) and *NYPD Blue* (1993–), although the ensuing controversies, propagated in particular by jittery advertisers and religious pressure groups, tend to encourage a diffident and timid spirit. Environmental issues have perhaps managed to pervade more successfully, although the programmes' implied criticism of governmental policies and unrestrained capitalism make them no less controversial – see for example the *Lois and Clark* episode 'Man of Steel Bars' (1993), the *Star Trek: The Next Generation* episode 'Force of Nature' (1993), the *Casualty* episodes 'No Cause for

Concern' (1993) and *Tippers* (1994), or the valiant BBC eco-thriller serials *Doomwatch* (1970–72), *Threads* (1984), *Edge of Darkness* (1985), *Natural Lies* (1992), and *Stark* (1993) – which, like parts of other contemporary serials, have successfully woven timely and important ecological messages into sympathetic social dramas. Indeed, 'green' concerns are increasingly normalized in some programmes, such as in the regular jokes around Homer's frighteningly unregulated work at a nuclear power plant in *The Simpsons* (1990–). Children's programmes have perhaps been the most persistent in emphasizing environmental themes over whole series, dating back at least as far as *Clangers* (1969–74), the charming British animations about small, knitted creatures who only wanted to live happily and peacefully together on their tiny planet, free from the interfering bits of baffling technology which occasionally fell from the sky. More recently, the surge of interest in environmental issues which began in the late 1980s was quickly reflected in a significant proportion of children's programming, from the explicitly 'green' American cartoons such as *Toxic Crusaders* (1991–92) and *Captain Planet* (1991–92), which both provided a critique of capitalist industrialism, nuclear technology and pollution to a surprisingly campaigning extent, to the repeated focus on ecological themes in the British *Blue Peter*, the dedicatedly eco-friendly *Go Wild!* (1992–93), and even in elements of *Sesame Street*.

In non-Western countries, however, programme-makers have become more ambitious in their self-appointed role as opinion formers or, it might be said, propagandists. As Singhal & Rogers (1989) note, some television producers in Third World countries have come to question the division of entertainment versus educational content, and have sought to promote development goals through soap operas. *Hum Log* (*We People*) is one such series, broadcast by India's government television system, Doordarshan, over 17 months in 1984–85. The 156 episodes of 22 minutes each were designed to promote a more equal status for women and smaller family size, whilst fulfilling the audience expectations – and Doordarshan's own stated prime objective – of entertainment. Rather blurring our increasingly pointless distinction between entertainment and 'educational' television, however, each episode was followed by an epilogue of 30 to 50 seconds in which a famous actor summarized the main concepts and provided viewers with 'appropriate guides to action' (p. 335). Whilst we might expect such a didactic approach might not appeal to all adult tastes, these segments were found to be very attractive to the viewers. Indeed, the programme had an average audience of 50 million viewers, the largest for a TV programme in India at that time. Singhal & Rogers conducted an audience survey of 1,170 adults in three different areas of India, 83 per cent of whom had seen at least one episode of *Hum Log*. Of these, in response to multiple choice questions, an impressive 96 per cent said that they liked it, 94 per cent found it entertaining, 83 per cent said it was educational, and 91 per cent agreed that it addressed social problems. Questions about whether the audience identified with characters as the programme makers had intended, however, show that responses cannot be so precisely planned: asked which was the best exemplar to copy in real life, the three female 'positive' role-model characters (hardworking and self-sufficient) were nominated by 37 per cent, 11 per cent and five per cent respectively, but a character intended as a negative role model for gender equality (a stereotype of the traditional Indian wife and mother) beat two of those into second place, scoring 18 per cent, whilst four per cent chose a drunken, chauvinistic father as their role model. The remaining selections were 'neutral' in terms of the programme's messages. Of course this does not necessarily show that the programme even partially failed: an analysis of 500 randomly selected viewers' letters showed that the traditional female character was admired for her tolerance, compromise and patience, particularly in the face of criticism from her husband and mother-in-law. Such responses show that, whilst not particularly advancing the programme's explicit goals, this character may have at least provided a point of empathy for similarly oppressed wives.

The survey also asked respondents to report how *Hum Log* had influenced their attitudes. Whilst subsequent self-reporting is a less desirable measure of change than having 'before' and 'after' surveys, the strength of claimed effects suggests that the reported influences must be valid to some degree: 70 per cent of respondents said that from their viewing of the series they had learned the message that women should have equal opportunities, 71 per cent that family size should be limited, 68 per cent that women should have the freedom to make their personal decisions in life, 75 per cent that family harmony should be promoted, 68 per cent that cultural diversity should be respected, and 64 per cent that women's welfare programmes should be encouraged. Of course, such stated beliefs do not always correspond to action, and we cannot tell how the programme influenced viewers' behaviour, if at all. Indeed, even these researchers note that 'Behaviour change is the bottom line in the hierarchy of media effects ... and one would expect it to occur only rarely as the result of a television soap opera' (p. 342). On the other hand, having been watched across India on such a massive scale, it is very possible that the programme made an impact on the culture, however small, in the direction of the programme's aims.

Whilst *Hum Log*, with its carefully planned role models and explicit educational epilogues, might sound quite unlike the kind of television show one might expect to see aimed at a prime-time adult or 'family' audience in Western countries, there are some not incomparable cases. The example covered by the most research literature is the US network drama series *Roots* (1977), and its sequel, *Roots: The Next Generation* (1978), based on Alex Haley's best-selling combination of fiction and biography which recorded his family's experiences in America, from their struggle as black people to gain freedom from slavery (in the first part) to their efforts to gain equality after the Civil War (in the sequel). Audiences have been estimated at 32 million households for *Roots* and 22.5 million households for the sequel (Ball-Rokeach, Grube & Rokeach, 1981, p. 58). Although they have been retrospectively criticized for diluting the power of Haley's books for a white TV audience (Tucker & Shah, 1992), the series were and still are regarded as cornerstones of quality, challenging entertainment television, forcing America to face its history of racial power abuse. In the process the series brought Maya Angelou, the celebrated feminist writer and poet who acted a supporting role, to the attention of a mass audience, and launched the careers of several black actors including LeVar Burton, later to become legendary as the blind Geordi La Forge of the USS Enterprise. The two original series were also followed by the successful sequels, *Roots – The Gift* (1988) and *Queen* (1992), and after Haley's death in 1992, viewers were delighted when two of LeVar Burton's *Roots* co-stars appeared in an episode of *Star Trek: TNG* (1993) as his parents, in a story about grief and loss.

The academic community could not have been expected to foresee the impact of the first series, of course, and so it is impressive that studies of audience reactions to the programmes were produced, even though assessed only by some rather limited single-wave surveys, mostly conducted by telephone interview around the time of broadcast (Balon, 1978; Howard, Rothbart & Sloan, 1978; Hur, 1978; Hur & Robinson, 1978). These studies generally showed that white viewers tended to be those with already more liberal values, who thought that the drama would improve racial tolerance, whilst some black viewers (who tended to have watched more episodes, and discussed it more) felt that it might increase hatred, bitterness and anger. They thought that viewers' own prejudices would affect their interpretation of the show, a suspicion which was supported by relationships found between general racial attitudes and appreciation of the programme. Nevertheless, reported reactions to the production were primarily sadness, then anger, and more than half of the population sample of 970 adults in one study (Howard *et al*) felt that their awareness of black history and culture had been enhanced, with three-quarters considering *Roots* to be relevant to modern race relations.

The media sensation and public debate sparked by the commitment of so many people to set aside several hours to watch the first series over an eight day period meant that the opportunity for more elaborate research offered by its sequel could not be ignored. Ball-Rokeach *et al.* (1981) therefore set up a 'before' and 'after' separate sample survey design to assess the impact of *Roots: The Next Generation*. Telephone interviews were conducted with samples randomly selected from telephone directories for two cities in Washington county, in the guise of audience research calls from the television station, as with the *Great American Values Test* study by the same researchers, so that respondents would not associate the questions about their viewing of a particular programme with the mail survey which they would receive separately, and apparently from a different organization, about their racial attitudes. Thus the telephone survey ascertained whether respondents had watched the programme, the number of episodes they had seen, and some basic demographic information. Meanwhile, 642 of these people had been sent a questionnaire about their personal and social values and attitudes one to five weeks before *Roots: TNG'* was aired, and 1,341 different people received it five to nine weeks after the series was shown. Demographic questions on the forms meant that the researchers could check that the same respondent in a household had completed both the telephone and mail surveys, and non-white respondents could be excluded from the analysis; this left 276 subjects in the 'before' sample, and 530 in the other. The mail survey measured attitudes toward black people using questions (amongst others, and with multiple choice responses) about the right of whites to keep black people out of their neighbourhoods should they want to, the right of black people to be assertive, predicted feelings if a son or daughter wanted to date someone of a different race, the reasons for black people's unemployment, and the use of positive racial discrimination in job appointments. In addition the survey asked about such factors as the desirability of equality as an American value, and the anticipated level of social support from friends if the respondent were to join a pro-minority civil rights organization.

The researchers found that the data showed significant effects of egalitarian values on selectivity and avoidance – that is, that those with more egalitarian or anti-racist attitudes and values would specifically select the series for viewing, whilst those with less egalitarian or more racially discriminatory views would deliberately avoid the programmes. This finding persisted even when demographic and personal factors (including sex, age, education, amount of TV viewing, income, and religious preference) were controlled, strongly suggesting that pre-existing prejudices significantly influenced the decision to watch, and so the opportunities to challenge the views of more bigoted indiciduals would have been limited. Accordingly, it was evident that egalitarianism was systematically related to the number of episodes viewed, with those most 'already egalitarian' watching most comprehensively. The main test of the series' social impact – whether the egalitarianism of viewers increased compared to that of those in the pre-broadcast sample or who didn't watch – found no evidence that this had occurred. Whilst it is of course possible that *Roots: The Next Generation* may have had more subtle positive influences, either more long or short term, than could be measured by such a study, it does however seem unlikely that the single mini-series had a direct effect.

Nevertheless, we can speculate that a more continued and less isolated appearance of such programmes might lead over time to have a cumulative influence on attitudes or beliefs. As Wander (1977) argues, *Roots* broke with the TV convention which usually shows people victimized by other individuals rather than by social institutions. Rather than taking the more common 'rotten apple' thesis with regard to social problems – that the removal of one bad cop, doctor, soldier, executive or other official will make everything alright – *Roots* deliberately 'explore[d] the institution of slavery through the eyes of the victim' (p. 66). In addition, Wander argues that the series demonstrated that the American audience can respond to challenging, 'quality' programmes shown in prime-time; media moguls would be wrong to assume that a diet of predictable and formulaic shows are all that is desired (p. 69). Moreover, 'edutainment' dramas can have a life beyond their network airings through use in the classroom. Singer & Singer (1983) note that guides for teachers and parents, independently published but supported by the US television networks, have usefully focused on series such as *Roots*, and others. By accepting rather than trying to ward off children's enjoyment of television, and in recognizing the pro-social and educational potential of such programmes for children, these guides offer a means to help increase their benefits by providing support for adult attempts to concentrate the potential influence of the programmes through positive evaluation and discussion of the issues. Indeed, in 1983 Singer & Singer wrote that:

> Publishers are becoming more interested in developing workbooks for use in language arts curricula that focus on television stories and characters in order to motivate students to develop critical thinking skills, increase vocabulary, learn

correct grammatical usage, summarize, use analogies, and in general develop expressive language (p. 204).

Whilst we can see that in the intervening time this vision has not come greatly to fruition, the authors are undoubtedly right that television entertainment could easily be embraced by teachers to help teach these basic skills – particularly since most children are going to watch television anyway. The reluctance of teachers and educationalists to appear to be recommending television over books is understandable, but the use in *part* of the curriculum of television programmes which are being watched at home to launch discussions and present skills could be a constructive way of getting more not just from school time but from the time children regularly spend viewing at home.

Social learning and morality

Despite the vigorous assertions of a minority who do not want to see any depictions of 'violence' (often bundled incongruously in with 'sex') on their screens, television programming is usually characterized by a notable emphasis on morality – at least in a basic, broad sense. (The reader who finds the invocation of 'morality' too emotive may wish to substitute, with some loss of meaning, a term such as 'social conventions'). For every character in a soap opera or situation comedy who rebels against social norms, for example, there is usually another asking if it is a good idea; for most sexual activity outside fixed relationships, a broken heart; for the typical unkindness, a consequence. With the whole range of TV behaviours, as with 'violence', critics and academics can be seen as misguided to fuss about depicted actions without looking at the associated contexts and consequences, which almost always will either ultimately reflect outcomes and results correspondent to what society generally regards as the moral domain – whether 'realistic' or not – or else, less commonly, will be part of a more sophisticated (usually single) drama where the lack of morality is implicitly acknowledged and presented as 'thought-provoking' (as often seems to be the intent of some *Screen Two* and *Film on Four* presentations), or as stylish and interesting – and therefore conspicuous (as in, for example, *Shallow Grave* (1995), or the films of Quentin Tarantino). It is therefore legitimate and indeed necessary, although not entirely common, to discuss the role of television drama (and other forms) in disseminating and debating moral norms in our culture.

Socialization is, of course, a complex process which cannot readily be broken down into constituent parts. Although Berry & Mitchell-Kernan, for example, wrote in 1982 that researchers 'are on the threshold of understanding the techniques and processes by which television functions as a socializing agent' (1982, p. 5), they were plainly at a loss to do so themselves, and the intricate, interconnected processes which must be involved have perhaps unsurprisingly remained more or less elusive. There is nevertheless interesting work to consider on children's responses to the morality of TV characters, and discussions of the interaction between television, morality and the social world.

Grant Noble (1983) contends that certain fictional programmes can be better teachers than well-intentioned documentaries. He argues that like all good learning:

... television today does guide viewers along the path of life. It gives some folklore which is representative of society's mores; it provides examples of appropriate behaviours for social settings beyond the viewer's direct experience, and it exposes viewers to people, places and events from the wider society. Such knowledge marks membership of the society (p. 102).

Of course it is this very act of bringing the outside world into the living room which upsets those who would rather be ignorant of it and 'protected' from it. Noble, however, believes that rather than intruding and corrupting, television drama is able to convey moral messages and thereby establish moral values.

To demonstrate that children acquire the values 'given off' by regular entertainment programming, Noble surveyed 240 children aged seven to eleven from two schools in Australia, about a series of nature programmes, *Australia Naturally*. Questions responded to each week on the day after transmission showed that viewers (compared to non-viewers) not only learned factual information given by the programmes, but also acquired the moral, pro-environmental values implicit within them. These messages were not always spelt out explicitly on screen, but the intended value position was verified for Noble by the TV programme's producer. Moreover, it was found that these moral lessons were learned with greater force than the straightforward factual information, and that more sophisticated messages (such as 'being careful not to upset the delicate balance of nature') actually had a greater impact than simpler ones (such as that we should not 'throw rubbish in the rivers'), which tended to be part of the children's conservation repertoire already (p. 105).

Another study, also described by Noble (1983), suggested from the self-reports of 136 teenagers in Melbourne that the popular series *Happy Days* had shown viewers how to 'be cool' (57 per cent very often, 11 per cent often), how to ask for a date (40 per cent very often, 20 per cent often) and how to get on with friends and be popular (various measures around 35 per cent very often, 26 per cent often). These self-reports are partly validated by the fact that few said that *Happy Days* had helped them do well at school work (10 per cent very often, eight per cent often). Whilst the 'how to' information which this study suggests was learned from the programme may seem oppressively prescriptive, this is of course only knowledge voluntarily picked up by the teenagers on subjects which concerned them, and Noble asserts that 'It is precisely this surrogate experience with events likely or imagined to be encountered which constitutes social learning from everyday television' (p. 111). *Happy Days* in this way fulfilled just the same function for older children as the social interaction elements of *Sesame Street* had performed – albeit rather more self-consciously – in earlier years.

One other study by Noble demonstrates the complicated relationship between children, television and individual morality, one which baldly contradicts the notion that 'good' children are those who have avoided 'bad' programmes, and vice versa. The research picked up from work by Wolfe & Fiske, who in 1949 had published their argument that normal young children used comic books as a means of successfully coping with reality, by projecting their desires which parents found unacceptable on to comic characters. The children in that study had singled out Bugs Bunny, whose ability to get away with clever tricks was much admired, and Noble found exactly the same responses emerging in some pilot research he was conducting thirty years later. To investigate further, 158 children aged between eight and eleven from two schools were asked, on separate occasions, to complete two questionnaires, one which measured the child's real-life morality, the other assessing their television exposure and identification, imitation, and perceived morality of selected TV characters. It was found that those children who were regular viewers of Bugs Bunny cartoons were those most obedient to authority in real life, and that those who wanted to be like Bugs were those who most strongly obeyed the letter (rather than the spirit) of the law. Therefore, quite contrary to the notion that such cartoons are most enthusiastically consumed by would-be delinquents, it was those who were most obedient and law-abiding who actually enjoyed Bug's 'tricky' antics best, whilst others, including those with what may be considered a maturer sense of morality, were not so interested. Meanwhile those who said they behaved like Bugs (who we should remember used cunning tricks to evade those who want to capture or kill him, but was not malevolent), showed real-life altruism to a highly significant degree. In addition, analysis of the full survey suggested that characters such as J.R. of *Dallas* (1978–91) were most regularly watched by viewers who were non-selfish, but who recognized J.R. as selfish; this association remained strong even when other factors such as age, sex and socio-economic status were controlled. It would therefore appear that – again quite contrary to the claims of some critics – viewers routinely engage in 'negative identification', taking such characters as models of how not to behave, and perhaps strengthening their moral self-identity through pride that they are *not* like certain disagreeable TV characters. Noble concludes that, 'Television characters thus seem to be critically observed for contiguity between them and the child's life space, rather than imitated' (1983, p. 121). Whilst it is difficult to assess the veracity of the viewers' responses and identifications indicated by this research – particularly since the use of questionnaires is at best a shallow method – such studies show that questions about moral learning from television are far from settled.

Having to some extent established that television can contribute to social learning, and that children are able to apply basic moral standards to television characters and so have their own morality, if anything, augmented rather than corrupted by television, it is worthwhile to look at some of the small body of work on the morality of television content.

The question of how television has grown to have such prominence in Western (particularly American) cultural life, and how such a vast audience manages to find meaning in programmes 'despite their artistic shortcomings', is the concern of Victor Lidz (1984). His answer is that television programmes 'participate deeply in American *moral* culture' (p. 267, emphasis in original), sustaining a secular moral framework which underlies all programmes, regardless of whether they are set in a family home, the newsroom, the Old West or outer space. The heroes of prime-time dramas, of course, are commonly highly committed to the ideals of justice and hard work, even to extremes such as Dr Sam Beckett in *Quantum Leap*, who was not only sentenced to a lifetime of 'putting right what once went wrong', but actually had this spelled out for him in a breathy voiceover on the titles each week. Lidz's contention is that 'it has been television's standing as an agent of conventional moralism that has made it so meaningful within the routines of daily life as well as integrative of popular social experience as a whole' (p. 288). The assertion that morality is at the very heart of television entertainment, whilst absolutely at odds with those who argue that morality is not to be found there at all, is certainly closer to the often-expressed claims of programme-makers themselves, and is clearly better able to explain the popularity of most TV dramas, sit-coms and soaps.

Newcomb & Hirsch (1984) take a slightly different view of television's role, describing it as a 'cultural forum' in which issues of the day are discussed. They argue that 'conflicting viewpoints of social issues are, in fact, the elements that structure most television programmes' (p. 65). Television should be studied as cultural ritual, they argue, with an emphasis on process rather than product: programmes produce a multiplicity of meanings, and views from the most traditional or repressive to those which are subversive or empancipatory are discussed and examined on screen. Television programming, when taken altogether, cannot be seen to offer any coherent conclusions or solutions to social issues, and that does not matter; instead of coherence there is confusion and contradiction, which means that television is more of a diverse seminar – within certain limits – than a pedagogic lecture.

The point, for Newcomb & Hirsch, is that 'in popular culture generally, in television specifically, the raising of questions is as important as the answering of them' (p. 63). The introduction and discussion of social issues, particularly topical or contemporary ones, and even within the limits which obviously exist in television, is at least just as important as their screened conclusion, whether traditional and normative or not. Television content in its entirety is seen to constitute a varied symposium on modern life; even banal programmes with no obvious 'argument' will contain submerged assumptions about values and lifestyle. Of course all programming can be received in a multiplicity of ways by the viewers, and it is this very richness and diversity which the cultural forum model embraces – although as Fiske (1984) notes, whatever one may say about audiences bringing their own interpretations, the fundamental morality of much TV drama is closed and fixed in such a way that the 'preferred reading' can hardly be avoided. The model recognizes that television is sufficiently complex that it can attract a diverse audience, and that its influence cannot be reduced to any simple deductions about straightforward 'effects'. Indeed, the cultural forum model is particularly useful precisely because it suggests that television has an influence in a way which absolutely cannot be quantified in the simplistic terms of 'effects' researchers, although it is the continual translation and discussion of moral and social issues in television entertainment which would be most likely to have an impact on a growing child.

More complexities of 'pro-social' television

The complexity of television – whether intentionally 'pro-social' or not – is illustrated in this section by two brief examples of work where attempts to capture the pro-social aspect of programmes have not met with success. The first is provided by Barbara Lee (1988), who reports the findings of a content analysis which examined four weeks of network prime-time television entertainment programmes, spread across the 1985–1986 season. The sophisticated definition of 'pro-social' behaviour used included altruistic actions (from heroic acts to sharing, cooperation and helping), socially approved affective behaviour (showing affection, empathy, sympathy or remorse), and control over negative inclinations of oneself or others (including controlling aggression, use of reasoning, and resisting temptation). This showed that 97 per cent of the programmes included at least one pro-social incident.[*] More interestingly, the analysis went beyond individual scenes and looked at each whole programme for an overall pro-social theme or moral. About a quarter (60 of the 235 analysed) were judged to have such pro-social themes, although Lee admits that the coding of themes would only have recorded quite conspicuous 'morals', and so have been likely to under-count other general acts of goodness, and would not have taken account of the underlying values of programmes. Thus, Lee notes, 'for example, several episodes of *The Cosby Show*, even though they generally promoted positive family relations, did not qualify as having a specific pro-social theme' (1988, p. 244). However, this approach is a significant improvement on the usual use of content analysis, which is generally to count incidents of violence or some other act without any reference to its context or meaning.

Lee sought to take this method further, attempting to identify the implicit values of programmes by asking coders to select the three instrumental values (means) and three terminal values (end goals) that guided main characters and were most favoured in the programme. This failed because the coders were unable to agree about these values to an acceptable level of reliability. This is unfortunate, since the analysis was an unusual and interesting attempt to get at the meanings of whole programmes, instead of individual scenes taken in abstraction; however, it is perhaps inevitable that the rather simple and unreflexive method of content analysis would be unable to cope with the full complexity of programmes. However, this study does illustrate the important point that the treatment of television programmes in many of the studies discussed in this review is far too simplistic: the very fact that the research can be sorted into studies of 'violence' (the 'bad' programmes) and 'pro-social' content (the 'good' programmes) clearly reflects this. Lee shows that the pro-social possibilities of television, when conceived in more sophisticated terms than in most of the studies, become very difficult to explore with traditional 'scientific' methodologies such as formal content analysis: television content is simply too complex to be understood in this manner.

Harold Fairchild (1988) provides us with the second example, a curious case of an academic who sought to make his own 'pro-social' television series. However, Fairchild was only able to get one 30-minute pilot programme made: *Star Crusaders*, a live-action science fiction drama with a multi-ethnic group of five heroes (although oddly, considering the author's expressed anti-sexist as well as anti-racist intentions, there is only one woman

---

[*] This may have been even higher if the analysis had covered only drama and fictional television programmes, but it should be noted that the sample of entertainment programmes used would include game shows, quizzes, variety shows, etc.

in the group, and the leader is male). The proposed series, *Star Crusaders: An Animated Space Adventure*, sounds like a languid imitation of *Star Trek: The Next Generation* (1987–1994), which was already being shown and highly popular. The author describes what his series 'would' be like, and tells us about a massive and complex study which 'should' be done to research its impact. However, Fairchild has not succeeded in transforming this dream into reality. It does not seem surprising that television producers have not taken up his idea, which begins with its good intentions and then sketches in some characters to try to convey them. The lesson of a successful series like *Star Trek: TNG* is that moral and philosophical concerns can be introduced and illustrated, but only when founded around properly developed characters who must be central to any dramatic conflicts of ethics or conscience. To have good intentions alone does not seem to be enough, as is illustrated by Stipp's (1993) analysis of Saturday morning American network programming over 20 years, 'which shows that many attempts to expose children to "better" programs were frustrated by children's lack of interest in watching them' (1993, p. 299).[*]

Finally, it is disappointing to note that very few of the studies reviewed in the earlier parts of this chapter looked for positive effects of any programme which was not made for explicitly and self-consciously 'pro-social' purposes. Johnston & Ettema (1986) write that, 'Whether effects are intended or not, television that models socially valued behaviors, responses, attitudes, or beliefs is pro-social television'. However, thus far very few researchers have sought to quantify the effects of the regular daily diet of programmes where positive effects are not the primary intention of the programme, and so the possible effects of the thousands of programmes which are not deliberately made as 'pro-social television', but which nonetheless feature good, moral heroes, or friends and families caring for each other, or any other ruminations about how best to go about life, have been generally ignored by effects researchers. It might be comforting to think that this is because they have accepted the arguments of Noble (1983) and Newcomb & Hirsch (1984) that television is too sophisticated and complex an influence on culture and consciousness to be assessed by such simplistic means. However, it seems that if anything these writers have been ignored and marginalized, and the absence of empiricists seeking to quantify television's positive effect is more likely due only to the fact that few of them appear to believe such an outcome to be possible.

---

[*] This is based on a study by Stipp, Hill-Scott & Dorr (1987). The main exception is *Sesame Street*, which consistently has achieved high ratings among two to five year olds (Stipp, 1993, p. 298).

65

6 Campaigns and advertising

Public information campaigns

The studies which have been discussed in previous chapters generally concerned effects which are either unintended, or which (in a smaller number of cases) are the hoped-for pro-social offshoots of particular programmes, usually for children. Running parallel to this tradition of research has been another which involves the evaluation of planned campaigns which seek to affect the consciousness of the public in a particular way – usually to influence behaviours which pertain to their health or safety. Many of these studies have been developed by those working in the health education field, and have only a small apparent interaction with the effects studies produced by communications researchers. Nevertheless, the pattern of the evolution of effects studies is mirrored in the development of campaign studies. As will be seen in the first section below, the research again began in an initial frenzy about possible large effects, to be replaced by a view that the potential effects were much more limited, followed by a renewed (albeit more cautious) belief that certain effects are possible.

Today, there are a number of campaigns which appear to have had some degree of effect; however, as Dervin (1989) notes, 'practitioners and academics alike acknowledge that public communication campaigns are effective only at great cost and within very definite constraints' (p. 67). Even in situations which are most conducive to the message being conveyed, the success of a campaign is measured in small degrees of change. In addition, there is not a consensus about which groups a campaign should be aimed at; whilst many campaign planners seek to address as many members of their target population as possible, the executive director of a public interest advertising agency told Alcalay & Taplin (1989) that the real focus of their campaigns was 'the two or three per cent of that audience who are opinion leaders and change agents, the influential and attentive public' (p. 114). However, all of the campaigns described in this section were aimed directly at the target population.

The development of campaign studies

Fears that society is or will become a 'mass society' with a corresponding 'mass culture' can be traced back as far as the eighteenth century (Hall, 1982). These views came to seem particularly relevant with the spread of mass communications and the apparently extreme effect of fascist propaganda in the early part of this century. The fears about the displacement and 'debasement' of high culture did not amount to more than the predictable anxiety of the traditionalists and upper classes; however, that mass communications could seemingly unite people behind causes which we might otherwise expect them to find reprehensible brought much force to these concerns. We can therefore understand the origins of the simultaneous hopes and fears for the new mediums of film and, later, television: the panic about possible effects of television on violence and crime was matched by an optimism that it might be a force for good, by conveying persuasive 'positive' messages to a receptive and malleable public. Early campaign studies, like the experimental effects studies which were to follow, were firmly rooted in the (often American) belief in positivistic social science, which sought 'scientific' predictions and conclusions about the social world. Cause and effect were often conceived oversimplistically; political campaign studies, for example, took voting patterns as their results, and saw these as the product of campaign influences. Political campaigns and subsequent election results were viewed in the same way as advertising and product sales, with all other potential contributory factors not merely excluded but rather wholly overlooked. Thus all of the other possible social influences, decisions and prejudices which led to each vote were ignored, as was the fact that many people would have known who they would vote for before, and quite regardless of, any campaigns. The two-step flow model (Katz & Lazarsfeld, 1955) introduced the notion that messages could be mediated and conveyed through social interaction between those who first receive and are affected by information – opinion leaders – and others whom they communicate with. Whilst this model went some way to breaking apart the notions of the audience as unconnected individuals, and media messages as guided information-missiles with an objective consistency of meaning and power, it still left other social factors out of the picture, and in any case was left aside by many behaviourists who seemed to favour only models which could be drawn using a single arrow.

As Hall (1982) notes of this period, 'Larger historical shifts, questions of political process and formation before and beyond the ballot-box, issues of social and political power, of social structure and economic relations, were simply absent, not by chance, but because they were *theoretically outside the frame of reference*' (p. 59, emphasis in original). The decontextualized pluralism implicit in this model of media and society – that any number of views (within a certain range) might develop and be popular, if only their proponents could market them properly – gradually came to seem particularly naive, however, and certainly was not able to survive the more socially conscious counter-cultural 'revolutions' and movements of the late 1960s.

Meanwhile, the findings of more carefully designed research had begun to replace the concerns propagated by the simplistic studies and apprehensive speculation, and communications researchers began to believe that the original hopes and fears of strong direct effects of mass media were unfounded (Rice & Atkin, 1989). From the late 1940s to the early 1970s a 'minimal effects' paradigm came to be dominant – at least amongst those who had hoped to be able to use the mass media to mount large-scale pro-social campaigns.

The study by Star & Hughes (1950) typifies the emerging findings which helped to establish this mood.

Star & Hughes describe a six-month 'crusade' to make the population of Cincinnati conscious of the United Nations, and aware of its aims and objectives. This information campaign was accompanied by a 'before' and 'after' survey, conducted by the American National Opinion Research Centre, to determine its success. The campaign itself was massive, with every effort made to meet the objective of reaching every adult among the 1,155,700 residents of central Cincinnati through numerous radio spots, hundreds of documentary films, intensified newspaper coverage, and exhibition of the campaign slogan, '*Peace Begins with the United Nations – the United Nations Begins with You*', in every conceivable place and form. Every school child was given literature about the United Nations to take home, and teachers were specially trained to keep the subject constantly before their pupils; churches and church schools preached the message to their followers, and 2,800 clubs were addressed by speakers supplied by a dedicated bureau. 59,600 pieces of literature were distributed in all, and there can be little doubt that this campaign was vigorously promoted on an enormous scale.

Before the campaign, in September 1947, a representative sample of 745 adults were interviewed, as were a different representative sample of 758 six months later, in March 1948. As many of the first group as could be contacted again were also reinterviewed at this time (592 respondents). There was also an 'approximate control' in that some of the questions were also asked of the national samples which were periodically surveyed by the National Opinion Research Centre. The surveys were designed to identify changes in interest, information and opinion about world affairs in general and the United Nations in particular.

The findings showed an apparent increase in interest in international affairs, but the development of the 'cold war' with Russia in the intervening time was alone found to account for this difference, and so the increased interest could not be attributed to the campaign. When asked what could be done to make war less likely, only three per cent of the 1948 sample proposed action by the United Nations – even less than the six per cent who had suggested it the previous year, *before* the campaign. Other solutions, such as 'Turn to God' (11 per cent before and after), were considerably more popular. Opinions about the United Nations seemed similarly unaffected: the organization was praised and blamed for the same things, and in virtually identical proportions, both before and after the campaign, whilst the proportion of 'don't knows' remained high throughout. For example, 44 per cent before and 41 per cent after the campaign were unable to name one good thing the United Nations had done – and this does not include the 12 to 14 per cent who expressly stated the opinion that the UN had not done *anything* good so far.

Most important of all should be the findings on changes in known information, since this was the main purpose of the campaign. By 'even the most liberal interpretation of replies' (p. 392), 30 per cent had to be classified as having no idea as to the main purpose of the United Nations before the campaign, and 28 per cent were the same after. Of the rest of the population, who 'knew something' about the purposes of the UN, their scores for more precise identification of the organization's aims remained remarkably constant over the two surveys, the only notable changes being five per cent increases (within the not wholly ignorant subgroup) in knowledge of the UN's mission to improve health conditions and equal rights across the world. Star & Hughes admit that 'The inescapable conclusion is that in the six months the local level of information did not alter very much' (p. 393). As mentioned above, Cincinnati was metaphorically carpet-bombed with masses of information about the United Nations, and a more extensive campaign would be difficult to imagine or, indeed, finance. Nevertheless, the main campaign slogan was not recalled by 51 per cent of the people, whilst an encounter with newspaper and radio items about the UN were recalled by only 50 and 53 per cent of the population respectively. Those who had gained the most information and interest from the campaign were found to be those who had been informed and interested to some degree already, and tended to be younger, better educated, and male. 'The conclusion is that the people reached by the campaign were those in least need of it and that the people missed by it were the audience the plan hoped to gain' (p. 397). Whilst the effects on those who were interested cannot be dismissed – those people may have gone on to be keen supporters of the United Nations, and acted as 'opinion leaders' to rally further support, for example – it does seem to be the case that the campaign, despite aiming its efforts elsewhere, was only able to catch the involved attention of those who were already interested. Whilst this study was able to contribute the worthwhile insight that campaigns would somehow have to present information as 'functional' or directly relevant to the targeted individuals' lives and concerns, its more straightforward effect was to set a tone of pessimism for prospective campaign planners which would last for well over a decade.

However, as the 1960s and 1970s progressed, a carefully qualified optimism began to be accepted, that the media could be used to influence people within carefully planned and limited parameters (Mendelsohn, 1973), perhaps rather indirectly by working through a complimentary mix of particular mediated and interpersonal channels, and cumulatively through repeated exposure to particular kinds of messages (Rice & Atkin, 1989; Alcalay & Taplin, 1989). It is these generally more recent studies which will be the focus of the rest of this chapter.

It can be noted that these newer campaigns and associated studies are generally closely grouped around themes of personal health and safety, as these are the issues which researchers have concluded are most likely to be (at least measurably) affected by carefully designed campaigns. The interest in 'propaganda' *per se* has always primarily centred around its rather unique use in the World Wars, and research into new propaganda (in the narrow definition which does not include 'public service' campaigns or the more general output of politicians and their 'information' offices) was virtually given up by the 1960s (Jowett, 1987). Indeed, the consensus today seems to be that the American propaganda effort in World War I was much more important to the development of the film industry than it ever was to the war effort (*ibid*, p. 110). Evaluation studies of political campaigns also quickly dwindled once it was realized that voting results could not be taken as the direct consequence of the relevant campaigns, since the effects of such campaigns are otherwise rather difficult to assess. As Meadow (1989, p. 257) notes, political candidates are unlikely to spend their budgets on campaign evaluation when in their terms there is only one poll which really counts; are 'reluctant not to try everything' in terms of campaign method and technique; and would not want to withhold their campaign from a control group of voters for understandable reasons. In addition, it would be very difficult to determine the independent contributions of each campaign source – not to mention the effects of negative campaigning by other candidates – and so an evaluation of more specific use than the simple election would be rather hard to devise. It is for reasons such as this that the most rigorous and successful campaign evaluations have been on personal issues which usually have an end-product behaviour (or lack of, where mortality rates are concerned) which can be readily measured.

Heart disease and anti-smoking campaigns

Campaigns seeking to reduce the prevalence of cardiovascular disease (fatal and non-fatal heart attacks and strokes) and cigarette smoking are those most frequently assessed by rigorous evaluative research, and tend to be amongst the best designed and executed, in part because large amounts of government funding are on occasion given over to such campaigns in a bid to improve a nation's standard of health. As will be seen, these campaign studies tend to find that massive campaigns are capable of producing a degree of change, particularly if the programme involves some direct, interpersonal contact, although there are exceptions and variations to this rule. In this section we will consider two sets of highly regarded large-scale campaign projects, the Stanford programmes in the USA and a set of comparable programmes in Finland, and then a selection of other smaller-scale campaigns in this area.

Researchers at Stanford University ran the Stanford Three Community Study (TCS) from 1971 to 1975, followed by the more ambitious Five Cities Project (FCP) from 1978 to 1991. The TCS sought to measure the effect of a large-scale 'intervention' on the knowledge, attitudes and risk-related behaviours of the populations of two communities compared to the changes in a matched, untreated control community (Flora, Maccoby & Farquhar, 1989). One of the two experimental towns was treated with a campaign which used the mass media alone, whilst in the other this campaign was supplemented with face-to-face skills training, support and incentives which were given to a randomly selected sample of high-risk participants and their partners.

The media campaign involved television and radio spots, newspaper coverage, and literature including health booklets and cookery books. A representative sample of adults aged between 35 and 59 in each town was surveyed, and then the media campaign began two months later, running for nine months. A second survey was taken, and then the campaign ran for a further nine months at a reduced level. A year later, a final survey was conducted to measure how the effects of the previous two years had been maintained.

The findings showed a general improvement for most variables in both treatment towns compared to the control community (or, more accurately, 'reference' community, since on a project of this scale obviously not all variables can be controlled). The results for the individuals for whom the media campaign had been supported with interpersonal contact were generally stronger than those for the media-only subjects. Indeed, there was 'considerable success' when the mass media was supplemented by intensive instruction, although the media campaign alone was able to effect significant changes in almost all of the knowledge measures (pp. 237–238). The individuals who had received additional instruction showed knowledge gains twice those of the media-only subjects, however. It was found that the media-only campaign was able to bring about small but significant changes in behaviour which depended to a greater degree only on increased knowledge, such as improved eating habits, but other behavioural changes such as smoking cessation required 'a considerable amount of skills training, self-monitoring and feedback' (p. 239).

Encouraged by the relative success of the TCS project, the team of investigators went on to create the Stanford Five City Multifactor Risk Reduction Project. This project, involving a six-year campaign within a 13-year total surveillance period, improved on the previous study not only in its greater scale but also by extending the age range surveyed to all those between 12 and 74 years; having an educational programme maintained throughout; employing an extensive community mobilization component; and by monitoring cardio-vascular disease related morbidity and mortality (heart attacks and strokes) in addition to risk factors. Two of the five communities received the campaign; two others served as controls for possible effects of the survey administration and disease monitoring; and one was a monitoring control only. The communities were in Northern California, and were roughly matched; subjects were randomly selected from the 92,000 eligible in the treatment cities and 141,000 in the reference cities. Data was collected using four cross-sectional surveys of the population, and four surveys of an unchanging panel of individuals, spread over six years. The campaign itself was substantially more extensive than in the TCS and involved both spots and special programmes on television and radio, considerable newspaper coverage, vast quantities of informational literature, and mass mailings. In the FCP the media campaign was not supplied to any group who did not also receive other more interpersonal treatments; these included more than 800 direct education sessions, promotions in workplaces, relevant curricula in schools, the participation of restaurants and grocery stores in specially designed healthy food programmes, and contests and lotteries designed to induce changes in smoking, exercise, nutrition and weight control (Flora, Maccoby & Farquhar, 1989, pp. 247–248).

The ultimate findings of this programme, which of course were only to emerge in the 1990s, are astonishing – but not for the anticipated reasons. The effects of the enormous and very comprehensive campaign seem to have been marginal at best, and in several aspects were non-existent.

Nutritional knowledge tended to increase over time in all cities (treatment *and* reference) and for both sexes, although the increase was significantly greater for women in the campaign cities (Fortmann, Taylor, Flora & Winkleby, 1993). Cholesterol levels tended to decline across the board, and there was no evidence of any difference in the rate of decline between treatment and reference cities. Amongst the cohort sample, there was no evidence of the campaign making a difference to either nutritional knowledge or choles- terol levels. An analysis for possible effects on those particular individuals who were at a higher risk also found no significant treatment effect.

Changes in body mass were also measured, but again significant differences between the treatment and reference cities were few (Taylor, Fortmann, Flora, *et al*, 1991). The average body mass index for both experimental and reference cities rose over time, although the increase was always less in the treatment cities. However, significant differences only occurred in comparisons of the first and last samples for the overall group, and for the women aged 25 to 34 group. Whilst the 'overall' result sounds promising, it is not reflected in the more precise comparisons of the various sex and age groupings, and a regression analysis of all subjects combined found no significant differences between the treatment and reference groups. The cohort sample similarly showed no significant overall dif- ferences. The independent samples suggest that although there was no relative improve- ment in their behaviour concerning physical exercise or weighing themselves, people in the treatment cities had a greater intention to lose weight, and dined at fast-food restaurants significantly less than their reference city equivalents. However, these differences do not appear in the cohort sample results. The authors appear disappointed at the lack of changes in the cohort sample, which is theoretically best equipped to detect treatment effects, and note that almost all of the changes suggested by the independent samples are due to a large apparent effect in one treatment city and within one time period.

Changes in cigarette smoking prevalence were also studied (Fortmann, Taylor, Flora & Jatulis, 1993). Smoking cessation had been encouraged through group programmes, self-help kits, contests, events, and school-based prevention activities, as well as via a television series and several public service announcements on both television and radio. In this case, there were significant results for the cohort sample, where smoking decreased at a greater rate in the treatment than in the reference cities, but not in the independent samples, where smoking decreased at a similar rate in both treatment and reference cities. However, since ex-smokers were asked when they quit, we can find from the final cross-sectional survey that over 22 per cent of people who were smokers at the start of the campaign had quit in the treatment cities, compared with under 18 per cent in the reference cities over the same period. Much more impressive is the finding that in the cohort group, almost 40 per cent of those initially smoking quit in the treatment city, compared to 23 per cent of reference city smokers.

Taken together, then, these Five Cities Project findings are surprisingly slight. The researchers found 'little evidence of a differential trend between treatment and control cities for nutritional behaviour, diet, or plasma cholesterol ...[;] we were unable to find any significant, lasting, nutritional effects of the Five-City Project' (Fortmann, Taylor, Flora & Winkleby, 1993, p. 1051). The findings for effects on body mass were partial, and small at best, whilst the smoking cessation findings were mixed but suggested that the campaign had made some effect. It is also very important to note that this campaign consisted of many parts, only one of which involved the mass media, which the previous study (and others discussed below) have shown to make a limited contribution to behavioural change, compared to the other more effective interpersonal methods. Therefore even the rather limited effects found here cannot be read directly as effects of the media; rather, the lesson is that even with these additional persuasive supports, the campaign was only able to achieve its aims to a small degree.

The North Karelia Project was a broadly similar, ten-year programme to reduce coronary heart disease in Finland, where the heart disease mortality rate for males in 1975 was the highest in the world (Puska *et al*, 1985). North Karelia is a county in eastern Finland where rates were particularly high. The study, like the Stanford studies, was 'quasi-experimental', comparing the 180,000 population of North Karelia with a similar reference community of 250,000, who were not exposed to the campaign.

The project cost over 1.75 million US dollars and involved an immense campaign, again only part of which was directed through the mass media. The media component involved radio, newspapers, health education literature, and support for various community meetings and campaigns; television health campaign programmes were also running nationally at the time (see below), but would of course be available to both treatment and reference groups in this regional study. The campaign also involved training for doctors, nurses, teachers, social workers and others; reorganization of the health services, with an improvement of relevant preventive activities; community organization activities involving a large number of voluntary organizations, the food industry and grocery stores; and the development of various information systems to monitor progress (Puska *et al*, 1985, pp. 166–167). Evaluation was conducted through independent, cross-section samples taken in 1972, 1977 and 1982, in which random samples of 6.6 per cent of the populations (of both treatment and reference counties) aged between 25 and 64 completed a questionnaire and their height, weight, blood pressure and cholesterol level. In addition, mortality data was collected.

The findings here were more impressive than those for the Stanford Five Cities Project. Cigarette smoking for North Karelian men declined by 34 per cent between 1972 and 1982, although the (overall much lower) rate of women's smoking increased slightly. However, the net change (change in the treatment area minus the change in the reference area) when the treatment and reference areas are compared were a highly significant 28 per cent reduction for men and 14 per cent for women. The self-reported smoking data was verified by reference to the thiocyanate levels in the 1982 blood samples, which correlated satisfactorily with the self-reports.

Dietary changes in line with the campaign objectives, particularly concerning fat intake, were found to have taken place. Cholesterol levels declined in both areas, but significantly more so (three per cent) for men in the treatment county. The reductions in the blood pressure of North Karelians were also significantly greater than those in the reference area.

Mortality due to coronary heart disease decreased significantly in North Karelia when compared to that for the rest of Finland, particularly for men (who suffer around five times more such deaths than women); the annual decrease between 1969 and 1979 in North

Karelia (2.2 per cent) was twice the figure for the rest of Finland (1.1 per cent). Incidence of angina pectoris among men aged 50 to 59 shot down from 10.4 per cent in 1972 to 5.6 per cent in 1982, whilst in the reference area it was unchanged (6.1 per cent to 6.2 per cent). The mean self-reported days of illness among North Karelian men was cut from 32 in 1972 to 25 in 1977, compared to a smaller decline from 27 to 24 days for reference area males. Similar but smaller decreases occurred for women.

In all, the apparent effects of the campaign were substantial, particularly for men, who were at highest risk: reductions in the risk factor of 36 per cent for smoking, 11 per cent for cholesterol concentration and five per cent for diastolic blood pressure. Such changes are particularly impressive since it is generally found that lifestyle behaviours are steadfastly difficult to alter even when the arguments in their favour are strong. Importantly, however, it should again be remembered that these changes were due to a multi-faceted campaign which involved reorganization of the area's health provision, as well as improvements in food products available and in training for many influential individuals. We cannot know the extent of the media's impact, but the structural changes as well as interpersonal persuasion available in the region are likely to have been crucial, and the fact that measures of knowledge about risk factors and attitudes towards health hardly changed at all (p. 177) suggest that the media's contribution was smaller rather than greater.

As mentioned above, however, there were also national television-led health projects being conducted at the same time in Finland, where the significance of the media element should be less in question. Firstly, there was a series of seven 45-minute smoking cessation programmes shown on Finnish evening TV over four weeks in February and March 1978 (Puska *et al*, 1979). Much hype preceded the series, including numerous articles about it in the press and substantial on-screen advertising in the two weeks prior to its launch. Smokers were strongly encouraged to follow the course in organized groups, and print resources were made available to group leaders. The programmes involved a group of ten smokers in the studio, who discussed their experiences and together sought to quit smoking. The first six programmes were recorded six months before transmission, but this fact was only revealed just before the final programme, giving viewers the opportunity to see the half-year experience of the group. The effect of the campaign programmes was measured using 'before' and 'after' mail surveys, with a representative random sample of approximately 2,550 people aged 15–64 being successfully polled each time. This sample was supplemented by a further 978 drawn from North Karelia, to assess the effects of the programme when supported by the increased health promotion activity taking place in that county. When the series was repeated a year later, a further 5,000 were polled nationally; this survey also gave one-year follow-up data on the original viewers. Also collected were the reports from self-help group leaders in North Karelia and a comparable reference county, and additional data on samples of middle-aged male smokers in these two counties.

The surveys found that 45 per cent of the population saw at least one programme, with seven per cent watching four or more. A respectable 2.2 per cent of the whole population reported having given up smoking with the programme, and 0.8 per cent were still non-smokers one year later. The repeat of the series had an even greater effect, with 3.9 per cent of all smokers (some 40,000 people) giving up with the programme. Although one year follow-up data on these 1979 viewers is not available, if long-term results matched those for the original showing then the programme would have produced 10,000–20,000 new ex-smokers. Therefore although the percentage changes may appear small, in a national population they represent significant numbers of people. The additional support available to North Karelians would appear to have effectively doubled the impact of the programmes in that county. Predictably, those who followed the programme in self-help groups were much more successful at giving up smoking, with 41 per cent stopping entirely, and the rest reducing their quantity dramatically; the very fact that they chose to join such a group before the television series began shows that a certain motivation was already there, and the group support would obviously have been of considerable help.

In the spring of 1980 the same team sought to consolidate their success with a new TV campaign series aimed at promoting all-round better health, with particular emphasis on the causes of cardiovascular and other chronic diseases – diet, physical inactivity, obesity, high blood cholesterol level, high blood pressure and, again, smoking (Puska *et al*, 1981). The series of nine 30-minute programmes was shown on Finnish TV every other week from February to June, and again preceded by coverage in the press and on-screen advertising. In addition, the series was accompanied by widely distributed printed guides and reference materials. The researchers sought to evaluate the effects with a mail survey of a random national population sample of ages 15 to 64, receiving 4,700 responses. In addition an extra sample of 1,500 in south-west Finland were polled, and 1000 in North Karelia. These surveys was conducted in April and May, towards the end of the course of programmes, and required viewers to self-report on its effects. Whilst this method is not ideal, at least the effects asked about – smoking cessation, weight loss, dietary changes – were of a visible, unambiguous nature which individuals could be expected to report with relative accuracy. In addition, claims to have stopped smoking were verified where possible by telephone interview or letter.

Significant findings were that 6.6 per cent of women and 3.4 per cent of men in the whole population reported reducing fat consumption and increasing their vegetable intake, and 5.2 per cent of women and 2.8 per cent of men reduced their salt consumption. A non-significant 2.2 per cent of women and 1.1 per cent of men reported losing weight with the aid of the programme. The telephone verification of smoking cessation claims found a degree of over-reporting, mainly by those who had given up with the earlier TV programme in 1978–9; the real effect of the 1980 programmes was estimated at 0.5 per cent of all smokers quitting smoking and maintaining this for at least six months. Personal interviews verified the weight loss claims, and found that an average of 4.5 kg had been lost by six months after the start of the programme. Again, the effects in North Karelia, where a much wider campaign was in progress, were almost double for the dietary changes, although only somewhat larger for smoking cessation, and roughly similar for weight loss. Once again, considering that the audience size was large for Finland (500,000–1,000,000 viewers), the effects as percentages of the population are small, but when considered in numbers of people – such as that 60,000 people lost significant weight with the aid of the television programme – the apparent effect becomes quite impressive.

The effect of a large-scale anti-smoking campaign in Sydney, Australia can be traced more readily back to the media since it depended primarily on television commercials. This television campaign (Pierce, Dwyer, *et al*, 1986; Dwyer, Pierce, *et al*, 1986) drew attention to the additional supports, such as information and treatment services, which were available. Of course, whilst such other sources of persuasion can be frustrating to the researcher who wishes to assess the impact of media alone, these other supports are extremely helpful to the aims of the health campaign; it is a recognition of the importance of supplementing a media campaign with print resources and support activities which makes more recent campaign planners reluctant to mount a campaign without them. Here, the 'Quit – For Life' campaign (with a budget of 620,000 Australian dollars) involved three commercials which were aired on prime time television in 1983. These spots all ended with an exhortation to telephone the specially-established 'Quit Line', which gave recorded information about the 'Quit Centre' established at Sydney Hospital, and about the 'Quit Kits' (a booklet and audio cassette) created to help would-be non-smokers.

Surveys of approximately 750 randomly-selected people in Sydney and 200 in the untreated reference city, Melbourne, were conducted in each month of the campaign, June to November (Pierce, Dwyer, *et al*, 1986). These showed that the TV commercials had an excellent reach, with the most often broadcast spot being recalled by 87 per cent of smokers. In the first three months of the campaign over 50,000 calls were made to the 'Quit Line', a massive increase on the 8,600 which had been expected based on previous call rates to similar lines; and an impressive 3,000 people joined stop-smoking classes, compared to about 500 the previous year. In addition, 19,200 'Quit Kits' were sold (compared to 'no significant sales' of similar materials to the public in the previous year). To evaluate effects, 'before' and 'after' surveys were conducted in Sydney, and in the rest of Australia for comparison (Dwyer, Pierce, *et al*, 1986). In May 1983, approximately 4,000 randomly selected people aged 14 and over in Sydney, and 5,100 in the rest of Australia were interviewed, and then a separate sample of 4,000 in Sydney and 4,300 elsewhere in Australia was surveyed a year later, in May 1984. In addition, a cohort of 570 subjects from Sydney and 364 from the comparable city of Melbourne who had responded to the 1983 'before' survey were successfully followed up a year later.

An overall decrease in smoking of 2.8 per cent was found in Sydney, compared to a decrease of 1.6 per cent in the rest of Australia; this difference was not statistically significant. Nor were there substantially different or significant effects in subgroups based on age, sex, education, income or other factors. Number of cigarettes smoked per day also changed in the direction aimed for by the campaign, but to a non-significant degree. The cohort study, however, found a significant positive campaign effect in Sydney, where smoking prevalence decreased by 3.4 per cent compared to a slight increase in Melbourne. It is concluded that in all the campaign had a significant 2.8 per cent effect – that is, it led to an additional 2.8 per cent reduction over the general Australian smoking cessation trend at the time, or 83,000 fewer Sydney smokers in 1984 than in the previous year.

In all, the studies of anti-smoking campaigns seem to consistently find effects which do not represent major behavioural revolutions but which nevertheless seem to help a significant minority to stop smoking each time. Further evidence is provided by a study in Houston (McAlister, Ramirez, Galavotti & Gallion, 1989), which found that television and newspaper campaigns in 1985 and 1986, when supplemented by training for retailers and teachers and a mass of printed materials intended to support community-based encouragement of smoking cessation, led 10 per cent of smoking viewers to quit for at least three months. The authors note that such campaigns are therefore easily 'cost effective', since smoking cessation typically increases life expectancy for one or two years and saves medical costs of $1,000 US on average.

A comprehensive review of anti-smoking campaigns by Flay (1987) synthesized the findings of 14 different mass media campaigns and programmes which sought to change knowledge and attitudes through the provision of information and motivation, and a further 17 which were more explicitly designed to promote smoking cessation. With the exception of high quality community-based studies such as the Stanford and North Karelia campaigns discussed above, Flay notes that 'Most of the evaluations reviewed here [are] very simple and of "pre-scientific" designs' (p. 115), with about half of the cessation promotions being assessed simply through a single survey of the targeted group after the campaign. Because of this it is preferable that we attend to Flay's compiled findings rather than the results of individual studies. Most of the information campaigns produced significant changes in the targeted knowledge areas, but all of the studies supported the conclusion that only extensive national campaigns were able to produce 'convincing behavioural changes' (p. 111). Novelty, widespread dissemination, high saturation, and persistence were all crucial for national public service advertising campaigns to have any demonstrable effect. In addition, once again, anything involving or likely to produce interpersonal interactions favourable to the campaign aims substantially improved the chances of success. Overall, however, it was clear that the attraction or addiction to smoking had a much firmer grip on most smokers than the persuasive messages supplied by the campaigns even when supported by potentially frightening medical research.

In their overview of anti-smoking campaign results, McAlister *et al* (1989), themselves campaign designers, were also forced to note the general modesty of effects even where all of the metaphorical stops had been pulled. Of course, campaigns which are limited to communication through the media, without additional supporting activities and information, have had even less success, but McAlister *et al* contend:

> On the basis of these failures to demonstrate strong and specific communication effects when media-only campaigns are employed, one might conclude that the many informational and persuasive events and campaigns of the past 30 years have had only temporary or limited impact on smoking behaviour. Actually, these efforts have achieved their immediate objectives quite well. People are now well informed about the health consequences of smoking. (1989, p. 295).

The evidence that virtually everyone today knows that smoking is bad for you, and that most smokers have tried to quit at least once, has not always translated into the 'desired' behaviour of total smoking cessation, of course, and again reflects the current 'unmistakable consensus' (Hornik, 1989, p. 309) that the mass media may be effective for providing information and creating awareness, but that face-to-face channels are essential for behaviour change to be produced.

Other campaign studies

Of course, campaigns have been conducted and evaluated on many issues other than heart disease and smoking, and although many of these are still health or safety related it is important to consider the full range of persuasion programmes, where the levels of potential benefit to self may vary. These studies tend to reinforce the view that knowledge gains are relatively easy to achieve (although even straightforward educational messages are sometimes found to have almost entirely evaded a population), whilst behavioural changes are far more difficult to effect. It also becomes more clear that individuals are likely to conduct a cost-benefit analysis, whether with conscious calculation or more at the level of gut reaction ('oh, I can't be bothered with that'): the more readily some campaign-recommended benefit can be gained with the least amount of personal expense – whether of money, pleasure or comfort – the more likely it is that the appropriate actions will be adopted.

O'Keefe (1985) reports the findings of a study of a crime prevention campaign featuring an animated trenchcoated dog, McGruff, who exhorted Americans to 'Take a bite out of crime' on TV public service announcements (PSAs), as well as on the radio and in newspaper and magazine adverts. The campaign was run by the Advertising Council from October 1979, and was aimed at promoting public involvement in crime prevention efforts, primarily through burglary self-protection and cooperative neighbourhood action. A national sample survey of 1,200 adults who were interviewed for 45 minutes each in November 1981, two years after the campaign had been launched, found that over half of the respondents (52 per cent) recalled having seen or heard one of the campaign PSAs, and a third had encountered them at least ten times. 88 per cent of those exposed were able to verbalise a main point of the ads, so these were clearly taken notice of, and nearly a quarter said that they had taken preventive actions due to having seen or heard the ads, including improving household security and helping neighbours with such measures. We should note, however, that this figure could be exaggerated, since a proportion of people who have admitted to having seen the ads may then claim to taken some degree of the recommended action so as not to seem foolish or ignorant.

To gain a better estimate of the effects, a panel survey was also conducted. A probability sample of 1,049 adults in Buffalo, Denver and Milwaukee were first interviewed in September 1979, before the campaign began. The three locales were selected to provide a diverse mix of regional characteristics and crime rate profiles. 426 of these respondents were successfully reinterviewed again in November 1981. Although the wide distribution of the campaign PSAs meant that an untreated control community was not available, the researchers used the 'next best' solution of dividing the respondents into those who recalled seeing the PSAs (the treatment group) and those who did not (control) – which conveniently fell into similar-sized groups of 48 per cent and 52 per cent respectively. Those who recalled the campaign showed a significant increase in how much they thought they knew about crime prevention, significantly more positive attitudes about the effectiveness of citizens taking action to prevent crime, and a significantly greater feeling of personal crime prevention competence. However, the campaign did not appear to have affected feelings of personal responsibility for helping to prevent crime, or on personal concern regarding crime prevention; however, it is not surprising that these two factors, which relate more to *concern* about crime, were unchanged, and indeed this adds credibility to the other findings of increases in the measures which the campaign targeted.

More importantly, the campaign had significant effects on behaviour. Of the seven behaviours advocated by the campaign, six increased significantly – leaving outdoor lights on, using timer lights, having neighbours watch the house, keeping watch on the neighbourhood, reporting suspicious incidents to the police, and joining with others to prevent crime – whilst the seventh, locking doors when out of the house, was something which most people did anyway. A number of crime prevention activities which the campaign had not directly advocated were found not to have increased significantly, suggesting that the campaign had a focused effect only on the particular targeted behaviours. It was also found that all of these changes occurred across the board rather than in specific subgroups, and that the behavioural effects were not limited to a particular attentive group who were already interested in crime prevention, but rather occurred most of all amongst those who had initially indicated lower levels of knowledge, perceived crime prevention effectiveness, and prevention competence – although they felt themselves to be at risk. It also seems that exposure to the PSAs aroused a moderate degree of fear in 22 per cent of the panel subjects (Mendelsohn, 1986, p. 135), but that this also increased the attention they paid to the information, and enhanced their crime prevention skills and competence accordingly. Whilst the study authors believe it much more likely that it was the subject of crime itself which was frightening, rather than the specific content of the ads, we can see that a small degree of fear arousal is not necessarily a bad thing, in terms of the campaign's efficacy.

Unfortunately, the methodology of this study is problematical since, as mentioned above, the 'treatment' group were not actually a sample of the whole population who may potentially (and would be likely to) have encountered campaign messages, but were rather the much more specific group of those who already reported recall of a campaign PSA. Even the 'control' group in this study would in other studies have been included in the 'treatment' category, since they were part of the group whom the campaign messages were aimed at, even though these individuals couldn't recall them. An estimate of the effect size on the whole population, therefore, can only be gained by halving the percentages related to those who recalled exposure. The control population, whilst not ideal, is at least only flawed in that it may have been 'infected' by the community-based activities of its PSA-watching neighbours who had been inspired by the campaign – so that differences between treatment and control should be, if anything, underrepresented. There can therefore be little doubt that the campaign had an impressive effect on crime prevention activities, a conclusion upheld by the mutually supporting findings of the cohort and national samples. Although based on an issue which calls for minimal self-sacrifice (except perhaps for a small financial outlay) whilst offering a universally desirable reward (freedom from crime and burglary), it is noteworthy that this campaign was run through the media only, and yet achieved behavioural changes.

In contrast, a television campaign promoting safety belt use in motor vehicles, studied by Robertson, Kelley, *et al* (1974) in the USA, failed to produce any detectable effect at all. A set of six short dramatic television spot films were shown over nine months beginning in June 1971, with the different ads being placed at suitable times for their target audiences (children, fathers, parents). The spots were shown on one cable of a special dual cable system designed for marketing studies; whilst both cables carried the same range of channels to a county population of 230,000 people, cable A carried the safety belt messages to 6,400 homes, whilst cable B, serving 7,400 homes, did not. Previous marketing studies had found no significant differences between the cable A and B receivers in demographic characteristics, car ownership or other relevant factors. The cable A homes received the campaign messages 943 times over the nine-month period, giving an expected average per-person exposure of two to three times per week. To find whether the safety messages were having an impact, the refreshingly direct (but labour-intensive) approach of actually observing people in cars was employed: 14 observation sites were chosen in all, and records were taken daily from May 1971 to March 1972, from one site watching cars go into the city in the morning, and another watching them come out in the afternoon. Observation was initially for 12 hours a day, but was cut to nine hours a day in mid-October because of shortened daylight; observations were also then halved, with recording alternating between the morning and afternoon sites. Observers tape-recorded the driver's sex, racial appearance and approximate age as the vehicle approached, their use of safety belts as the vehicle passed, and its license number as it went away. The license numbers were used to identify the driver's address, and this was matched to the records of whether their home received cable A or B. This method meant that the subjects did not know they were in an experiment, and even the observers were unable to know which drivers were in the treatment or control groups.

The results are stark. Despite the numerous, repeated showings of the emotive campaign spots over nine months, 'The campaign had no measured effect whatsoever on safety belt use' (p. 1077). There were no significant differences between drivers on the experimental and control cables in any time period, nor between sex or age sub-groups. Indeed, the use of safety belts declined noticeably in all groups during the period of study, from around 15 per cent in May 1971 to seven per cent in March 1972. This media-only campaign, which sought to promote personal benefits at minimal cost to the individual, was clearly a failure.

Geller (1989), although accepting this study as 'classic and rigorous' (p. 201), notes that the fear tactic used by four of the six TV spots, highlighting the negative consequences of disfigurement and disability, has been shown by more recent research to be less effective than other approaches, since the negative images can interfere with viewer's attention and retention, or can lead them to avoid the messages altogether. On the other hand, we can note that the repeated showings would have made it very difficult for viewers to avoid the images or their meaning altogether. It is also noteworthy that similar British TV campaigns about safety belts, speeding and drink-driving in the mid-1990s are still heavily reliant on fear-inducing images not just of injury, but of death. Geller himself believes that role models are likely to have a more profound effect, and with his students initiated a nationwide campaign in 1984 to bring to public attention TV characters' non-use of safety belts. Letter-writing campaigns encouraged stars to 'buckle up' on TV, and were rewarded with 'thank you' notes when they did so. Mr. T received more than 800 'buckle up' letters in 1984, and as a consequence his character in *The A-Team*, B.A. Baracus, increased on-screen usage from one per cent of all driving scenes in 1984 to 20 per cent in 1985; and by 1986 the entire A-Team were wearing their safety belts in 39 per cent of all driving scenes. (Regular *A-Team* viewers will recall that in the remaining 61 per cent of driving scenes, the Team would be liable to be firing guns harmlessly from their van, or else would probably be riding a vehicle hastily welded together out of old bits of farm machinery in the final section of the programme, and thus not equipped with seat belts, nor even, on the whole, seats.) Unfortunately, however, and as is quite common in work on campaigns, Geller does not have data on the effect of these increased portrayals.

A much more established and long-running campaign is the 'Smokey Bear' crusade against forest fires in the United States (McNamara, Kurth & Hansen, 1981). Since these wildfires ravage around five million acres of US land a year, and 99 per cent are caused by people or their equipment, it is a problem of much concern, and one which could be avoided. The campaign began in 1942 (proclaiming 'Careless Matches Aid the Axis'), with Smokey being introduced a couple of years later. By the 1970s the campaign had an allocated annual budget of $50 million and involved numerous mailings and messages on television, radio, magazines and newspapers, as well as a popular Junior Forest Ranger Program sending fire prevention information to over six million children. There has not been a systematic evaluation of the campaign's effect, and this would be difficult in any case (questionnaires asking respondents if they have started any major forest fires are hard to envisage). However, before the program began in 1942, 30 million acres were lost to wildfires each year, but by the 1970s this was down to less than five million. A 1976 public awareness survey showed a near-universal 98 per cent aided recall awareness of Smokey Bear, who is credited with saving some $17 billion in resources over his first 30 years. Whilst the steep decline in forest fire prevalence may have been helped by other factors, including the interactions with parents and teachers both prompted and unprompted by the campaign, it is likely that Smokey must deserve much of this praise.

Returning to the sphere of personal health, campaigns have of course focused on concerns other than the heart disease and smoking studies described in the previous section, although those large-scale programmes do tend to be the most systematically evaluated. In recent decades sexual health and more recently, of course, AIDS has grown as an important area of campaign communications, although here it has been perhaps more difficult to evaluate the effects of different campaigns. In addition, it is clear that AIDS information should be disseminated as widely as possible, and that establishing unin-formed 'control' groups to contrast with 'treatment' groups for research purposes would be highly irresponsible.

An early television attempt to break traditional taboos about venereal disease was a 1972 programme, *VD Blues*, which used a 'fast-paced variety show' format to provide candid information and to break the media silence on the subject (Greenberg & Gantz, 1989). The programme achieved some notoriety at the time, and was aired several times on public television but was 'too strong' for the commercial networks; one reviewer described it as 'educational entertainment, a sort of *Sesame Street* for the sexually active' (p. 204). A central aim of the programme was to bring taboo topics into the public arena, in order to stimulate interpersonal conversations on such subjects. Therefore the programme sought not only to educate in itself, but also to encourage further learning beyond its specific content by reducing inhibitions about the venereal disease problem, whilst raising its social visibility.

A field study was conducted in 1974 to test the success of these aspirations. The night after the programme was aired in a region of Michigan, 923 adults were interviewed by telephone. Of these, 135 (15 per cent) said they had watched the show the previous evening or when it had been first broadcast several months earlier. These viewers demonstrated greater knowledge about VD, particularly in regard to more detailed information such as how diseases can and cannot be transmitted, and their long-term effects. They also showed significant differences in the number of situations in which they thought it would be 'okay to talk about VD', 93 per cent of the programme viewers agreeing to at least six of seven suggested contexts, compared to 77 per cent of equally loquacious non-viewers. However, we should also note that the group of people who had chosen to watch the programme were found to be younger, more educated, and to have more prior media-based information about VD, compared to the non-viewers. In other words, similar results may have been produced simply by comparing a general population with a group of people who would *potentially* choose to watch such a programme, without the programme itself needing to exist. Nevertheless, it is not unlikely that at least a part of the viewers' increased knowledge about venereal disease, and some of their broader perception of how acceptable it would be to discuss it, can be attributed to the programme.

Concern about escalating population levels has led to family planning campaigns in a number of developing countries. Since the 1970s the social marketing approach has been introduced, which seeks to promote the concept of birth control and to sell contraceptives through existing and expanding market networks at subsidised prices (Atkin & Meischke, 1989). Interpersonal promotion and explanation from salespeople is combined with mass media publicity, which combines information and motivational messages in a commercial (rather than a formal governmental) style. In Bangladesh these social marketing strategies saw condom sales rocket over just seven years from 10 million in 1976 to 82 million in 1983. In India, a 'massive' campaign increased the sales of a condom brand by almost 400 per cent from 1969 to 1973, and by 1984 these had almost doubled again to 200 million per year. The crucial importance of the interpersonal and field support to social marketing is emphasized by a campaign in Peru where the commercial mass media communications alone failed to produce any apparent effect on contraceptive use (*ibid*). Once again we come to the conclusion that the media only begins to be an aid to persuasion where its messages are reinforced by direct, face-to-face communications.

The innumerable mass media AIDS campaigns which have been produced since the early 1980s have not on the whole been subjected to rigorous evaluation. Some of the reasons for this are obvious: budgets are invested in the attempt to get the message out to as many people as possible, and using proportions of those budgets to measure their effectiveness could easily be seen as wasteful and unproductive. Whilst such research might help save lives by identifying groups who have not been reached by the campaigns, such findings can be anticipated by field workers from their experience, and by campaign planners on the basis of previous health campaign research, and so money tends to be pumped entirely into campaigns, both general and targeted, without much going into evaluation. In addition, people are likely to receive information about AIDS from a wide variety of sources, ranging from personal friends and contacts, to professionals such as teachers and doctors, to media information in the form of campaigns, news, TV and film drama. Even for those who do not know someone who is HIV+, actual planned campaigns might therefore be less affecting than such media experiences as the sensitively handled and very moving story of Gill and Mark Fowler in *EastEnders* for British viewers (culminating in Gill's death in 1992), or the AIDS death in *Grange Hill* (1995), the mini-series *And the Band Played On* (1993) in America, the more elegiac Pet Shop Boys songs, or the movies *Longtime Companion* (1990) and *Philadelphia* (1993). This multiplicity would make it very difficult to assess the contribution of any single source. A search of the latest comprehensive medical abstract CD-Roms shows that there are many evaluation studies of programmes which involve workshops and face-to-face education, in some cases among sub-groups such as intravenous drug users (e.g. Feucht *et al*, 1991; Martin *et al*, 1990), or for school or college students (Lustig, 1994; Alteneder *et al*, 1992; Brown *et al*, 1991; Dommeyer *et al*, 1989), youth groups (Kipke *et al*, 1993), in the workplace (Barr *et al*, 1992) or local communities (Flowers *et al*, 1991; Miller *et al*, 1990). However, there are very few studies of specific media campaigns.

Rhodes & Wolitski (1989) sought to test the effectiveness of four commercial videotape presentations in changing the knowledge and attitudes about AIDS of 584 college students. A 'before' and 'after' survey showed that all four videotapes significantly increased the subjects' knowledge, compared to a control group, and this was still the case at the time of a follow-up survey four to six weeks later for all but one of the tapes. Attitudes, however, were not affected, with the exception of a significant improvement in the perceived effectiveness of AIDS prevention methods. Interestingly, there was no difference in the follow-up results between groups who followed the video presentation with a discussion and those who had not. No attempt was made to record actual behaviour, but we can perhaps surmise from the relative lack of attitudinal changes that the videotapes were unlikely to have made the students become much more responsible than they already were.

A similar study was conducted by Scott, Chambers *et al* (1990), although it did not feature a media-only condition, and a videotape formed only one part of a seminar which also involved an oral presentation and discussion. 1,898 Canadian secondary school students completed questionnaires about the usefulness of the seminars, and there was strong agreement that they were valuable and informative. However, it should be clear that such studies are only of marginal value in ascertaining the real-life effectiveness of such campaigns, even without attempting to isolate the contribution of the media element. Whilst we can understand the reasons why the major mass media AIDS campaigns have not generally been comprehensively evaluated, there can be little reason for complacency, particularly since studies have found that despite a measurable rise in AIDS knowledge amongst young people, a very small percentage actually changed their own behaviour, and were generally confident that they themselves would not become HIV+ (Reardon, 1989, p. 275).

Throughout its history, the mass media has of course been used to promote the messages and campaigns of an almost unimaginable number of causes, agencies, charities and governments; obviously we cannot consider them all here. An additional problem is that, with disappointing frequency, many academic articles discuss the design and aims of a campaign at length but are not able to follow this with a research evaluation of its actual success. A report on a carefully designed TV campaign to encourage the French to decrease their alcohol consumption – with the necessarily non-hardline slogan 'One drink alright, three drinks, hello troubles' (Vilain, 1986) – tells us that it reached and was recalled by a very high percentage of the sampled population, and was judged 'necessary' by 86 per cent, but beyond this we cannot tell whether the campaign had any effect or not. Similarly we hear that television promotion of a cancer information phoneline led to calls shooting up from 600 to 13,500 a month (Stein, 1986), but have no idea of its actual effect, such as on smoking cessation, or whether it led to the public more often identifying the symptoms of cancer at an earlier stage. Flay, Pentz, *et al* (1986) continue this penchant for somewhat perfunctory information by measuring the 'effectiveness' of some health-promoting television programmes simply by noting how many children watched them, and finding that they were most likely to do so when told to for school, and when the programmes were supported in the curriculum. Despite the weaknesses of some published studies, however, there is clearly an emergent consensus amongst the numerous evaluated campaign studies which have been covered in the above sections: the media alone are unlikely to have more than a marginal influence, even on issues which carry clear social or personal benefits, without the direct support provided by persuasive interpersonal contact. This, of course, is not good news for commercial advertisers, as we shall see in the next section.

Advertising

It is not to be denied that advertising campaigns do, on the whole, increase or maintain sales of a product – which would seem to suggest that the public (or at least wholesalers, then shopkeepers, then the public) have somehow been brought to want to consume them. In this section, we will consider the evidence regarding advertising's apparent effects, and it will be suggested that the impact of advertising is a subtle and complex process which cannot simply be connected to the rather more straightforward conceptions of cause-and-effect under consideration elsewhere in this review.

The effect of television advertising in a modern, western capitalist society is inherently very difficult to assess. This is quite apart from any of the previous arguments that the media is extremely unlikely to make people do anything which they do not want to, and that media-only campaigns are notoriously poor at producing behavioural changes. It must be remembered that advertising does not generally seek to make individuals do anything which they would not previously have done, for advertising is about shopping, and shopping is something which most people do anyway. Advertising is therefore only really aiming to change the *detail* of our behaviour: precisely what it is that we buy when we shop. The product brands which are stocked in stores are more likely to be the ones advertised on television, making it impossible to simply compare the sales of advertised and unadvertised products with the assumption that the advertising causes any difference; it *might* be the ads, but it might be the packaging, or the taste, or the amusing free gift. It is certainly true that people prefer to buy familiar products to ones which they have never heard of, and so advertising, by raising *awareness* of a product is likely to have an effect on sales. But whether this counts as an 'effect' on the purchaser is another matter, and certainly a headache for the would-be researcher. Quite simply, in a capitalist society people expect to be sold things, and expect to buy them. The potential unexpected 'effects' here are hard to see, but possible hypotheses that we must consider include that people will be made to buy things which they don't want or need, that children who do not understand what advertising is will feel instructed to demand products, or that children will be led to desire things, such as illicit drugs (as some have argued), which society may not want them to have.

The first of these can be discounted straight away, since there is no evidence that television has the kind of direct line to consciousness that would 'make' people act against their own nature. Advertising can certainly make some products seem more attractive than others, even where they are substantially the same, and thus influence our purchasing decisions. However, this kind of effect is radically different from the other alleged 'effects' of television, such as the promotion of violence, which are generally of concern. The choice between soap powders A and B can in no way be compared to the 'choice' of whether or not to go out and commit a violent act. The first is a question of almost trivial detail in an action – buying soap powder – which would be done in any case, whilst the second is a decision to instigate an entire act which is not socially approved, nor 'advertised' on television. The only parallels advertising could ever have for these much more dramatic 'effects', therefore, would be along the lines of the choice between punching someone with the left or right hand. This distinction between the scale of alleged effects is important, because it is often argued, 'if the media has no effect, why is so much money spent on advertising?'. The effect of raising a person's recognition and opinion of a product to the level where they might consider buying it, when the decision is usually only as opposed to another, similar brand, and almost always at the expense of much ingenuity, repetition and money by the advertiser, is wholly different from the much more serious effects which are of genuine concern. Nevertheless, the fears that children may be the dupes of advertisers are understandable, and worthy of consideration. In addition, if we find that television advertising does not have a such an effect on children, it can be anticipated that its impact on adults will be no more grave.

First of all there is the basic question of whether children can tell the difference between television commercials and programmes, since possible 'effects' are perhaps more worrying if children are not aware of such a distinction. A study by Levin, Petros & Petrella (1982) sought to examine this with a sample of 72 children, equally divided between ages three, four and five. Three videotapes were prepared with a randomly-ordered sequence of 10 second clips, each tape containing 14 clips from TV programmes, plus seven from commercials aimed at children, and seven from those aimed at adults (making a total of 42 programme and 42 advert excerpts). The children, drawn from urban lower-middle class families, were studied individually, and were told that they must identify each segment as a 'commercial' or as a 'programme', although these terms were not defined. The first tape was shown with both sound and picture, but the second was shown with sound only, and the third with picture only. The results show that the children did very well indeed. For the clips shown with both audio and video, the three year olds made 66 per cent correct identifications, the four year olds 69 per cent, and the five year olds got 80 per cent correct. Their scores for the further clips with either sound or visuals switched off were virtually identical, from 66 per cent again for the three year olds to 79 per cent for the five year olds. Furthermore the children were even better at distinguishing between the programme clips and the ads aimed particularly at children, the age groups getting 72, 78 and 89 per cent correct respectively. These results are even more impressive when we note that the study relied on the young children already understanding the terms 'commercial' and 'programme', and that seeing TV programmes in swift 10-second chunks is unusual and unfamiliar. Whilst this particular study cannot demonstrate that children *understand* advertising or its intent, it does show – to a degree so impressive that the relatively small sample size is of less concern – that they are aware of a difference between commercials and programmes, and can tell one from the other.

Other studies have more directly attempted to find if children understand the commercial intent of advertisements. Early studies on this question, conducted by Scott Ward and colleagues for the 1972 Surgeon General's report on television effects in the USA, have become well-known despite their shortcomings. The two relevant studies (Blatt, Spencer & Ward, 1972, and Ward, Reale & Levinson, 1972) involve samples of just 20 and 67 upper-middle class children respectively. When divided into age groups, these become very small, a problem which is exacerbated when the findings are carelessly reported elsewhere: Liebert & Sprafkin (1988, pp. 167–169), for example, report the findings of the first study without mentioning that the four age groups are only represented by five children each, whilst for the second study they deceptively convert the results into percentages without stating the sample sizes, so that just one person in the age eight to ten group responding in a particular way to a question in the study, appears as a whole 10 per cent of the population on their table. These studies have also been criticized, as we shall see below, for their reliance on young children being able to verbalise what they know to a stranger. In any case, the findings were as follows. Blatt, Spencer & Ward's five kindergarten children seemed at least partly aware that ads promoted goods for sale, although they tended to see this as a helpful public service, but the seven to eight year old group were clearly aware of commercial intent, responding that ads were 'to make you buy (the product)', so that the advertisers 'can get more money and support the factories they have' (p. 457). The older children were even more keenly aware of, and somewhat cynical about, advertisers' techniques. Ward, Reale & Levinson found that almost half of their five to seven year olds recognized the selling motive of adverts to some extent, although very few mentioned that the ads also paid for the programmes (p. 473). By the ages of eleven and twelve, this fact was mentioned by a quarter of the subjects, whilst almost all recognized the selling intent. Ambiguous questioning about whether or not adverts are 'true' found that about one in five of the five to eight year olds volunteered opinions that ads are deceptive and cannot be trusted because 'they just want to make money' (pp. 484–485).

Various other studies have generally found that between the ages of five and nine years, the majority of children have been able to articulate the selling intent of advertising (Wartella, 1981). However, an imaginative study by Donohue, Henke & Donohue (1980) found that when children are given the opportunity to demonstrate their understanding in ways which do not rely on verbal ability, they can do so at a much younger age. The authors note that children younger than six years may well know the answer to questions but lack the verbal skills to respond, and additionally have a tendency to be shy when confronted by unfamiliar adults, particularly those asking unusual questions. Studies which depend on open-ended interviewing are likely to 'grossly underestimate what the child understands' (p. 52). For their own study, Donohue *et al* selected an animated commercial (because critics have alleged that cartoon-like adverts are particularly deceptive), in which 'Toucan Sam' discovered Froot Loops, a breakfast cereal, in a haunted house. The advert contained no suggestion that children request or acquire the product, and was six years old, so that none of the children would have seen it. A total of 97 children aged from two to six years, from middle and lower-middle income households in Chicago, were individually shown this commercial. They were then shown two pictures, one of a woman taking a box of Froot Loops from a supermarket shelf, the other of a child watching television, and were asked to indicate which picture best indicated 'what Toucan Sam wants you to do'. The correct picture was selected by a very impressive 75 per cent of two to three year olds, and 95.5 per cent of the six year olds (p. 54). Such significant results, based on a relatively subtle advert involving no mention of product purchase, clearly show that childrens' level of understanding of the intent of commercials is more developed than the verbal interview studies had suggested.

The studies above show that children are generally aware from an early age that television adverts are trying to sell them something, then, and many other studies have shown that children have a distrust of commercials ranging from the unease of a minority at ages five to seven, to over 80 per cent of 10 to 13 year old children who say that adverts do not always tell the truth (Wartella, 1981). The subjects of David Buckingham's (1993) illuminating qualitative interviews, aged around eight to ten, are fluently critical of advertising, humorously mimicking the imagined reactions of the stupid people who would fall for advertising, but clearly distancing themselves from such gullibility (pp. 246–249). Indeed, Buckingham's research supports that conducted by the advertising industry itself, which is becoming increasingly anxious that the young audience of today has become so TV literate, consuming commercials independently of the product being marketed, that they are becoming ever more difficult to reach (p. 261). The findings of such studies suggest that young people are likely to be resistant to the intended influence of commercials, but cannot confirm this for us specifically. However, the attempts of researchers to measure 'effects' more directly tend to be poorly designed at best. A review of these studies by Atkin (1981), several of them his own, reflects a field populated by a range of surprisingly uninformative and bizarre studies, many of them failing to recognize the point mentioned at the beginning of this section that people are bound to prefer products they have heard of to ones which they have not. For example, one of his studies was an experiment in which children were shown one of two versions of a Pop Tarts advert, one with and the other without mention of a free gift offer (a 'premium'). He reports, 'When asked after viewing to indicate why kids like to get Pop Tarts, relatively few of the children referred to the premium but almost all of those who did were in the condition in which they had viewed the premium version of the commercial' (p. 294). The finding that children are only able to pass on information if they have been given it is, of course, entirely obvious, and it was found that the premium made no difference to the percentage of children who wanted the product in any case. Other cited studies show that mothers and children rate television as an important source of information about products; and that people would prefer a previously unknown product which they have at least been shown one advert for, to one which they have never heard of – none of which is surprising. Competing with these in the absurdity stakes is the study in which children were asked if they would like to have most of the things shown on commercials (p. 289); since this sounds an offer too good to refuse, the surprise is that as few as only two-thirds of kindergarteners and half of eight to twelve year olds said yes. Atkin's finding of a moderate relationship between higher exposure to candy advertising (which must be part of a higher overall amount of television viewing) and frequency of eating candy *might* show that some brands were being successfully promoted, but is explained by his own evidence that television viewing in general is correlated with snack consumption (p. 291). To give them their due, some of Atkin's studies do show that particular products are a little more likely to be consumed by those who have seen more adverts for them, although this again may only reflect an increased awareness of the products, even if we ignore the possible explanation that heavier TV viewers will already be the kind of people more likely to consume the kinds of convenience foods advertised on TV.

Experiments conducted by Goldberg & Gorn (1983) at least manage to more convincingly demonstrate that advertising can increase the appeal of advertised products. For example, a commercial for a 'Ruckus Raiser Barn' toy was shown to an experimental group of pre-school children but not to a control group, although they were familiar with the toy and had seen it. All of the children were told that their mother would prefer them to have a (less appealing) tennis ball, and were then asked which toy they would prefer. About 80 per cent of the control group deferred to their mother's judgement, but only half of the group who had seen the commercial did so (p. 137). Other studies showed that children were more likely to pick foods which they had just seen advertised, when offered a choice in both hypothetical and real situations (p. 147). This function of children being led to appreciate and even desire an item by certain, successful advertising seems to be the strongest 'effect' we can find. In these studies the effect was in the reasonably short-term, though we might even concede from our own experiences that adverts can lead to longer lasting desires. But this kind of 'effect' does not lead directly to any behaviour, and is certainly not a function of all adverts for all people. It would be wrong to deny that television advertising can have the power to make products appealing – the particular ways in which it may do this will be discussed briefly below – but also wrong to suggest that this is something which is 'done' to viewers over which they have no control, and cannot resist. This case is generally supported by the studies relating to the other feared effect which we must consider – that of drug advertisements. In the 1970s, there was much concern that television advertising of legal drugs such as headache cures and pain relievers may lead children to believe that drugs are the answer to life's problems, and unwittingly promote illicit drug use. (The term 'illicit' drugs is used here to indicate a range of psychoactive drugs; these vary with regard to legality, since some are wholly illegal to sell or possess, whereas others may not legally be used except under medical authorization). Whilst the journey from Aspro-Clear customer to crack-head may seem a long and indeed unlikely one, a number of studies were conducted in this area.

Much the best study in terms of methodology is a longitudinal panel study by Milavsky, Pekowsky & Stipp (1975), conducted as an additional part of the study of television and aggressive behaviour (Milavsky *et al*, 1982) described in chapter three. The sample was the older group of 800 boys aged initially between 12 and 16, from low and middle-income black and white families in two cities. Over three and a half years, the boys were interviewed on five separate occasions, 300 of them responding to all five of the waves. The boys were asked if they had ever used various named drugs, and were presented with a list of almost 50 television programmes against which they were asked to indicate how many episodes of each they had seen in the past four weeks (or two weeks for daily programmes). These responses were compared with records of when adverts for ingested drugs (medicines and pills for headaches and colds, sleeping aids, throat lozenges etc.) had been broadcast, producing an index for each subject of how much drug advertising he could have seen. Analysis of this data found a weak positive relationship between exposure to drug advertising and the teenage boys' use of *proprietary* drugs (legal, commercial drug products such as those advertised). However, the relationship between drug advertising exposure and the use of illicit drugs was *negative*. In addition, exposure to drug advertising made no difference to the subjects' readiness to take drugs or see them as a solution to problems. This extensive and carefully conducted study therefore found that the fears about drug advertising on television were unfounded; indeed, on the contrary it was those who saw less TV drug advertising who were more likely to use illicit drugs.

A study by Atkin (1978) of 256 girls and boys aged between 10 and 14, whilst less in-depth, found similar results. The children completed questionnaire booklets which described and illustrated four typical TV drug ads and asked 'how much' they watched the commercial when it appeared (on a four-point scale from 'always' to 'never') and how many hours of television they watched on average between 8pm and 11pm (when most drug commercials are shown). These scores were multiplied together to produce a drug advertising exposure index for each child. The measures can be criticized for their level of precision, but should at least have sorted out lighter from heavier drug ad viewers. The questionnaires also asked several questions about the subjects' attitudes to various drugs. The results showed weak positive relationships between exposure to drug advertising and a belief in the helpfulness of drugs in combating colds and stomach aches, in the speed with which they would take effect, and in approval of drug use to tackle illness. However, there was no significant effect on belief in the efficacy of sleeping pills, or approval of the use of sleeping pills or aspirin. Most importantly, exposure to television drug advertising made absolutely no difference to approval of 'uppers' and 'downers' (illicit pills), and again had a *negative* relationship with approval of cannabis-related substances: once more, heavier viewers of TV drug ads were *less* likely to approve of these illicit drugs.

Finally, a similar study, but involving younger (and more) children, and only concerning proprietary drugs, was conducted by Rossiter & Robertson (1980). A sample of 668 children aged between eight and thirteen, from a range of socio-economic backgrounds, again answered questions about their attitudes towards and usage of various drugs, and their drug advertising exposure was measured by the method devised by Milavsky *et al* (see above). Once again, small positive correlations were found between exposure to TV drug commercials and belief in the efficacy of proprietary drugs, and intention to use them when ill; however, the authors say that 'this influence cannot be regarded as substantial' (p. 327). The older children felt even less favourably disposed towards the drugs. Rossiter and Robertson conclude that 'TV drug advertising does not seem to influence children to an extent that may be regarded as socially harmful or worthy of further legislative attention' (p. 328). In the light of these findings, and particularly Milavsky *et al*'s detailed longitudinal results, we can conclude that the fears about television drug advertising are unfounded.

On the whole, then, and particularly in terms of concerns about the effects of particular bits of television, advertising does not seem to warrant concern. Marketing studies funded by advertisers themselves, such as the study of the impact of 1,000 commercials by Stewart & Furse (1986), certainly reflect the advertisers' pragmatic lack of ambition to persuade, being concerned with trivial differences in subjects' levels of product recall and differentiation which can be of little interest outside the industry. Evidence brought together by Cashmore (1994) suggests that advertisers continue to pour money into advertising not because research has unambiguously demonstrated that it is able to persuade us to buy products in the simple cause-and-effect sense, which it hasn't, but rather because companies simply have no better way of reaching a mass market and raising awareness of their products (p. 95), and since a competent advertising campaign clearly is able to attract sales to a product, away from its competitors. Estimates of how much advertising fails, however, range from 90 to even 99 per cent; advertisers have to spend so much money because the power of ads is so weak, and substantial effort has to be made just to inspire a minority to consider purchasing a product. Of course, advertisers recognize the limits of the simple 'buy this, it's good' line, and link their products to attractive or desirable situations, values and experiences in an attempt to give products meaning beyond their function. Advertisements therefore invest goods with meanings connected to the other, less material things which we desire and need (Williamson, 1978; Cashmore, 1994): the embedded suggestion is that the product will make the purchaser feel loveable, secure, daring or fashionable, and that others will share this view. Thus what is ultimately sold is not just the product but a whole package of values. It is no great surprise that advertising is likely to work by these more complex means, rather than the traditional, cause and effect view of advertising held by some critics and researchers. It also suggests that attempts to quantify the effects of advertising in any but the crudest of ways would be rather difficult.

We should also deal very briefly with the broader argument that advertising can be seen as propaganda for capitalism, cultivating consumerism, and promoting materialism as a dominant value. Goldman (1992), for example, lucidly argues that the concern with the 'effects' of individual ads only serves to obscure the structural role of advertising in the reproduction of social domination and the normalization of consumerist conformity. The escalating sophistication and 'knowing winks' to the audience of recent postmodern advertising are only doing what is necessary to retain the attention of today's viewer/consumers, and so rather than actually creating distance between individual and product, serve to continually rejuvenate consumerism as something fresh, thrilling and clever. This type of argument, painting a picture of a broad, hegemonic influence of the media, can certainly be regarded as viable, but is not limited to advertising or to television, let alone to particular instances which, when removed, would make everything all right. In other words, it is just one part of a critique of the role of the mass media in late 20th century capitalism, and, consequently, capitalism itself, an argument which is far too wide-ranging to find a place within our focus of concern on the question of whether particular things on television have effects on viewers, and if so, what they are. If we accept our shopping-bag culture, at least for the moment, then television advertising would not appear to hold any nasty surprises.

Synthesis of campaign study implications

It should by now be clear that health and safety campaigns, and other targeted attempts at persuasion, have generally rather staggering failure rates considering that they usually seek results which are widely regarded as desirable and set out, explicitly and determinedly, to produce them. It should also be obvious that since the mass media has such an apparent inability to lead people to do things for which they will be positively rewarded, it should be far less likely to induce 'wrong' or criminal behaviour which is neither socially approved nor (despite the assertions of some) marketed by the media.

This chapter began with the Cincinnati campaign to promote the United Nations, which unleashed a mass of media information upon the city, in every conceivable form, and yet signally failed to achieve its aims. Almost no-one could have failed to encounter the massive campaign, and yet those who knew little or nothing about the UN before were generally just as clueless afterwards. The number of people who thought of the UN as a possible remedy to growing international problems actually declined, whilst it was largely only those who already knew something about and were interested in the organization who went on to learn something more from the programme.

Such findings initially produced a degree of consensus that media campaigns were barely worth the effort. Once this had passed, the revived interest in the potential of campaigns, represented by the many more recent studies discussed above, might lead us to think that researchers had found reason to be more optimistic. However, the results of their evaluations suggest not so much that campaigns had been found to be effective, but rather that planners had come to terms, in a way, with their only marginal chance of success. Some change, after all, is better than none, and when people are aware of the dangers of smoking, poor diet or not wearing a seatbelt, then at least they have made an informed choice when they carry on. Of course other actions such as unsafe sexual activity and firestarting can have more direct consequences for others, and effective campaigning therefore becomes even more important, although no easier.

Whilst the Stanford Three Community Study seemed to produce some notable changes, the enhanced and more ambitious Five Cities Project only managed a mix of failure and some partial, small changes. In North Karelia the successful massive campaign effort included so many interpersonal aspects and structural changes – with important modifications being made not only to healthcare provision but also to the availability of food products in line with the campaign's aims – that the mass media element was reduced to a supporting rather than central role. Nevertheless, a Finnish national TV series was able to have a small but significant impact on smoking cessation, and another seemed to have similarly limited but worthwhile effects on diet. The TV anti-smoking campaign in Sydney had a small effect on a cohort group but this was not reflected in independent cross-sectional samples. Other anti-smoking campaigns seemed only to have an effect when they managed to smother a population without being too boring, and ideally when supported by as much interpersonal contact as possible. The 'McGruff' media-only crime prevention campaign appeared to have a greater impact than most of the programmes about personal health, perhaps because it called for very little self-sacrifice; however, a TV campaign promoting use of safety belts had no observable effect at all. In general, the consensus that campaigns are unlikely to have a substantial effect unless omnipresent and supported by face-to-face contact, particularly if a change in personal behaviour is called for, is inescapable.

We should note that, as with the studies of less desirable alleged effects, the paradigm of campaign designers and researchers is individualistic and tends not to see problems as part of a larger, more complex whole. Wallack (1989) observes that cigarette smoking, for example, is viewed in terms of numbers of people who choose to smoke, rather than tracing it to the giant corporations that keenly market the product. He argues:

> Public health problems are rooted in basic social structures that contribute to inequality and differential access to opportunities for health and well-being. It is fairly typical for people to see the mass media as an able agent in the effort to facilitate a more equal and just society through the ability to impart information to large numbers of people. Yet mass media health promotion efforts focus on symptoms, not causes; emphasize the most obvious (and politically safest) point of intervention, the individual; and ignore the social roots of disease (p. 365).

Whether the mass media is seeking to 'save' individuals from their own failings, or is itself being accused of causing failings in individuals, then, possible social explanations for the respective problems are neatly avoided.

The studies of advertising were similarly rather flawed by their implicit model of a relationship between advertising and the individual which ignored the wider demands and constraints of capitalist society. However, even given that life in such a society is bound to involve both advertising and consumerism, and that the former only seeks to alter our performance of the latter in limited ways, the commercials were found to have an undistinguished impact. Children were able from an early age to identify advertising and its purpose, and quickly became cynical about its methods and power to persuade. Studies were unable to demonstrate much of an 'effect' beyond that people would be a little more likely to select products which repeated advertising had made them aware of, compared to less advertised products. Drug advertising did not foster an interest in illicit drugs – quite the reverse, in fact – whilst the mild increase in positive views about proprietary drugs, which exposure to drug commercials was correlated with, was of a size more recognisable as a usefully informed rather than drug-crazed state.

On the whole, deliberate efforts to cajole and persuade the public via television have met with what might be considered a remarkable lack of success. Since those who have worked in the field for years apparently find it so hard to produce minor but socially beneficial results, it becomes difficult not to think that the idea of negative effects accidentally 'slipping out' is equally unlikely.

7 Towards an understanding of influences?: 'New' directions in effects research

New angles on old problems?

The deficiencies of the traditional approach to television effects have not, of course, gone unnoticed by researchers, and some attempts have been made to find new angles on the old problem, and new avenues of enquiry. However, this research has not generally succeeded in advancing knowledge about the kinds of potential effects which have previously been of concern in this field. The new work has tended to fall short of this undertaking in one of two ways, by either failing to escape from the old paradigm, or else moving so far away from the study of effects that the work falls into a different field altogether.

The first type of work is still basically concerned with the same old question of direct effects, which we have already established is redundant; whilst these studies may attempt to take a more sophisticated approach by looking at effects on specific groups, or at less obvious, non-imitative effects, they are nevertheless wedded to the old idea that television may have a direct effect on viewers. For example, Halloran's (1978) argument that advertising on television may lead to dissatisfaction and frustration amongst some viewers, and so cause them to commit crimes – which undoubtedly is a more complex conception of how television may have an effect – is still founded in a relatively traditional expectation of effects. Although Halloran rightly accepts Klapper's (1960) argument that television is just one factor working amid other influences, his conception of television creating a psychological terrain of false needs, which then lead to crime, is entirely speculative and still involves the idea of the medium, in relative isolation, creating social problems. Whilst the evidence in support of this hypothesis may be as strong as that weak evidence offered in support of other effects (Feilitzen, 1994, pp. 152–153), it is still likely that television advertising is not even *one of* the most significant causes of any crime, and the research has not demonstrated that it is. Once again, if television had any effect it would be likely to be very small in comparison to a wide range of other possible contributory factors. The focus on the possibility of a minor and almost certainly subordinate television effect, rather than the many other far more severe structural causes of crime, seems almost perverse – after all, as Halloran himself has noted (1990, p. 571), to use television as a scapegoat for problems with other causes is not only misguided but potentially dangerous, as it can obscure social problems which have genuine and serious consequences.

In a similar way, Dervin's (1994) relatively sophisticated approach to television's possible impact, in which she argues that we should not presume that effects are predictable even within specific demographic groupings, ultimately reveals itself to nevertheless be rooted in the traditional effects assumptions as Dervin concludes not that effects cannot be found, but rather that we have been looking for them in the wrong place. Whilst her arguments that viewers make their own meanings, and do so flexibly in different ways at different times, are fully justified, she still presumes that significant direct effects of television on viewers are there to be found. If the body of research into effects has shown us anything, it is that this simplisitic notion carries no weight, and the paradigm has to be left behind.

The other direction which research has taken as the weaknesses of earlier research have become more apparent, is to investigate effects or influences which, whilst no more readily detectable, and are so far from most concerns about television effects that they constitute a significant break from the effects tradition, forming a new and separate field of enquiry. For example, Noelle-Neumann's (1994) analysis of the possible effect of the media on individuals' perceptions of public opinion, and Murdock's (1994) discussion of the ways in which particular discourses are reinforced by their use in the mass media – for example, how governments may seek to define particular groups and their actions as 'terroristic', so that they appear transparently unjustifiable – are examples of work which deliberately seeks to explore new research questions in the light of the inadequacies of the old ones. Whilst the investigation of new areas is always interesting, these studies obviously no longer have anything to do with the central question of the impact of television on the behaviour of viewers, which is of concern in this review, and is commonly understood to be the basis of effects research. These studies can perhaps be seen as new approaches to television's *influences*, however, and as such are welcome; but they nevertheless focus on perceptions of things external to most viewers' lives – events happening elsewhere, other people's opinions – and so are not able to tell us about the media's impact on immediate concerns or behaviours.

The 'uses and gratifications' tradition of media research is also seen by some as the successor of effects research (for examples, see Rosengren, Wenner & Palmgreen, eds, 1985; Bryant & Zillmann, eds, 1991). Concerned with the question of *why* people like to watch particular programmes and genres, and what they get out of the experience, this school has produced some interesting work; however, the question of why people are drawn to certain programmes clearly cannot provide answers about what the material *does* to them in terms of the behavioural consequences which are of concern in traditional effects research. In a sense, of course, this is an advantage, freeing researchers to investigate the 'internal effects' of pleasure, entertainment and stimulation which televi-sion produces. Understood in these terms, the uses and gratifications approach is poten-tially much more constructive and noticeably less basic than most of the straight effects research. On the other hand, the school has not always fulfilled this potential, at times reproducing the same flaws which crippled the effects tradition. Researchers who aim, for example, to identify the cognitive processes which inspire 'the audience' to watch TV violence, apparently fail to appreciate that the depictions of violence on television are not generally encountered by viewers who have sat down 'to watch violence', but rather occur as components in dramas which contain many other emotional and involving elements.

However, with sensitive and qualitative research focused on particular cases, the opposite becomes true. Recent research which is less swift to make simplistic assumptions about young people's media preferences has been able to show that the connections are complex, and quite unrelated to the cause-effect models. Examination of an aggressive and trouble-some adolescent's interest in horror videos, by Derdeyn & Turley (1994), for example, revealed that the horror stories intersected with his own worries, fears and fantasies which were in turn a product of his emotionally deprived and abused childhood. The frightening situations and ultimate resolution of the films were seen to be analogous to the fairy tales enjoyed by younger children; and by understanding and discussing the horror films with the boy, both therapist and patient were better able to comprehend his past troubles, and to help him for the future. By taking on board the boy's media use as a symptom, rather than a cause, the researchers were thereby able to produce the kind of valuable insights which are rarely found in effects studies.

Nevertheless, whilst carefully conceived uses and gratifications research can provide this kind of useful insight into viewers' preferences and psychological needs, it clearly cannot contribute directly to our knowledge of the kinds of *effects*, beyond pleasure or emotional responses, which are the focus of this book.

Cultivating a new approach to influences?

The failure of direct-effects research to produce results showing clear consequences of media consumption does not mean that we must look for alternatives so far removed from the previous primary concerns; some form of study of television's influence on the way people view the whole texture and tapestry of their lives should still be possible.

An approach to the possible influences of television fitting this requirement could be based on the method of cultivation analysis developed by Gerber and colleagues – although not in the oversimplistic form in which it has generally been used in the past and is still deployed today. The basic principle at the root of the approach is a promising one: that exposure to television programmes will, over time, have a cumulative influence on viewer's perceptions of the world and their place in it. This basic assumption underpinned the useful and intelligent approaches to television and the development of moral values, and the notion of television as a 'cultural forum', which we have already discussed in chapter five. Recent formulations of the cultivation perspective certainly make it seem like an important and sophisticated advance in research; for example, Morgan & Signo-rielli (1990, pp. 18–19) state:

> Cultivation analysis looks at [television's] messages as an environment within

which people live, define themselves and others, and develop and maintain their beliefs and assumptions about social reality ... The cultivation process is not thought of as a unidirectional flow of influence from television to audiences, but rather part of a continual, dynamic, ongoing process of interaction among messages and contexts.

Unfortunately, however, the assumptions and methods which have supposedly been built upon this promising theoretical basis leave much to be desired. It is argued, for example, that television, by showing women and members of minority groups as victims more often than others, subdues people of those groups and tells them a 'message' about their place in the world – that other dominant groups have power, whilst they are powerless – which they come to accept (for example, Gerbner & Gross, 1976; Gerbner, 1994). This is a possible outcome, but not one which is obviously more likely than that such portrayals would demonstrate the injustices of the world to viewers of those groups and others, and so raise their political consciousness and lead them to seek social changes. The conclusion that viewers would *accept* a victimized, submissive position simply because they had seen it demonstrated a number of times on television does not have an obvious logic. It seems more likely that if viewers were regularly subjected to depictions of their unjust treatment in society, they would be roused to seek change; however, of course, television entertainment – particularly in America – tends not to dwell on explicit or intense depictions of social injustice in any case, and if Gerbner's methods allowed for a more sophisticated reading of programmes beyond a content analysis which simply identifies the demographic characteristics of victims, it would be likely to find that such victimization is rarely shown in anything other than a sympathetic light which reflects, at least to some degree, its unfairness. It might then be concluded that portrayals which remind society of the unjust treatment of minorities actually help to generate sympathy and awareness of their plight. This was clearly the aim of *Roots* and its sequels, and the legitimating rationale for the racial abuse storylines of the British soap operas *EastEnders* and *Brookside*, and the depictions of racist violence in the medical drama series *Medics* and *Casualty*, which escalated to repeated, explicit racial confrontations in both series in the mid-1990s (see, for example, *Medics: Going West* (1994), and the race riot in *Casualty: A Breed Apart* (1994)). It could even be argued that television output should therefore devote *more* time to portrayals of such victimization – although, of course, the arguments for more positive, empowering images of minorities are just as strong.

The assumption that television projects one 'mainstream' message and viewpoint, which is adopted by heavy viewers, is itself severely flawed. Television output is characterized in this approach as 'a particularly consistent and compelling symbolic stream' (Gerbner, 1990, p. 249), and even Morgan & Signorielli, quoted above, see television as 'an essentially repetitive and stable system of messages' (1990, p. 18). The idea of television depicting a perpetually 'mean and dangerous world' has also become a cultivation analysis catchphrase (for example, Gerbner *et al*, 1986, p. 26; Gerbner, 1988, p. 26; Signorielli, 1990), despite its great oversimplification of the broad range of television output. The notion of television projecting a particular worldview may be partly applicable to

America's commercial networks, seeking to appeal to as many viewers as possible in their endless battles for ratings, although even in that case no singular set of political or other values could be identified as receiving consistent support. In other countries such as Britain, the diversity of programmes available, whilst generally restricted within particular cultural and political boundaries, make it impossible to describe a singular 'TV opinion' or 'TV world'.

In addition, the discourse about television 'mainstreaming' its viewers strongly recalls the assumption of the inactive viewer, the proverbial potato who happily absorbs anything that hits their couch, and is unable to regard programmes critically or ironically. Indeed, the 'heavy viewer' is roundly (if unintentionally) demonized in the cultivation literature, and the cumulative picture which the research reports themselves cultivate is one of people who watch larger amounts of television as edgy, zombified individuals who are in a category quite removed from the researchers themselves, and who watch television in an entirely unselective way. Even if this has any partial relevance to some American viewers, the model is little able to cope with either the typically more selective behaviour of viewers in other countries such as Britain (Wober, 1990), or the many viewers of more specialized cable channels in the United States and elsewhere (Perse, Ferguson & McLeod, 1994). In particular, the widespread ownership and use of video recorders very clearly reflects the discrimination of viewers (Levy & Gunter, 1988; Dobrow, 1990; Perse *et al*, 1994), whether using the machines to timeshift particular programmes to more convenient times (Gray, 1992), or for the pleasure and empowerment of curating and controlling one's own sequence of viewing (Cubitt, 1990; Canning, 1994). After all, video recording, the VideoPlus system, and the multitude of TV schedule guides would never have become popular if it was wholly the case, as Gerbner *et al* suggest, that 'most viewers watch by the clock and either do not know what they will watch when they turn on the set or follow established routines rather than choose each program as they would choose a book, a movie or an article' (Gerbner, Gross, Morgan & Signorielli, 1986, p. 19). Statements such as this clearly also reveal the researchers' elitist and disrespectful stance towards television viewers, and their deliberately failed attempt to apply a 'high culture' usage model to the medium (which in any case is unable to fit the serial nature of many programmes) is not only patronizing, but also shows a degree of ignorance and contempt for popular television and its audience.[*] As Newcomb & Hirsch (1984) suggest, researchers might gain a better understanding of their subject by beginning with the assumption that to be capable of attracting a mass audience in a complex culture, television must be 'dense, rich and complex, rather than impoverished' (p. 71), and being accordingly unsurprised to find that the audience has sophisticated and heterogenous responses to the medium. However, Gerbner and colleagues tend to weaken their argument by unnecessarily conflating the

---

[*]   This also recalls Jenson's (1992) comments on the false distinction made between enthusiasts and academics concerned with 'high' culture, and 'fans' concerned with popular culture. Whilst they communicate in different types of discourse, Jenson argues, both groups are basically people with comparable interests, enthusiasms and attachments to figures in, or aspects of, their chosen field, although one group is better able to define and take advantage of notions of 'respectability' than the other.

feeling that television may have an influence on its viewers with the view that its output is overtly repetitive, similar and simplistic.

The research methods adopted to explore the possibility of cultivation influences or effects also have severe limitations, as we have partly seen in chapter four. The bland and inherently unrevealing correlational methodology, where amount of TV viewing is simply compared with a measure of some belief or attitude, is apparently handed down by the 'founding father' Gerbner on tablets of stone, and seems to be taken for granted even by those of his followers who take an otherwise more sophisticated approach (such as Morgan & Signorielli, 1990). Cultivation studies in Signorielli & Morgan's state-of-the-art collection (1990) such as those by Hall Preston on pornography, Perse on involvement in local television news, Signorielli on fear of crime, and Hoover on religious programming, are all severely weakened by their method of simply correlating television exposure with particular attitudes, and presuming that the former causes the latter. The need for evidence of this causation is imperative, particularly since in many cases the suggestions of a causal link otherwise appear extremely unlikely. For example, Hoover's data shows that pro-Christian and conservative attitudes are more strongly correlated with the viewing of Christian religious programmes (in the United States) than they are with viewing of non-religious television, and although the article acknowledges that religious television has an obvious appeal to already-religious people, the data is interpreted as demonstrating an effect of viewing on attitudes in much the same style as the most outdated of simple correlation studies. Similarly, Zimmerman Umble's evidence (in the same volume) that the most devout and conservative Mennonites watch least television, whilst more liberal and less strict Mennonites watch more, is unsurprising and provides little reason to believe that this is an *effect* of television, as the author concludes.

Murdock (1994) notes that Gerbner's approach, whilst differing from the standard effects model in some ways, nonetheless shares the same '*transportation*' model of meaning, in which the media are simply seen as vehicles for shifting messages from sender to receiver. Murdock himself proposes 'a *translation* model, which sees television as an organizational system for converting social discourses into completed programs through the mediation of specific cultural forms' (p. 173). However, even this model seems to suggest that discourses are funnelled into programmes and then (presumably) *transported* into the world by those programmes. The idea that viewers unproblematically absorb television content, whether this is conceived as a set of messages or as the undoubtedly more sophisticated notion of discourses, remains in both models. A third model can be considered, which concerns discourse as it is produced *about* television programming *by* the audience, with any intended transported meanings, or discourses translated into television output, of interest only in terms of how they have come out on the 'other side' of the broadcaster-viewer relationship.

Beyond simple surveys: listening to the audience

The cultivation researchers' rigid adherence to the practice of not informing subjects that the study of their attitudes is being conducted in the light of their television exposure – a technique elevated to one of high cunning in some reports – means that any opportunity to find their reactions and meanings derived or developed from their television viewing is lost. The researchers do not seem to have considered that instead of simply stockpiling correlational data, they could actually ask the respondents about the possible mediation and formation of their attitudes through television; whilst this would make it impossible to investigate the connection between viewing and attitudes without respondents being aware of the research topic, it presents opportunities to better understand television influences beyond the uninformative correlations and their speculative results. The idea of valuable research being found in such interaction with subjects might seem alarming to the more 'scientific' psychology and communications researchers, but their own failure to produce many genuine insights is one of the strongest arguments in favour of the alternative methods.

David Buckingham's qualitative interviews with groups of children, for example, reported in his *Children Talking Television* (1993), amply demonstrate the benefits which can be gained from in-depth exploration of children's knowledge, attitudes and perceptions by simply sitting down and *talking* with them. Patricia Palmer (1986) combined loosely structured interviews with individual children, lengthy observation of their viewing in the home environment, and a survey to test the generalisability of certain findings, in a study which was thereby able to reveal children's sophisticated, interactive approach to television. The interview component of such studies show that the volunteered, verbal responses of subjects can tell us what they really think and feel in ways which convey information in greater detail and, importantly, with much greater precision than many a set of questionnaire responses. This point is also extensively illustrated in Ann Gray's fascinating interview-based study of womens' use of videocassette recorders, *Video Playtime: The Gendering of a Leisure Technology* (1992); in Schlesinger, Dobash, Dobash & Weaver's *Women Viewing Violence* (1992) in which groups of women watched and then discussed several complete programmes; and in Hagell & Newburn's (1994) interviews with young offenders, discussed in chapter one.

The value of more qualitative research has also been demonstrated by Tulloch & Tulloch's (1992) study in which groups of Australian school students were shown sequences involving violence from two different programmes: scenes of domestic violence from the Australian soap, *A Country Practice*, and of conflict between police and miners from a British documentary about the 1984 miners' strike, Ken Loach's *Which Side Are You On?*. After each twenty-minute screening, the children were asked to write up to a side of A4 on 'what it was about', providing the researchers with the written interpretations of almost 400 students (aged nine, twelve and fifteen) to analyse – an amount of data sufficient to impress any quantitative researcher. The study was able to show, for example, that the children could all readily understand and make inferences about the soap narrative, but that the non-linear documentary caused problems for some of the younger viewers, with its less familiar (and foreign) 'arts programme' format, and unusual portrayal of the police not as benevolent helpers but as instigators of violence. Almost all of the children condemned the violence in the scenes (the only exceptions being a small number of younger children who did not understand the documentary, and assumed that the miners must have been 'naughty'), and many developed complex responses to what they had seen. The study was able to provide 'massive endorsement to the notion that (reformist-type) "feminist" readings are common among adolescents – boys as well as girls – in the area of domestic violence' (p. 230), and the children's responses show that whilst they in no way approved of the fictional acts of violence, they believed that such depictions were important – in the words of one 12-year-old girl – 'to show people what is happening to people' (p. 213).

Another method, developed by Morrison & MacGregor (1993; also MacGregor & Morrison, 1995) has taken the idea of confronting subjects with the media issues in question one step further, through encouraging focus groups to actively edit video material into preferred television programmes or reports for themselves. The task of actually producing their own 'cut' evidently brings into the open the participants' most deeply felt responses and thoughts about television content, which are not necessarily recorded by the 'gut reaction' responses given to interviewers, or even revealed in focus group discussions.

Qualitative research into the media sophistication of young adults is perhaps as much-needed as study of the intersections between deprivation, violence and media use. Research with children (Buckingham, 1993) has already suggested that media literacy is generally underestimated to a substantial degree. Viewers may well, for example, keenly look forward to a *Cracker* story about a serial killer motivated by the 1989 Hillsborough football stadium disaster (more specifically, blaming police for the deaths of the 96 fans, and bitter about the treatment of the victims and their families by a British culture which held them in low regard – Jimmy McGovern's *To Be A Somebody*, 1994). The viewers' reaction to the existence of such a killer in *real life*, we can hypothesize, would be similar to anyone's – most likely of horror and shock. Indeed, the television fiction (deliberately) produces such emotions, particularly in having a well-developed central character, DCI Bilborough, murdered before our eyes. Nevertheless, the drama's production and 'high concept' can at the same time be quite separately enjoyed for its imagination, gripping realization, and audacity in tapping into the open wound of a relatively recent event in British history. The ability of viewers to recognize screen entertainment for what it is would mean not so much that they are 'media educated' enough to avoid the supposed temptations of imitating screen violence, but rather that their naturally developed media literacy means that any potential links between the screen fiction and their own behaviour would be severed at source. Indeed, the work of researchers such as Livingstone (1994) suggests that the very differences between the views of some clearly genuinely worried researchers, and the many quite unconcerned viewers, is because familiarity with TV *genres* is central to their appreciation. In other words, the researchers' greater level of concern about television's effects might be due not only to differences in sensibilities and expectations, but also a discrepancy in the levels of contemporary media literacy held by researchers as compared to the young people who have grown up with recent television output, and so whose media sophistication has been cultivated over considerable viewing time. Clearly, however, more research is needed into such degrees of viewing literacy and modes of consumption. One way forward is to put video production resources into the hands of children themselves, and see what is produced – giving young people the power to directly refute the notion that they are naïve and incompetent in their media encounters (Gauntlett, 1995a, 1995b).

The more sophisticated, qualitative approaches discussed in this section have clearly shown that research which engages respondents with the focus of study, such as television depictions of violence, are much more likely to reveal their actual feelings, concerns, interpretations and preferences about television output, than simple surveys which seek to keep television separate from the other questions in respondent's minds. A more dynamic and imaginative interpretation of what are supposedly the tenets of cultivation research – the influence of television over time as it is actively watched and interpreted by viewers within the full environment of their lives – would perhaps produce research which manages to break free of the apparent pull of the stimulus–response effects tradition, and would enable researchers to better understand viewers' uses and interpretations of television, and its place in their lives.

8 The context: Panic versus programmes

he television effects research, of course, is not an area of abstract academic
discourse, and needs to be firmly grounded in the realities of its existence and
purpose. We therefore have to pay close attention not just to the research results,
but to the mass media concern which has helped to keep the research alive for so many
years, a moral panic firmly rooted in both history and class fears, and to the actual
television content which is supposed to be the basis of all the commotion.

Why the alarm? Effects research and moral panic

Whilst the history of television effects research has often been interpreted in the light of
the development of mass communications study, it can be understood just as well in its
place as part of an enduring moral panic. Indeed, it is now perhaps more interesting not
to ask what the effects of television are, but rather why there is so much concern about the
question.

There is nothing like history to put a social 'problem' into some perspective. Whilst critics
today often suggest that television has helped to bring about a sudden and rapid moral
decline from the stable traditions of the past, Geoffrey Pearson (1983) has shown that
similar fears have been commonplace throughout history, and that contemporary perceptions about the state of the world in no way represent a disjuncture with historical
precedent, as these campaigners would have us believe. Music Halls in Victorian Britain,
for example, were held at the time to promote lawlessness, immorality and violence
(p. 63), whilst violence at football matches, rather than being just an artefact of a lack of
discipline in the late twentieth century, was rife 100 years earlier, complete with pitch
invasions, attacks on players and referees, and battles between fans (p. 64). Bicycles, too,
were seen as symptomatic of moral decay in the 1890s, with the 'Cyclist Terror' (*The
Daily Graphic*, 1897) – or 'Cyclomania' (*News of the World*, 1898) – being seen as the
cause of chaos in town and country, endangering the health of riders and the very lives of
innocent passers-by. 'Hit-and-run' cyclists were prosecuted for deaths and injuries which
they may or may not have caused; one jury, returning a verdict of 'heart disease from
natural causes' on the death of a 70 year old man, was lambasted in an angry *Daily Mail*

editorial of 1898: 'There were cyclists on the jury, we read, and this fact has a grim sound ... Steps should be taken to put these people down' (p. 68). Whilst such slices of history can be regarded with amused affection now, we should remember that at the time they were treated with the same seriousness and fervour which is applied to concerns about television content and effects today.

The relatively simple concept of moral panic may be unable to explain the fears which underlie the expressions of concern (which would be a book in itself, with the account perhaps involving anxieties about the breaking of taboos and the loss of social order), but nevertheless serves as an at least partial explanation of *what happens*. Stanley Cohen, in his noted study *Folk Devils and Moral Panics* (1972, p. 9), describes the moral panic as a situation in which:

> A condition, episode, person or group of persons emerges to become defined as a threat to societal values and interests; its nature is presented in a stylized and stereotypical fashion by the mass media; the moral barricades are manned by editors, bishops, politicians and other right-thinking people; socially accredited experts pronounce their diagnoses and solutions; ways of coping are evolved or (more often) resorted to; the condition then disappears, submerges or deteriorates and becomes more visible.

The moral panic about television violence fits exceptionally well into this definition, although it has not been a sudden, short-lived social problem which something is ultimately 'done' about. The moral panic about so-called 'video nasties' in Britain in the early 1980s fits more neatly into that particular category, since the panic was swiftly followed by the hasty introduction of the Video Recordings Act 1984, which imposed a formal system of video classification to be operated by the BBFC, with tougher criteria than for cinema certificates, and made it a criminal offence to supply or possess for supply an unclassified video, thereby effectively banning most 'video nasty' titles, amongst others (this moral panic is well documented in Barker, (ed.), 1984. A similar controversy and rush for legislation occurred in other countries – see, for example, Shuker's (1986) account of the same phenomenon in New Zealand). The revival of this moral panic in 1993–94 similarly led to the British government announcing even tighter legislation and censorship of videos, in April 1994.

The alarm about general television violence is different from the more usual short-lived panic in two ways. First, there is its very longevity – the controversy, whilst coming in waves of more vigorous concern at various times, has remained reasonably stable and constant, relatively unaffected by research or counter-arguments, and not terminated by a major act of censorship or restriction imposed on the cause of the panic in Britain or the United States. Second, moral panics have at least usually developed in reasonably close relation to the subject of concern – for example, Cohen's (1972) study of the moral panic about Mods and Rockers in the mid-1960s shows how the media and its subject interacted, leading to a degree of escalation of the feared activity. However, the continuing panic about television violence has had little to do with changes in the actual cause of concern, the level of violence on television, which has remained reasonably constant over past decades. Particular instances of violent depictions can always be called upon by the critics and 'moral entrepreneurs' (Becker, 1963) who wish to promote the controversy, of course, but actual television content is left more or less on the sidelines of this particular, and very persistent, moral panic – in this sense, it is quite literally 'pure' panic. The escalation and reinforcement of concern can be (simplistically) illustrated as in Fig. 1.[*]

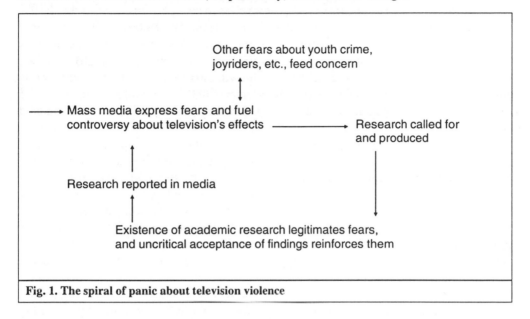

Fig. 1. The spiral of panic about television violence

The initial media panic generates and provides a means of expression for public concern about television violence, which leads to academic interest and research funded by broadcasters, government or other bodies. The claims and findings of this research are then interpreted and reported by the media, and so may fuel more expressions of moral panic, leading to further (but usually similar) research, and so on. Studies which suggest that effects occur are clearly more 'newsworthy' than those which do not, and so more sophisticated academic approaches to the problem are unlikely to have the media impact necessary to entirely halt the spiral, although it may be their restraining influence which means that the spiral does not escalate out of hand, but rather remains reasonably constant in the magnitude of its recurring waves of concern.

Class fears and the 'video nanny'

Assumptions about class are another factor central to the moral panics about screen violence in general, and 'video nasties' in particular. In his work discussed above, Cohen (1972) suggested also that moral panics are particularly likely to develop where their

---

[*] Of course, social processes cannot really be represented in diagrams – this illustration is obviously a slightly ironic and highly simplified 'ideal type' model.

implications can be placed at the door of the working-class, whilst middle class moralists and politicians feel that they can pontificate about the subject with relative impunity. Television violence has become a classic example of this for right-wing politicians, critics, and others, who plainly seem to believe that the presumed effects will not happen to them or their children, but will turn working-class adolescents into unruly savages. The British Board of Film Classification's decision-making has at times reflected this, with the subtitled (but extremely violent) *Man Bites Dog* released on video uncut, whilst the similar *Henry: Portrait of a Serial Killer* was cut for video release, and *Reservoir Dogs* was held for an extended period in that video limbo occupied by other tape-unclassified movies such as *Straw Dogs* and *The Exorcist*. The assumption, made explicit in the BBFC's own statements on the subject, is that the foreign film will only be watched by a middle-class elite, rather than the corruptible masses (see Ferman, 1993).[*] The thinking mirrors that of D.H. Lawrence's publishers who queried whether they could publish the then-banned *Lady Chatterley's Lover* if they promised never to bring it out in paperback (Edwards, 1994). The rhetoric of certain politicians, academics and the tabloid press at the time of the renewed British video nasties panic make it no surprise that representatives from *Living Marxism* magazine complained at a debate that working-class parents were being scape-goated, caricatured as 'folk devils, down in the pub every night whilst the kids are stuck in front of the video machines' (Anwar, 1994). Whilst not always as explicit as *Crime-watch* presenter Sue Cook (1994), who expressed shock that even some 'middle-class professional people' would allow their children to watch the 15-certificate *Terminator 2: Judgement Day*, most of the self-appointed cultural commentators seemed to be basing their arguments on a picture of working-class children left in front of their 'video nanny' to watch a diet of peculiarly horrible films. The repeated concern that new legislation would not affect 'artistically valid' or 'serious' films – *Schindler's List* rapidly becoming a widely-accepted test case – reinforced this impression.

The 'mass culture' of television and video seems still to be regarded with the same kind of distaste accorded to the 'masses' themselves. For example, although there is substantial evidence that media education can help children to recognize the constructedness of screen images, and be critical and resistant to their impact (Singer & Singer, 1983; Cumberbatch, 1989a, p. 47; Buckingham, 1993), the British Conservative government only made moves to remove the subject from the school curriculum in the mid-1990s, suggesting a rather 'schizophrenic' attitude to the supposed danger of television. However, it is likely that right-wing politicians do *believe* their own rhetoric about television, and they have been reasonably successful in constituting its portrayals of violence as a threat to civilized society, and a cause of social ills. The notion of the individual as the unfettered determinator of their own destiny, as celebrated in right-wing ideology, is an ideal place for notions of television effect to be incubated, free from concerns about the possible influence of structural factors such as poverty and unemployment, which are seen as mere conditions

---

[*] James Ferman, director of the BBFC, commented in 1993: '*Man Bites Dog* is not the same kind of issue [as the American hit *Reservoir Dogs*] because it will have a fairly narrow release, it's a subtitled film and I don't expect it to go very wide'. (Quoted in *Empire*, June 1993, p. 7).

which it is the individual's responsibility to escape. A survey of a representative sample of 974 people in Britain (Docherty, Morrison & Tracey, 1988) has shown that working-class people are more likely to perceive sociological factors such as poor housing, poverty and unemployment as responsible for violent crime, whilst the middle classes strongly favour more individualistic explanations, such as lack of discipline in the home (p. 116). For middle-class politicians, therefore, who are relatively safe from both the social problems of poor living conditions and rising crime in their localities, the 'radically individualist view' of television as a direct cause of crime (Docherty *et al*, p. 115) is likely to seem more tenable. Fears of working-class youth are likely to feed into this ideology, and this is reflected in the discourse about the 'other people' who are going to be affected by television, who are portrayed as those who have not had the 'decent' middle-class upbringing which would presumably enable them to filter out television's damaging effect. However, the finding of Docherty *et al*'s survey, and the 44 discussion groups that they conducted, is that the notion of 'the people' needing to be protected from television's effects is not shared by the audience themselves (p. 115):

> As our research has demonstrated overwhelmingly, in the particular case of television 'the people' claim that they have no need of [such protection]; most people think that it is ludicrous to ignore the social sources of their behaviour in favour of claiming that their attitudes and actions are formed by television.

This common view, and the potential offence caused by the patronizing attitude of many politicians to viewers of popular television, has not, of course, substantially curbed the expressions of moral panic about television effects, which seem to thrive in an atmosphere quite removed from the specific details of public concern and, indeed, television content, which is discussed in the following section.

Researchers' assumptions versus television content

Television effects research has deficiencies beyond the internal inconsistencies and poor design of individual studies, of course; television is all too often written about by psychologists and communications academics whose ideological (or other) reservations about the medium – and consequent ignorance or selective interpretation of its pro-grammes – lead to a rather stunted discussion of the potential consequences of actual TV material. Within the confines of this section, a limited attempt is made to redress this imbalance.

The discussion inevitably begins, once again, with the concerns about violence, followed by a brief consideration of television's alleged role as a propagator of sex stereotypes. These areas are not unconnected: the decline of violent machismo in 1990s television means that the space available for the 'gratuitous violence' which so concerns the critics and researchers is ever more squeezed out.

First of all, it is instructive to recall here the research of Hagell & Newburn (1994), described in chapter one, which found that the viewing habits of young offenders were no different from those of a general sample of non-offenders of the same age, except that the offenders had watched *less* television than their 'ordinary' counterparts and were generally less involved with and engaged by it. Such findings do not, of course, put a stop to the alarm so frequently expressed about television content and its presumed or implied consequences. The academic and political discourses about television violence, as well as the more popular forms of moral panic, tend to present a picture of television as filled with a never-ending array of gratuitously violent programmes. Paik & Comstock (1994, p. 517), for example, note simply that 'Television content has not changed – it continues to be violent', whilst Gerbner (1994, p. 133) more spectacularly writes that 'We are awash in a tide of violent representations unlike any the world has ever seen ... drenching every home with graphic scenes of expertly choreographed brutality'. Even without such pronouncements, the effects studies can easily carry the reader along with their tacit assumptions about the world and about television programming. Their discourse assumes that it is 'obvious' that prime-time television is full of sickening, gratuitous and unjustified violence, and that this is likely to be a primary cause of violence in society. The assumptions about television content may in part be due to the fact that most of these studies are produced in America, where television programming may be considered to be more violent and less diverse than in Britain (Halloran, 1978, p. 823; Murdock, 1994, p. 179). To consider the situation on either side of the Atlantic, however, it is important that we do not consider the question of television effects in terms of the impressions generated by any kind of hysteria, moral panic, or research which is not related to TV output, but rather assess it in the context of the kinds of material which are actually shown on television.

Of course, it would ultimately be most desirable to be able to draw on a research literature describing the perceptions of programmes containing 'violence' or other controversial content, held by 'ordinary' viewers. In the absence of any amount of such up-to-date material, however, the following passages can be taken as an argument that it is both useful and indeed necessary that the researcher or commentator on supposed media effects at least make some effort to relate their argument to what they consider likely to be common readings of relevant popular mass media (Gauntlett, 1994).

As previous chapters have shown, the effects research as a whole has tended to keep very closely to the notion that effects could only be imitative, such as that the portrayal of violence could only lead to real-life violence. This assumption presumably derives from the view that television's portrayal of violence is always promotional. The paucity of careful thought behind this extremely generalized and monolithic conception of screen violence is particularly apparent when we consider the kind of material which has prompted public expressions of concern. In the United States the first episode of the police drama series *NYPD Blue* (1993–) had not even been broadcast when the American Family Association took out full-page newspaper advertisements declaring that 'This time TV has gone too far', and lambasting the show for 'blood and guns and racy language'; the series was swiftly banned in Texas. No matter to them that the occasional violent scenes and (actually quite tame) language occur in the context of detectives Kelly, or, now, Simone and Sipowicz passionately seeking justice, and even a better quality of life, for the New York population. Gratuitous violence, whether by criminals or police officers, far from being condoned, is opposed and resisted, particularly by the young lead. As Keane (1994) notes, 'Detective Kelly is straight as a die, bending the rules only on the very rare occasions when his natural sense of justice overrides the law. Although this occurs about once every other episode it is not something he undertakes lightly. A Catholic, Kelly is acutely aware of the danger career cynicism might inflict on his mortal soul'. Those in favour of moral standards, except perhaps in the fundamental religious sense, should have nothing to fear.

An even more baffling confusion between portrayal and promotion of violence occurred in the controversy surrounding the *Casualty* episode, 'Boiling Point' (1993), which critics claimed would inspire young people in the audience of 17 million to engage in violent activities against innocent people, and to burn down hospitals, as depicted in the programme (for this debate, see Broadcasting Standards Council, 1993; *Radio Times,* 1993a, 1993b; Barker, 1993; Douglas, 1993; Kingsley, 1993). However, months went by, and riots did not break out, and the hospitals remained standing. The programme's critics, in their knee-jerk, alarmist reaction, had failed to understand the point made by some viewers on the letters page of *Radio Times* (20 March & 10 July 1993), whose argument is typified by a Mrs McKeown, who noted that the episode 'actually made clear how mindless behaviour can escalate into tragedy. At least one young offenders' group I know of was shown it and was appalled to see what can happen.' (10 July 1993, p. 105). This possibility that the portrayal of violence on television may have the effect of turning viewers *against* violence in real life – not through 'catharsis' but simply by showing its unpleasantness – is almost never considered in the academic literature, or tested for in research, even though there seems little reason for considering it less likely than the popular reverse hypothesis. Noble (1975) seems almost alone in the academic community for taking this notion seriously, although it is likely that the possibility has always been obvious to many viewers, as demonstrated by the women in the Schlesinger *et al* (1992) study (see chapter one), and the children surveyed by Tulloch & Tulloch (1992 – see chapter seven), who recognized the potential positive side to the distressing depictions of domestic violence in *EastEnders* and *A Country Practice*.

Only the crudest reading of television programmes could suggest that violence and killing is 'celebrated', as is sometimes alleged. In almost all cases, the most common reading of such portrayals is likely to be that the acts depicted are, at the very least, unpleasant and painful, and that is not an impression which one would expect the anti-violence campaigners to want banned. The film *Terminator 2: Judgment Day* (1991), for example, which is regularly and routinely picked on by people who appear not to have seen it, ultimately contains a strong anti-violence and anti-war message, the leading characters (including the 'Terminator' played by Arnold Schwarzenegger) pointedly finding solutions other than killing people – which they at no point do – in their attempt to avert a devastating nuclear war. It is certainly the case that both of these examples, mentioned here because of the controversy which erupted about their violent content, were written with pro-social intentions, *Casualty: Boiling Point* to demonstrate how tragedy can develop from small and pointless acts of violence prompted by unemployment and poor living conditions (see interview with writer Peter Bowker in Kingsley, 1993, pp. 40–42), and *Terminator 2* to bring a mass audience to face the horror of nuclear war (see interview with writer/director James Cameron in Shay & Duncan, 1991, p. 19). In addition, it is curious that those who are concerned about television's effects complain about the more visceral and unpleasant screen violence which reflects the seriousness of the acts – such as may occasionally be seen in the drama series *Cracker* (1993–), Dennis Potter's *Lipstick on Your Collar* (1993), *NYPD Blue*, or any number of televised feature films – whilst the cheerful, 'clean' and more frequent killings featured in films such as *Top Gun* (1987) and the James Bond series (1962–89) are excused from such criticism, and seen as somehow more wholesome. These considerations give credence to Martin Barker's (1989, 1994) argument that major controversies about violent content often develop when the depictions conflict with certain political values, rather than standards solely related to decency, taste, or feared effects. In any case, whilst other programmes and films certainly contain less justified and more visceral depictions of violence, cases where it is promoted as a solution to everyday problems are extremely rare, and the argument that British or American television is likely to encourage young people to be genuinely violent is not really supported by television content any more than it is by the effects research.

Related to this area – since depictions of violent machismo are central to the fears about television and aggression – is the sphere of criticism which complains that television promotes and maintains gender stereotypes and differences. Whilst this argument has a firmer grounding in television's history than the violence contentions, it is certainly another case where critics seem disappointingly out of touch with recent programming. Assuming that by this stage we can forget proposals of direct effects altogether, we can recognize that there is substance to the argument that television in the past has depicted rather extreme delineations of masculinity and femininity, and that some of the TV tradition of strong, heroic, breadwinning males and weaker, submissive females survives in part to this day. However, it is important to note that today this situation is sometimes presented with irony or occasional parody, and that television has not entirely failed to change with the times. Furthermore, in the 1990s there are many transformations taking place in TV gender portrayals which the critics who assume that nothing has changed since the 1970s or even the late 1980s embarrass themselves by failing to notice. To trace the changes, we can consider the example of *Lois and Clark: The New Adventures of Superman* (1993–), which has managed to translate the old macho superhero myth into a distinctly 'nineties' – and popular – package. Here, Clark Kent does possess 'super' powers and strength, but he is also sensitive, gentle, and confused; Lois Lane, meanwhile, is a genuine top reporter, more intelligent and successful than Clark, and noticeably more independent. ('Who on this side of the Atlantic', marvelled Chris Dunkley in the *Financial Times* (1994), 'would have guessed that the Americans were so far into post-feminism?'). The new series has at times fallen into the cliches of previous incarnations – Lois being saved from peril by Superman – but at least an effort is made not to show this as a consequence of feminine stupidity. Clark/Superman spends his episodes in emotional dramas, frequently turning to his parents and friends for help, whilst Lois gets on with the job. Significantly, Clark gains respect for his emotional honesty, just as Lois does for her careerism; whilst these types of characters may have been parodied as 'boy wimp' and 'career bitch' in the competitive dramas of the 1980s such as *Dallas*, that is certainly no longer the case. Similarly, the female and male FBI investigators of *The X-Files* (1993–), Scully and Mulder, whilst less concerned with their emotional troubles, accept each other as intellectual equals immediately and without a second thought. On the other side of the same coin are the dramas where men are still macho but are seen to suffer from it, rather than triumph in it. Fitz in *Cracker*, for example, is a man who most of the time takes a tough, no-nonsense, arrogant and aggressive line, but is clearly troubled by it both from within and in the shortcomings of his social relations. Sipowicz in *NYPD Blue* is similarly a man finding that his old-school macho style is increasingly inappropriate, ineffective and a lifestyle dead-end.*

A classic example of the interface between changing portrayals of violence and gender is the contrast between John Thaw's lead roles in *The Sweeney* (1975–78) and *Inspector Morse* (1987–93). As Regan in the earlier series, he had few qualms about injuring suspects, and pursued his duties with macho vigour. His casting as Morse perfectly caught what would soon be called the more 'nineties' preferences of modern audiences on both sides of the Atlantic: gentle, lonely and quietly intellectual, Morse had no stomach for violence. Facing a potentially fatal situation at the climax of the episode 'Promised Land' (1992), for example, where he must put right the mistake of a wrongful conviction for

---

* At the same time women are rapidly gaining promotions in the television world and can now be seen working assertively as central or leading parts of every professional team, in the police, fire and emergency services, in hospitals, on oilrigs, spacestations, as private detectives, and in every other classic TV genre situation. The female doctors and administrators in *Medics* (1992–) and *Casualty* (1986–), for example, can be just as nice and nasty (respectively) as their male counterparts, whilst the female private detective *Anna Lee* (1993–94) and duo *Chandler and Co* (1994–) are independent and assertive in a way that *Charlie's Angels* (1976–81), whose mild subordination and emphasis on glamour was underlined even within the title, rarely achieved. The creator of *Chandler and Co*, Paula Milne, had previously broken ground by tackling the sexism of 1970s crime drama from within in her contribution to the final season of *Z Cars*, *A Woman's Place* (1978), and the newer series successfully illustrate the thesis that the genre can not only do without lengthy chases and punch-ups – which had already been demonstrated by the gentler, usually morose male detectives of series such as *Inspector Morse* (1987–93) and *Wycliffe* (1993–) – but does not need men at all. Of course, some of the groundwork had been laid for this already in the series *Juliet Bravo* (1980–85) and *Widows* (1983, 1985), and later in DCI Tennison's notable struggles with sexism in the police force in the *Prime Suspect* series (1991–). The American contributions are also not to be ignored: whilst admittedly *Wonder Woman* (1976–79) has only become a feminist icon for those with some sense of irony, the arrival of *Cagney and Lacey* (1982–88) set an impressive and (relatively) early standard for female TV detectives, partly imitated in Britain by the rather less powerful *CATS Eyes* (1985–87). Importantly, too, for the first time openly lesbian characters have begun to appear on a regular basis and as *normal people* in the British series *Brookside* (from 1993), *EastEnders* (1994) and *Medics* (1994). In the United States, we can contrast the practical and witty women of *Northern Exposure* (1990–) with those who were often little more than ornamental 'bimbos' at Southfork, Hazzard County and many other fictional locales of the earlier 1980s, and note that the eponymous stars of *Ellen*, (1994–) *Grace Under Fire* (1993–) and *Roseanne* (1988–) respond to attempted subordination with a force which quite eluded that of *I Love Lucy* (1951–61).

which he feels responsible, his sense of duty and destiny is sorrowful rather than swaggering: 'I'm old, and – unmarried, and – I don't understand human nature; what does it matter?', he muses, with typical lyricism. Comparison of almost any of the 'masculine' crime dramas of the 1970s or early 80s with those of today shows that the old conception of 'action' has moved largely from the physical to the mental (Dunkley, 1993), with psychology replacing violence, dialogue supplanting demolition (again, see *Cracker*, and the increasingly complex moral dilemmas faced by the newly privatized protagonists in *Between The Lines*). Similarly at the cinema, whilst action movies retain their physical thrills, the emergent type of mid-nineties male action hero, as exemplified by Keanu Reeves in *Speed* (1994), is a sometimes-emotional hero who has a strong urge to protect – but who does not doubt women's ability to look after themselves.

The point here is not, of course, that *any* of these portrayals will have direct effects on behaviour, but simply that mainstream television output is unlikely to even provide models of the kind of pointless, amoral behaviour which would need to be depicted for many of the research conclusions, all too hastily drawn about television violence, to have foundation.[*]

---

[*] Not all of the changes in gender portrayal have gone unnoticed by feminist media commentators, of course, but most academic progress tends to have been concentrated at the cultural studies end of the field, rather than in the sociological areas which are more concerned with the audience (see, for example, Jeffords (1993) on the changing portrayal of masculinity in Hollywood cinema, Clark (1990) and D'Acci (1987) on *Cagney and Lacey*, Skirrow (1987) and Brunsdon (1987) on women in British 1980s TV crime drama, and of course the flood of work on Madonna's video image – start with Kaplan (1992), bell hooks (1992)). However, these rather specific exceptions do not alter the fact that in some quarters, the notion of television gender portrayals as hopelessly stereotyped and traditional – and persuasive – still persists. The arguments of Signorielli (1993) and Palmer, Smith & Strawser (1993), for example, were out of date well before they were published, and in particular are flawed in their reliance on studies from the 1970s and 1980s which have rapidly become antiquated. Whilst women undoubtedly are still used on television at times for little more than ornamentation, and that much programming could do better in terms of providing winning 'role models' for women, programme-makers are clearly making changes. Once again, the critics would do well to turn an unprejudiced eye to their screens.

9 Summary and conclusion

This review has demonstrated that the traditional effects research paradigm is redundant, and can now be left behind with confidence. The attempts to find direct effects of television on viewers' behaviour have had no success. This can of course be traced directly back to the inherently simplistic, determinist type of question being posed, which has been flawed from the start. Does television make viewers do things they would not otherwise have been inclined to do? No. To argue that screen violence causes real-life violence, in particular, is as Boston (1994) says, 'like suggesting that the wind is caused by trees shaking their branches'. But is television likely to have had any influence at all on viewers' perceptions of one thing or another? Of course. But the traditional research questions are not couched in these terms.

The cumulative 'message' of this monograph is not so much that there should be no concern about TV content – people have the liberty and imagination to worry about an infinite range of potential problems – but that, scientifically speaking, you're on your own. All too often the television effects research evidence is interpreted as 'inconclusive', or as showing nothing. In fact, if nothing else, it *has* answered its own question: television does not have predictable, direct effects. The mass of studies, which individually may be inconclusive or flawed, when taken as a whole must surely demonstrate that. The lack of 'positive' results showing effects in the real world do not constitute an informational void, but have to be taken as a conclusion in themselves.

The history and persistence of effects research can be much more easily traced back to the recurrent moral panic and associated political interest about television, than to any more intelligible process of thoughtful research development based on a growing body of knowledge. The research evidence has at least shown that this moral panic has little justification. As Barwise & Ehrenberg note, it is not simply that effects of televison on violence have not been proved, but that they are not usually even a consideration for those professionally involved in limiting it (1988, p. 139): criminologists do not concern themselves with television output when they seek to explain crime rates, any more than villains are genuinely likely to trace their illicit career back to Saturday evenings in front of *The A-Team*.

The point of defending television against the charges of its negative impact is not simply to protect a much-loved entertainment medium, but is rather to argue that it is irresponsible to blame important social problems such as crime and violence on the small screen. Television does not deserve to have the complex and deep-rooted troubles of society laid at its door. An emphasis on television as life's primary corrupter is a conspicuously shortsighted view which only provides a convenient excuse for the other, more genuine causes of social ills to be ignored.

Constructive study of television's possible influences or effects would have to combine rigorous audience research with some attempt to explain what is going on, and why. As we have seen, most of the effects studies, especially those claiming that television viewing produces violence or other undesirable outcomes, have generally made no attempt to suggest why the alleged effects might occur. Since the claimed results are usually very tenuous extractions from weak data, one would expect such justification to be doubly necessary.

The research into the possible effect of television depictions of violence on viewers' aggression, on its own terms, has produced a variety of results, some positive. However, we have seen that the studies which claim to find 'effects' tend to be methodologically flawed, and are often small-scale. Freedman (1986, p. 378) asks readers of these studies:

> 'If all of the results were precisely reversed, if every effect that showed an increase in aggression actually showed a decrease and vice versa, would the evidence be sufficient to convince you that television violence reduced aggression? I doubt that it would.'

The laboratory experiments are flawed in their measures of aggression, which generally take surrogates for aggression as being equivalent to the real thing, and by the artificiality of the material shown to subjects, which generally do not represent the kinds of programmes available for viewing in the home environment. There is also the extreme likelihood that experimenter demand influences the behaviour which children display following their exposure to the experimental TV material. In addition, there are inconsistencies in the experimental research findings which are difficult to explain: some experiments have found that aggressive responses are only produced in subjects who have been previously angered or frustrated, whilst others have shown that quite unrelated stimuli such as comedy films can produce aggression 'effects' in the laboratory which are just as significant as those produced by the violent films. The lack of consistency between these findings and the other laboratory evidence throws the validity of this whole type of research into question, and suggests that the effects apparently found in laboratory experiments may merely be the result of an arousal effect, the differences between control and experimental groups being simply the result of different levels of stimulation produced by the bland control films and the exciting experimental films. There is a strong case to be made that the results of the laboratory experiments, which must usually be 'positive' in order to be published, are a product of the unnatural and rarefied environment in which they are conducted, which has been deliberately designed to maximize the possibility of their occurrence. The capacity of these studies to represent effects as they might occur in the real world is highly questionable, and they are likely to be much less representative of natural situations than those studies which seek to study the world without intervention and manipulation. The field experiments suffer from similar problems, but in any case have failed to find consistent and positive effects. This fact in itself suggests that it is precisely the total control over the situation, possible only in laboratory experiments, which enables the production of positive experimental findings.

The natural or 'found' experiments, which retrospectively examine possible effects of television on crime in society at a macro level, have consistently found no evidence of any effect of television viewing on rates of reported violent crime. The methodological rigour of the Hennigan *et al* (1982) and Messner (1986) studies makes their findings highly persuasive. Even with the problems of using official statistics, which the researchers are aware of and take steps to avoid, there can be little reason to doubt that if television violence had an effect on aggression, the extensive data would in some degree have reflected this. However, none of the studies found any sign of such an effect, and Messner even found a significant inverse relationship between his television violence exposure and violent crime measures.

The correlation studies tend to reflect a relatively weak correlation between television violence viewing and aggressive behaviour. However, they do not provide any evidence for a causal link, and the correlation can be easily explained by the unsurprisingly greater attraction of more violent television programmes to those who are already more aggressive people. This view is supported by research which shows stability in these correlations over time, suggesting that television exposure does not increase aggression.

The longitudinal panel studies are those most likely to reflect effects as they might occur in the real world, since they study natural behaviours over a certain period of time. Of these, the Lefkowitz *et al* (1977) and Huesmann *et al* (1984) studies claimed to find some small and inconsistent effects, although methodological problems cast doubt upon even these minor findings. The most sophisticated, large-scale and rigorous study, by Milavsky *et al* (1982), concluded from very extensive analyses of data gathered in several waves over three and a half years, that exposure to television violence had no effect on aggressive behaviour. The findings of the well-designed three-year study by Wiegman, Kuttschreuter & Baarda (1992) firmly agreed with this 'no effect' result. A study in Australia (Sheehan, 1986) also found no effects at all, whilst replications in Israel (Bachrach, 1986) and Poland (Fraczek, 1986) found partial or weak relationships which the authors considered to be verging on the inconsequential.

These far more complex studies show clearly that viewing television violence has no significant or consistent effects on real-life aggression. Even if we do not consider the findings of the two former, less reliable panel studies to be incorrect in their interpretation of the data, the influence of television on aggressive behaviour which they purport to have identified is only around five per cent. This leaves us with the question of why so many researchers have devoted so much time to the investigation of a possible phenomenon which, even if we accept these questionable findings, is still unable to explain 95 per cent of the factors which contribute to aggression. Even if television were to contribute the claimed five per cent, its role would only be as a part, and a rather minor and dependent part, of the wider social milieu – the 95 per cent – which surrounds us, and which must hold the key to the far more substantial and significant causes of violence and aggression. Since effects of any size are only 'found' by flawed studies, and the best designed studies find no such effects, there can be little reason not to reject the aggression effects hypothesis on the basis of the available evidence.

The research into the possible pro-social effects of television similarly contains a disappointing number of unconvincing laboratory experiments which are likely to be affected by experimenter demand. It is also unfortunate that the empirical and quantitative research, flawed as it is, has so far focused almost exclusively on children's programmes which have a self-conscious educational intent, rather than looking for possible pro-social effects of more general, popular entertainment viewing. The one longitudinal study which sought to measure the pro-social effects of a general diet of programming over three years (Wiegman *et al*, 1992) did not find any significant impact on real-life behaviour, although the approach – as crude as any which isolates variables on screen and in real life, and seeks a relationship between them – was perhaps too simplistic to be of use. Interestingly, however, the study showed that viewers who saw more violence on screen were also those who saw more pro-social acts, partly demonstrating the lack of foundation in the fears about children watching specific 'violent' or 'bad' programmes which would offer no models of 'good' behaviour.

More specific field studies suggested that *Sesame Street* helped children to develop social skills and racial tolerance, as well as basic educational advantages – to a limited extent – even when viewed at home without additional support. The drama series *Freestyle* was able to influence only one of the several attitudes about sex-typed behaviours which were targeted, although its impact was improved when viewing was accompanied by classroom discussion. The study of the effects of one specially designed programme on adults by Ball-Rokeach *et al* (1986) suggested that the attitudes and related behaviours of certain viewers can be influenced towards 'pro-social' ends by a specific type of persuasive programme, although this case was somewhat unique. Viewers of the Indian soap opera *Hum Log* claimed to have been influenced in the intended directions, but a more objective study of the impact of *Roots: The Next Generation* in America found no effect. A number of studies by Noble (1983) suggested that children use television to gain useful social learning, and that the development of morality is aided rather than impeded through a kind of dialogue with television characters, good and bad. Other work (Lidz, 1984; Newcomb & Hirsch, 1984) supports this thesis, suggesting that television serves as a modern forum for the continual discussion of moral, social and cultural issues, reflecting contemporary concerns and developments even where its solutions do not 'agree' with the more challenging perspectives.

The studies of public information and persuasion campaigns, summarized at the end of chapter six, clearly point to an overall finding that campaigns which are communicated by the mass media alone tend to have a very limited impact. Interpersonal contact supporting the campaign seems to be almost essential for its influence to be magnified beyond the marginal. Advertising seems to be similarly impotent, requiring advertisers to be ever more innovative to even begin to get through to the TV-literate viewers of today.

We should note, of course, that even where studies have demonstrated that programmes or campaigns have had some small, positive effect on viewers, such findings do not suggest that antisocial effects might equally be produced, since no programmes are intentionally or even vaguely antisocial in the way that some programmes – like *Sesame Street* deliberately, and any number of programmes more generally – are pro-social. Of course, there is also a significant difference between persuading people to engage in socially-approved pro-social deeds, and causing them to commit deviant and possibly criminal antisocial acts, which makes it quite impossible to draw conclusions about television's effects on antisocial behaviour from the findings of the pro-social effects research.

It is clear that more sophisticated research into the possible pro-social and other *influences* of television is needed, particularly longitudinal studies which involve natural viewing habits and qualitative research methods. The search for direct effects of short sequences of programming upon the short-term behaviour of viewers has produced little dependable information about the influences which television might have; but a more in-depth and naturalistic mode of study, perhaps based on a more sophisticated version of cultivation analysis supplemented by interviews, diaries, video editing or other exploratory methods, might produce results of greater value. The pathological search for pathological effects, on the other hand, in its dogged pursuit of results which clearly are not going to show up, has already wasted quite enough research time and money.

In conclusion to the most vexed question in effects research, it must be observed that the causes of violence and crime seem much more likely to be found in poverty, unemployment, homelessness, abuse, frustration, personality traits and psychological background, than in television programmes. This review of the effects research has found that despite the apparent enthusiasm of some researchers to squeeze as much anti-TV argument as possible from some rather small, highly questionable, and sometimes startlingly convoluted findings, careful inspection of the evidence shows that such arguments simply are not tenable. Despite the exceptional *quantity* of research, no methodologically sound and consistent evidence of a significant effect of television violence on aggressive behaviour has been found. At the same time, the fact that a majority of generally non-violent and law-abiding people enjoy television, and feel that they get something from it, suggests that it may have positive long-term influences beyond those produced by specific educational programmes. However, the moral panic both outside of and all too often within the research arena has ensured that all of the most terrifying and apocalyptic possible effects of television viewing have been envisioned and claimed, not helped by many researcher's too-often apparent lack of awareness of actual contemporary television content. Television may *reflect* social problems, and may cause viewers to feel distressed about them, perhaps even compelled to challenge or change some of them, but the programmes are unlikely to actively reinforce them. Media and communications research surely has a place in recording, analysing and transforming the ways in which we share and develop understandings about the world through the powerful medium of television, but such complex and sophisticated processes will only ever be understood by correspondingly subtle and carefully-handled research.

The search for direct 'effects' of television on behaviour is over: every effort has been made, and they simply cannot be found. Television is likely to be one of the many hundreds of influences that touch people every day, however, and it is only with a conception that places television firmly in its place within the much wider social world that we might begin to understand the contribution made to consciousness by its emissions of sound and light.

References

I. Articles and books

Alcalay, Rina, & Taplin, Shahnaz (1989), 'Community Health Campaigns: From Theory to Action', in Rice, Ronald E., & Atkin, Charles K., eds, *Public Communication Campaigns: Second Edition*, Sage, Newbury Park, California.

Altenedcr, R.R.; Price, J.H.; Telljohann, S.K.; Didion, J., & Locher, A. (1992), 'Using the PRECEDE model to determine junior high school students' knowledge, attitudes, and beliefs about AIDS', in *Journal of School Health*, vol. 62, no. 10, pp. 464–470.

Andison, F. Scott (1977), 'TV Violence and Viewer Aggression: A Cumulation of Study Results 1956 – 1976', in *Public Opinion Quarterly*, vol. 41, no. 3, pp. 314–331.

Anwar, Farrah (1994), 'To censor or not to censor, that was the question they came to question', in the *Observer*, 24 April 1994, pp. 6–7.

Atkin, Charles K. (1978), 'Effects of Drug Commercials on Young Viewers', in *Journal of Communication*, vol. 28, no. 4, pp. 71–79.

Atkin, Charles K. (1981), 'Effects of Television Advertising on Children', in Palmer, Edward L., & Dorr, Aimée, *Children and the Faces of Television: Teaching, Violence, Selling*, Academic Press, New York.

Atkin, Charles K., & Meischke, Hendrika W.J. (1989), 'Family Planning Communication Campaigns in Developing Countries', in Rice, Ronald E., & Atkin, Charles K., eds, *Public Communication Campaigns: Second Edition*, Sage, Newbury Park, California.

Bachrach, Riva S. (1986), 'The Differential Effect of Observation of Violence on Kibbutz and City Children in Israel', in Huesmann, L. Rowell, & Eron, Leonard D., eds, *Television and the Aggressive Child: A Cross-National Comparison*, Lawrence Erlbaum Associates, Hillsdale, New Jersey.

Ball-Rokeach, Sandra J.; Grube, Joel W., & Rokeach, Milton (1981), '"*Roots*: The Next Generation" – Who Watched and with What Effect?', in *Public Opinion Quarterly*, vol. 45, no. 1, pp. 58–68.

Ball-Rokeach, Sandra J.; Rokeach, Milton, & Grube, Joel W. (1986), 'Challenging and Stabilizing Political Behavior and Beliefs', in Ball-Rokeach, Sandra J., & Cantor, Muriel G., eds, *Media, Audience and Social Structure*, Sage, Beverly Hills, California.

Balon, Robert E. (1978), 'The Impact of *Roots* on a Racially Heterogeneous Southern Community: An Exploratory Study', in *Journal of Broadcasting*, vol. 22, no. 3, pp. 299–307.

Bandura, A.; Ross, D., & Ross, S.A. (1963), 'Imitation of film-mediated aggressive models', in *Journal of Personality and Social Psychology*, vol. 66, pp. 3–11.

Bandura, Albert (1965), 'Vicarious processes: A case of no-trial learning', in Berkowitz, Leonard, ed., *Advances in Experimental Social Psychology*, vol. 2, Academic Press, New York.

Barker, Martin, ed. (1984), *The Video Nasties: Freedom and Censorship in the Media*, Pluto, London.

Barker, Martin (1984), 'Nasty Politics or Video Nasties?', in Barker, Martin, ed., *The Video Nasties: Freedom and Censorship in the Media*, Pluto, London.

Barker, Martin (1989), *Comics: Ideology, Power and the Critics*, Manchester University Press, Manchester.

Barker, Martin (1993), 'Sex, Violence and Videotape', *Sight and Sound*, vol. 3, no. 5 (New series; May 1993), pp. 10–12.

Barker, Martin (1994), 'Violence and the Media Prism', *The Times Higher Education Supplement*, 3 June 1994, p. 12.

Barr, J.K.; Waring, J.M., & Warshaw, L.J. (1992), 'Knowledge and attitudes about AIDS among corporate and public service employees', in *American Journal of Public Health*, vol. 82, no. 2, pp. 225–228.

Barwise, Patrick, & Ehrenberg, Andrew (1988), *Television and its Audience*, Sage, London.

Becker, Howard S. (1963), *Outsiders: Studies in the Sociology of Deviance*, The Free Press, New York.

Belson, William (1978), *Television Violence and the Adolescent Boy*, Saxon House, Farnborough.

Berkowitz, Leonard (1962), *Aggression: A Social Psychological Analysis*, McGraw-Hill, New York.

Berkowitz, Leonard, ed. (1965), *Advances in Experimental Social Psychology*, vol. 2, Academic Press, New York.

Berry, Gordon L., & Mitchell-Kernan, Claudia (1982), 'Television as a Socializing Force Within a Society of Mass Communication', in Berry, Gordon L., & Mitchell-Kernan, Claudia, eds, *Television and the Socialization of the Minority Child*, Academic Press, New York.

Blatt, Joan; Spencer, Lyle, & Ward, Scott (1972), 'A Cognitive Development Study of Children's Reactions to Television Advertising', in Rubinstein, Eli A., Comstock, George A., & Murray, John P., eds, *Television and Social Behaviour: Reports and Papers, Volume IV: Television in Day-to-Day Life: Patterns of Use*, National Institute of Mental Health, Maryland.

Borden, Richard J. (1975), 'Witnessed Aggression: Influence of an Observer's Sex and Values on Aggressive Responding', in *Journal of Personality and Social Psychology*, vol. 31, no. 3, pp. 567–573.

Boston, Richard (1994), 'Sense and Censorship', in the *Guardian*, 7 April 1994, section 2, p. 5.

British Board of Film Classification (1993), *Video in View: Public Attitudes to Video Classification*, British Board of Film Classification, London.

Brittan, Arthur (1989), *Masculinity and Power*, Basil Blackwell, Oxford.

Broadcasting Standards Council (1993), *Complaints Bulletin*, no. 28, May 1993.

Brown, L.K.; Barone, V.J.; Fritz, G.K.; Cebollero, P., & Nassau, J.H. (1991), 'AIDS education: the Rhode Island experience', in *Health Education Quarterly*, vol. 18, no. 2, pp. 195–206.

Brunsdon, Charlotte, 'Men's Genres for Women', in Baehr, Helen, & Dyer, Gillian, eds, *Boxed In: Women and Television*, Pandora, London.

Bryant, Jennings, & Anderson, Daniel R., eds (1983), *Children's Understanding of Television: Research on Attention and Comprehension*, Academic Press, New York.

Bryant, Jennings, & Zillmann, Dolf, eds (1991), *Responding to the Screen: Reception and Reaction Processes*, Lawrence Erlbaum Associates, Hillsdale, New Jersey.

Buckingham, David (1993), *Children Talking Television: The Making of Television Literacy*, The Falmer Press, London.

Canning, Claire (1994), interviewed in Benson, Richard, 'Video Nation', in *The Face*, vol. 2, no. 73 (October 1994), pp. 102–108.

Cashmore, Ellis (1994), *... and there was television*, Routledge, London.

Chaffee, Steven H. (1972), 'Television and Adolescent Aggressiveness (Overview)', in Comstock, George A., & Rubinstein, Eli A., eds, *Television and Social Behavior: Reports and Papers, Volume III: Television and Adolescent Aggressiveness*, National Institute of Mental Health, Maryland.

Clark, Danae (1990), 'Cagney & Lacey: Feminist Strategies of Detection', in Brown, Mary Ellen, ed., *Television and Women's Culture: The Politics of the Popular*, Sage, London.

Coates, Brian; Pusser, H. Ellison, & Goodman, Irene (1976), 'The Influence of "Sesame Street" and "Mister Rogers' Neighborhood" on Children's Social Behavior in the Preschool', in *Child Development*, vol. 47, pp. 138–144.

Cohen, Stanley (1972), *Folk Devils and Moral Panics: The Creation of the Mods and Rockers*, MacGibbon & Kee, London.

Comstock, George (1981), 'New Emphases in Research on the Effects of Television and Film Violence', in Palmer, Edward L., & Dorr, Aimée, *Children and the Faces of Television: Teaching, Violence, Selling*, Academic Press, New York.

Comstock, George, & Paik, Haejung (1991), *Television and the American Child*, Academic Press, San Diego, California.

Cook, Sue (1994), 'Teaching 10-year-olds to be Terminators', in *The Times*, 13 April 1994, p. 22.

Cook, Thomas D., & Curtin, Thomas R. (1986), 'An Evaluation of the Models Used to Evaluate Television Series', in Comstock, George, ed., *Public Communication and Behavior*, Volume 1, Academic Press, Orlando.

Cook, Thomas D.; Kendzierski, Deborah A., & Thomas, Stephen V. (1983), 'The Implicit Assumptions of Television Research: An Analysis of the 1982 NIMH Report on Television and Behavior', in *Public Opinion Quarterly*, vol. 47, pp. 161–201.

Cubitt, Sean (1990), *Timeshift: On Video Culture*, Routledge, London.

Cumberbatch, Guy (1989a), 'Overview of the Effects of the Mass Media', in Cumberbatch, Guy, & Howitt, Dennis, *A Measure of Uncertainty: The Effects of the Mass Media*, Broadcasting Standards Council Research Monograph, John Libbey, London.

Cumberbatch, Guy (1989b), 'Violence and the Mass Media: The Research Evidence', in Cumberbatch, Guy & Howitt, Dennis, *A Measure of Uncertainty: The Effects of the Mass Media*, Broadcasting Standards Council Research Monograph, John Libbey, London.

D'Acci, Julie (1987), 'The case of Cagney and Lacey', in Baehr, Helen, & Dyer, Gillian, eds, *Boxed In: Women and Television*, Pandora, London.

Daily Mirror (25 November 1993), 'Freaks of Nature', p. 1; 'Judge Blames Violent Videos', p. 4–5.

Daily Mirror (1 April 1994), 'At last, experts admit: Movie nasties do kill: Vidiots!', p. 1; 'You vidiots', p. 11; 'Now ban them: The Video nasties that shame Britain, p. 11.

The *Daily Telegraph* (1 April 1994), '"Naive" experts admit threat of violent videos', p. 1; 'MPs want a ban on horror for hire', p. 4; 'Suspected link with crime cited in three murder trials', p. 4; 'Long fight against offensive viewing', p. 4; 'Violent connection', p. 22.

The *Daily Telegraph* (2 April 1994), 'Howard to call for more cuts in videos', p. 1 & p. 3; '"I am not sure it is not too late"', p. 17.

Derdeyn, Andre P., & Turley, Jeffrey M. (1994), 'Television, Films, and the Emotional Life of Children', in Zillmann, Dolf; Bryant, Jennings, & Huston, Aletha C., eds, *Media, Children and the Family: Social Scientific, Psychodynamic and Clinical Perspectives*, Lawrence Erlbaum, Hillsdale, New Jersey.

Dervin, Brenda (1989), 'Audience as Listener and Learner, Teacher and Confidante: The Sense-Making Approach', in Rice, Ronald E., & Atkin, Charles K., eds, *Public Communication Campaigns: Second Edition*, Sage, Newbury Park, California.

Diener, Ed, & DeFour, Darlene (1978), 'Does Television Violence Enhance Program Popularity?', in *Journal of Personality and Social Psychology*, vol. 36, no. 3, pp. 333–341.

Dobrow, Julia R. (1990), 'Patterns of Viewing and VCR Use: Implications for Cultivation Analysis', in Signorielli, Nancy, & Morgan, Michael, eds, *Cultivation Analysis: New Directions in Media Effects Research*, Sage, Newbury Park, California.

Docherty, David; Morrison, David E., & Tracey, Michael (1988), *Keeping Faith?: Channel Four and its Audience*, John Libbey, London.

Docherty, David (1990), *Public Opinion and Broadcasting Standards: Violence in Television Fiction*, John Libbey, London.

Dommeyer, C.J.; Marquard, J.L.; Gibson, J.E., & Taylor, R.L. (1989), 'The effectiveness of an AIDS education campaign on a college campus', in *Journal of American College Health*, vol. 38, no. 3, pp. 131–135.

Donnerstein, Edward, & Berkowitz, Leonard (1981), 'Victim reactions in aggressive erotic films as a factor in violence against women', in *Journal of Personality and Social Psychology*, vol. 41, pp. 710–724.

Donohue, Thomas R.; Henke, Lucy L., & Donohue, William A. (1980), 'Do Kids Know What TV Commercials Intend?', in *Journal of Advertising Research*, vol. 20, no. 5, pp. 51–57.

Dorr, Aimée, & Kovaric, Peter (1981), 'Some of the People Some of the Time – But Which People?: Televised Violence and Its Effects', in Palmer, Edward L., & Dorr, Aimée, *Children and the Faces of Television: Teaching, Violence, Selling*, Academic Press, New York.

Dorr, Aimée (1986), *Television and Children: A Special Medium for a Special Audience*, Sage, Beverly Hills, California.

Douglas, Torin (1993), 'Is TV Going Too Far?', in *Radio Times*, 19–25 June 1993, pp. 59–61.

Dunkley, Christopher (1993), 'Up with sex, down with violence', in the *Financial Times*, 24 November 1993, p. 19.

Dunkley, Christopher (1994), 'Mass Appeal at its Best', in the *Financial Times*, 12 January 1994, p. 23.

Durkin, Kevin (1985), *Television, Sex Roles and Children: A Developmental Social Psychological Account*, Open University Press, Milton Keynes.

Dworkin, Andrea (1981), *Pornography: Men Possessing Women*, The Women's Press, London.

Dwyer, Terry; Pierce, John P.; Hannam, Cherie D., & Burke, Nick (1986), 'Evaluation of the Sydney "Quit. For Life" Anti-Smoking Campaign: Part 2: Changes in Smoking Prevalence', in *Medical Journal of Australia*, vol. 144, no. 7, pp. 344–347.

Edwards, Mark (1994), 'Censorship', in *The Face*, no. 69 (June 1994), pp. 62–66.

Everywoman (1988), *Pornography and Sexual Violence: Evidence of the Links*, Everywoman, London.

Fairchild, Halford H. (1988), 'Creating Positive Television Images', in Oskamp, Stuart, ed., *Television as a Social Issue*, Applied Social Psychology Annual no. 8, Sage, Newbury Park, California.

Feilitzen, Cecilia von (1994), 'Media Violence – Research Perspectives in the 1980s', in Linné, Olga, & Hamelink, Cees J., eds, *Mass Communication Research: On Problems and Policies: The Art of Asking the Right Questions*, Ablex Publishing, Norwood, New Jersey.

Ferman, James (1993), quoted in *Empire*, no. 48 (June 1993), p. 7.

Feshbach, Norma Deitch (1988), 'Television and the Development of Empathy', in Oskamp, Stuart, ed., *Television as a Social Issue*, Applied Social Psychology Annual no. 8, Sage, Newbury Park, California.

Feshbach, Seymour, & Singer, Robert D. (1971), *Television and Aggression: An Experimental Field Study*, Jossey-Bass, San Francisco.

Feucht, T.E.; Stephens, R.C., & Gibbs, B.H. (1991), 'Knowledge about AIDS among intravenous drug users: an evaluation of an education program', in *AIDS Education & Prevention*, vol. 3, no. 1, pp. 10–20.

Fiske, John (1984), 'Popularity and Ideology: A Structuralist Reading of "Dr. Who"', in Rowland, Willard D., Jr., & Watkins, Bruce, eds, *Interpreting Television: Current Research Perspectives*, Sage, Beverly Hills, California.

Flay, B.R.; Pentz, M.A.; Johnson, C.A.; Sussman, S.; Mestell, J.; Scheier, L.; Collins, L.M., & Hansen, W.B. (1986), 'Reaching Children with Mass Media Health Promotion Programs: The Relative Effectiveness of an Advertising Campaign, a Community-Based Program, and a School-Based Program', in Leathar, D.S.; Hastings, G.B.; O'Reilly, K., & Davies, J.K., eds, *Health Education and the Media II*, Pergamon Press, Oxford.

Flay, Brian R. (1987), *Selling the Smokeless Society: Fifty-six Evaluated Mass Media Programs and Campaigns Worldwide*, American Public Health Association, Washington DC.

125

Flora, June A.; Maccoby, Nathan, & Farquhar, John W. (1989), 'Communication Campaigns to Prevent Cardiovascular Disease: The Stanford Community Studies', in Rice, Ronald E., & Atkin, Charles K., eds, *Public Communication Campaigns: Second Edition*, Sage, Newbury Park, California.

Flowers, J.V.; Booraem, C.; Miller, T.E.; Iverson, A.E.; Copeland J., & Furtado, K. (1991), 'Comparison of the results of a standardized AIDS prevention program in three geographic locations', in *AIDS Education & Prevention*, vol. 3, no. 3, pp. 189–96.

Fortmann, Stephen P.; Taylor, C. Barr; Flora, June A., & Jatulis, Darius E. (1993), 'Changes in Adult Cigarette Smoking Prevalence after Five Years of Community Health Education: The Stanford Five-City Project', in *American Journal of Epidemiology*, vol. 137, no. 1, pp. 82–96.

Fortmann, Stephen P.; Taylor, C. Barr; Flora, June A., & Winkleby, Marilyn A. (1993), 'Effect of Community Health Education on Plasma Cholesterol Levels and Diet: The Stanford Five-City Project', in *American Journal of Epidemiology*, vol. 137, no. 10, pp. 1039–1055.

Fraczek, Adam (1986), 'Socio-Cultural Environment, Television Viewing, and the Development of Aggression among Children in Poland', in Huesmann, L. Rowell, & Eron, Leonard D., eds, *Television and the Aggressive Child: A Cross-National Comparison*, Lawrence Erlbaum Associates, Hillsdale, New Jersey.

Freedman, Jonathan L. (1984), 'Effect of Television Violence on Aggressiveness', in *Psychological Bulletin*, vol. 96, no. 2, pp. 227–246.

Freedman, Jonathan L. (1986), 'Television Violence and Aggression: A Rejoinder', in *Psychological Bulletin*, vol. 100, no. 3, pp. 372–378.

Freedman, Jonathan L. (1988), 'Television Violence and Aggression: What the Evidence Shows', in Oskamp, Stuart, ed., *Television as a Social Issue*, Applied Social Psychology Annual no. 8, Sage, Newbury Park, California.

Friedrich, Lynette K., & Stein, Aletha H. (1975), 'Pro-social Television and Young Children: The Effects of Verbal Labeling and Role Playing on Learning and Behavior', in *Child Development*, vol. 46, pp. 27–38.

Friedrich-Cofer, Lynette, & Huston, Aletha C. (1986), 'Television Violence and Aggression: The Debate Continues', in *Psychological Bulletin*, vol. 100, no. 3, pp. 364–371.

Gantz, Walter, & Greenberg, Bradley S. (1990), 'The Role of Informative Television Programs in the Battle against AIDS', in *Health Communication*, vol. 2, no. 4, pp. 199–215.

Gauntlett, David (1993), *Zapping Their Brains? Young People, Video Games and Gender*, MA dissertation, University of Lancaster.

Gauntlett, David (1994), 'Calling all couch potatoes', in *The Times Higher Education Supplement*, 8 July 1994, p. 13.

Gauntlett, David (1995a), 'Green, clean and on the screen', in *Green Teacher*, no. 33, Spring 1995.

Gauntlett, David (1995b), '"Full of very different people all mixed up together": Understanding community and environment through the classroom video project', in *Primary Teaching Studies*, vol. 9, no. 1 (Spring 1995).

Geen, Russell G. (1994), 'Television and Aggression: Recent Developments in Research and Theory', in Zillmann, Dolf; Bryant, Jennings, & Huston, Aletha C., eds, *Media, Children and the*

Family: Social Scientific, Psychodynamic and Clinical Perspectives, Lawrence Erlbaum, Hillsdale, New Jersey.

Geller, E. Scott (1989), 'Using Television to Promote Safety Belt Use', in Rice, Ronald E., & Atkin, Charles K., eds, *Public Communication Campaigns: Second Edition*, Sage, Newbury Park, California.

Geraghty, Christine (1991), *Women and Soap Opera: A Study of Prime Time Soaps*, Polity Press, Cambridge.

Gerbner, George, & Gross, Larry (1976), 'Living with Television: The Violence Profile', in *Journal of Communication*, vol. 26, no. 1, pp. 173–199.

Gerbner, George; Gross, Larry; Morgan, Michael, & Signorielli, Nancy (1980), 'The 'Mainstreaming' of America: Violence profile No. 11', in *Journal of Communication*, vol. 30, no. 3, pp. 10–29.

Gerbner, George; Gross, Larry; Morgan, Michael, & Signorielli, Nancy (1986), 'Living with Television: The Dynamics of the Cultivation Process', in Bryant, Jennings, & Zillmann, Dolf, eds, *Perspectives on Media Effects*, Lawrence Erlbaum Associates, Hillsdale, New Jersey.

Gerbner, George (1988), *Violence and Terror in the Mass Media*, Unesco Reports and Papers on Mass Communication No. 102, Unesco, Paris.

Gerbner, George (1990), 'Epilogue: Advancing on the Path of Righteousness (Maybe)', in Signorielli, Nancy, & Morgan, Michael, eds, *Cultivation Analysis: New Directions in Media Effects Research*, Sage, Newbury Park, California.

Gerbner, George (1994), 'The Politics of Media Violence: Some Reflections', in Linné, Olga, & Hamelink, Cees J., eds, *Mass Communication Research: On Problems and Policies: The Art of Asking the Right Questions*, Ablex Publishing, Norwood, New Jersey.

Goldberg, Marvin E., & Gorn, Gerald J. (1983), 'Researching the Effects of Television Advertising on Children: A Methodological Critique', in Howe, Michael J.A., ed., *Learning from Television: Psychological and Educational Research*, Academic Press, London.

Goldman, Robert (1992), *Reading Ads Socially*, Routledge, London.

Graves, Sherryl Browne (1993), 'Television, the Portrayal of African Americans, and the Development of Children's Attitudes', in Berry, Gordon L., & Asamen, Joy Keiko, eds, *Children and Television: Images in a Changing Sociocultural World*, Sage, Newbury Park, California.

Gray, Ann (1992), *Video Playtime: The Gendering of a Leisure Technology*, Routledge, London.

Greenberg, Bradley, & Gantz, Walter (1989), 'Singing the (VD) Blues', in Rice, Ronald E., & Atkin, Charles K., eds, *Public Communication Campaigns: Second Edition*, Sage, Newbury Park, California.

The Guardian (25 November 1993), 'Judge's remarks prompt MP's horror video curb call', p. 4.

The Guardian (26 November 1993), 'Indecent exposure?', section 2, pp. 2–3.

The Guardian (18 February 1994), 'Film advisers claim censor sacked them', p. 1; 'Why talk of penises, sado-masochism and erotic history of lingerie always ended in a row', p. 3; 'Film ratings fall-out led to showdown', p. 3.

The Guardian (1 April 1994), 'Video-crime link stronger than thought, say child experts', p. 1 & p. 26; 'Psychologists' rethink bodes ill for video nasties', p. 2.

The Guardian (2 April 1994), 'Video report author rejects "nasties" ban', p. 3; '"No absolute proof on violence link"', p. 3.

The Guardian (7 April 1994), 'Sense and censorship', section 2, p. 5; 'Letters to the Editor: Video ban would criminalise parents', p. 23.

Gunter, Barrie (1987), *Television and the Fear of Crime*, John Libbey, London.

Gunter, Barrie, & McAleer, Jill L. (1990), *Children and Television: The One Eyed Monster?*, Routledge, London.

Hagell, Ann, & Newburn, Tim (1994), *Young Offenders and the Media: Viewing Habits and Preferences*, Policy Studies Institute, London.

Hall, Stuart (1982), 'The Rediscovery of "Ideology": Return of the Repressed in Media Studies', in Gurevitch, Michael; Bennett, Tony; Curran, James, & Woolacott, Janet, eds, *Culture, Society and the Media*, Methuen, London.

Hall Preston, Elizabeth (1990), 'Pornography and the Construction of Gender', in Signorielli, Nancy, & Morgan, Michael, eds, *Cultivation Analysis: New Directions in Media Effects Research*, Sage, Newbury Park, California.

Halloran, James D. (1978), 'Mass Communication: Symptom or Cause of Violence?', in *International Social Science Journal*, vol. 30, no. 4, pp. 816–833.

Halloran, James D. (1990), 'Mass Media and Violence', in Bluglass, R., & Bowden, P., eds, *Principles and Practice of Forensic Psychiatry*, Churchill Livingstone, New York.

Hargrave, Andrea Millwood (1993), *Violence in Factual Television*, John Libbey, London.

Hawkins, Robert P., & Pingree, Suzanne (1986), 'Activity in the Effects of Television on Children', in Bryant, Jennings, & Zillmann, Dolf, eds, *Perspectives on Media Effects*, Lawrence Erlbaum Associates, Hillsdale, New Jersey.

Hearold, Susan (1986) 'A Synthesis of 1043 Effects of Television on Social Behavior', in Comstock, George, ed., *Public Communication and Behavior*, Volume 1, Academic Press, Orlando.

Hennigan, Karen M.; Del Rosario, Marlyn L.; Heath, Linda; Cook, Thomas D.; Wharton, J.D., & Calder, Bobby J. (1982), 'Impact of the Introduction of Television on Crime in the United States: Empirical Findings and Theoretical Implications', in *Journal of Personality and Social Psychology*, vol. 42, no. 3, pp. 461–477.

Hirsch, Paul (1980), 'The 'Scary' World of the Non-Viewer and Other Anomalies: A Reanalysis of Gerbner et al's Findings on Cultivation Analysis: Part 1', in *Communication Research*, vol. 7, pp. 403–456.

Hodge, Robert, & Tripp, David (1986), *Children and Television: A Semiotic Approach*, Polity Press, Cambridge.

hooks, bell (1992), *Black Looks: Race and Representation*, Turnaround, London.

Hoover, Stewart M. (1990), 'Television, Religion, and Religious Television: Purposes and Cross Purposes', in Signorielli, Nancy, & Morgan, Michael, eds, *Cultivation Analysis: New Directions in Media Effects Research*, Sage, Newbury Park, California.

Hornik, Robert C. (1989), 'Channel Effectiveness in Development Communication Programs', in Rice, Ronald E., & Atkin, Charles K., eds, *Public Communication Campaigns: Second Edition*, Sage, Newbury Park, California.

Howard, John; Rothbart, George, & Sloan, Lee (1978), 'The Response to "Roots": A National Survey', in *Journal of Broadcasting*, vol. 22, no. 3, pp. 279–287.

Howitt, Dennis (1989), 'Pornography: The Recent Debate', in Cumberbatch, Guy, & Howitt, Dennis, *A Measure of Uncertainty: The Effects of the Mass Media*, Broadcasting Standards Council Research Monograph, John Libbey, London.

Huesmann, L. Rowell (1982), 'Television Violence and Aggressive Behavior', in Pearl, David; Bouthilet, Lorraine, & Lazar, Joyce, eds, *Television and Behavior: Ten Years of Scientific Progress and Implications for the Eighties, Volume 2: Technical Reviews*, National Institute of Mental Health, Maryland.

Huesmann, L. Rowell; Eron, Leonard D.; Lefkowitz, Monroe M., & Walder, Leopold O. (1984), 'Stability of Aggression Over Time and Generations', in *Developmental Psychology*, vol. 20, no. 6, pp. 1120–1134.

Huesmann, L. Rowell; Lagerspetz, Kirsti, & Eron, Leonard D. (1984), 'Intervening Variables in the TV Violence-Aggression Relation: Evidence From Two Countries', in *Developmental Psychology*, vol. 20, no. 5, pp. 746–775.

Huesmann, L. Rowell (1986a), 'Cross-National Communalities in the Learning of Aggression from Media Violence', in Huesmann, L. Rowell, & Eron, Leonard D., eds, *Television and the Aggressive Child: A Cross-National Comparison*, Lawrence Erlbaum Associates, Hillsdale, New Jersey.

Huesmann, L. Rowell (1986b), 'Psychological Processes Promoting the Relation Between Exposure to Media Violence and Aggressive Behavior by the Viewer', in *Journal of Social Issues*, vol. 42, no. 3, pp. 125–139.

Huesmann, L. Rowell, & Eron, Leonard D., eds (1986), *Television and the Aggressive Child: A Cross-National Comparison*, Lawrence Erlbaum Associates, Hillsdale, New Jersey.

Hur, K. Kyoon (1978), 'Impact of "Roots" on Black and White Teenagers', in *Journal of Broadcasting*, vol. 22, no. 3, pp. 289–298.

Hur, Kenneth K., & Robinson, John P. (1978), 'The Social Impact of "Roots"', in *Journalism Quarterly*, vol. 55, no. 1, pp. 19–24.

The Independent (2 April 1994), 'Howard acts to curb video nasties', p. 1; 'Censorship laws among toughest in the world', p. 2; 'Letters to the Editor: The links between video nasties and particular crimes', p. 19.

Jeffords, Susan (1993), 'The Big Switch: Hollywood Masculinity in the Nineties', in Collins, Jim; Radner, Hilary, & Collins, Ava Preacher, eds, *Film Theory Goes To The Movies*, Routledge, London.

Jenson, Joli (1992), 'Fandom as Pathology: The Consequences of Characterization', in Lewis, Lisa A., ed., *The Adoring Audience: Fan Culture and Popular Media*, Routledge, London.

Johnston, Jerome, & Ettema, James S. (1982), *Positive Images: Breaking Stereotypes with Children's Television*, Sage, Beverly Hills, California.

Johnston, Jerome, & Ettema, James S. (1986), 'Using Television to Best Advantage: Research for pro-social Television', in Bryant, Jennings, & Zillmann, Dolf, eds, *Perspectives on Media Effects*, Lawrence Erlbaum Associates, Hillsdale, New Jersey.

Jowett, Garth S. (1987), 'Propaganda and Communication: The Re-emergence of a Research Tradition', in *Journal of Communication*, vol. 37, no. 1, pp. 97–114.

Kalis, Pamela, & Neuendorf, Kimberly A. (1989), 'Aggressive Cue Prominence and Gender Participation in MTV', in *Journalism Quarterly*, vol. 66, no. 1, pp. 148–154.

Kaplan, E. Ann (1992), 'Feminist Criticism and Television', in *Channels of Discourse, Reassembled: Television and Contemporary Criticism: Second Edition*, Routledge, London.

Kaplan, Robert M., & Singer, Robert D. (1976), 'Television Violence and Viewer Aggression: A Reexamination of the Evidence', in *Journal of Social Issues*, vol. 32, no. 4, pp. 35–70.

Katz, Elihu, & Lazarsfeld, Paul (1955), *Personal Influence*, Free Press, New York.

Keane, Stevan (1994), 'Blue Wednesday', in the *Guardian: The Guide*, 16 July 1994, p. 20.

Kenny, David A. (1972), 'Two Comments on Cross-Lagged Correlation: Threats to the Internal Validity of Cross-Lagged Panel Inference, as Related to "Television Violence and Child Aggression: A Followup Study"', in Comstock, George A., & Rubinstein, Eli A., eds, *Television and Social Behavior: Reports and Papers, Volume III: Television and Adolescent Aggressiveness*, National Institute of Mental Health, Maryland.

Kipke, M.D.; Boyer, C., & Hein, K. (1993), 'An evaluation of an AIDS risk reduction education and skills training (ARREST) program', in *Journal of Adolescent Health*, vol. 14, no. 7, pp. 533–539.

Kingsley, Hilary (1993), *Casualty: The Inside Story*, BBC Books, London.

Klapper, Joseph T. (1960), *The Effects of Mass Communication*, The Free Press, New York.

Lee, Barbara (1988), 'Pro-social Content on Prime-Time Television', in Oskamp, Stuart, ed., *Television as a Social Issue*, Applied Social Psychology Annual no. 8, Sage, Newbury Park, California.

Lefkowitz, Monroe M.; Eron, Leonard D.; Walder, Leopold O., & Huesmann, L. Rowell (1972), 'Television Violence and Child Aggression: A Followup Study', in Comstock, George A., & Rubinstein, Eli A., eds, *Television and Social Behavior: Reports and Papers, Volume III: Television and Adolescent Aggressiveness*, National Institute of Mental Health, Maryland.

Lefkowitz, Monroe M.; Eron, Leonard D.; Walder, Leopold O., & Huesmann, L. Rowell (1977), *Growing Up To Be Violent: A Longitudinal Study of the Development of Aggression*, Pergamon Press, New York.

Lefkowitz, Monroe M., & Huesmann, L. Rowell (1981), 'Concomitants of Television Violence Viewing in Children', in Palmer, Edward L., & Dorr, Aimée, *Children and the Faces of Television: Teaching, Violence, Selling*, Academic Press, New York.

Lesser, Gerald S. (1974), *Children and Television: Lessons from Sesame Street*, Random House, New York.

Levin, Stephen R.; Petros, Thomas V., & Petrella, Florence W. (1982), 'Preschoolers' Awareness of Television Advertising', in *Child Development*, vol. 53, pp. 933–937.

Levy, Mark R., & Gunter, Barrie (1988), *Home Video and the Changing Nature of the Television Audience*, John Libbey, London.

Leyens, J.P.; Parke, R.D.; Camino, L., & Berkowitz, L. (1975), 'Effects of Movie Violence on Aggression in a Field Setting as a Function of Group Dominance and Cohesion', in *Journal of Personality and Social Psychology*, vol. 32, pp. 346–360.

Lidz, Victor (1984), 'Television and Moral Order in a Secular Age', in Rowland, Willard D., Jr.,

& Watkins, Bruce, eds, *Interpreting Television: Current Research Perspectives*, Sage, Beverly Hills, California.

Liebert, Robert M., & Sprafkin, Joyce (1988), *The Early Window: Effects of Television on Children and Youth: Third Edition*, Pergamon, New York.

Liu, Alan P.L. (1981), 'Mass Campaigns in the People's Republic of China', in Rice, Ronald E., & Paisley, William, eds, *Public Communication Campaigns*, Sage, Beverly Hills, California.

Livingstone, Sonia M. (1990), *Making Sense of Television: The Psychology of Audience Interpretation*, Pergamon Press, Oxford.

Livingstone, Sonia M. (1994), 'Watching Talk: Gender and Engagement in the Viewing of Audience Discussion Programmes', in *Media, Culture and Society*, vol. 16, pp. 429–447.

Loye, D.; Gorney, R., & Steele, G. (1977), 'An Experimental Field Study', in *Journal of Communication*, vol. 27, pp. 206–216.

Lustig, S.L. (1994), 'The AIDS prevention magic show: avoiding the tragic with magic', in *Public Health Reports – Hyattsville*, vol. 109, no. 2, pp. 162–167.

Lynn, Richard; Hampson, Susan, & Agahi, Edwina (1989), 'Television Violence and Aggression: A Genotype-Environment, Correlation and Interaction Theory', in *Social Behavior and Personality*, vol. 17, no. 2, pp. 143–164.

MacGregor, Brent, & Morrison, David E. (1995), 'From Focus Groups to Editing Groups: A New Method of Reception Analysis', in *Media, Culture and Society*, vol. 17, no. 1.

McAlister, Alfred; Ramirez, Amelie G.; Galavotti, Christine, & Gallion, Kipling J. (1989), 'Antismoking Campaigns: Progress in the Application of Social Learning Theory', in Rice, Ronald E., & Atkin, Charles K., eds, *Public Communication Campaigns: Second Edition*, Sage, Newbury Park, California.

McIntyre, Jennie J., & Teevan, James J. Jr. (1972), 'Television Violence and Deviant Behavior', in Comstock, George A., & Rubinstein, Eli A., eds, *Television and Social Behavior: Reports and Papers, Volume III: Television and Adolescent Aggressiveness*, National Institute of Mental Health, Maryland.

McLeod, Jack M.; Atkin, Charles K., & Chaffee, Steven H. (1972), 'Adolescents, Parents, and Television Use: Adolescent Self-Report Measures from Maryland and Wisconsin Samples', in Comstock, George A., & Rubinstein, Eli A., eds, *Television and Social Behavior: Reports and Papers, Volume III: Television and Adolescent Aggressiveness*, National Institute of Mental Health, Maryland.

McNamara, Eugene F.; Kurth, Troy, & Hansen, Donald (1981), 'Communication Efforts to Prevent Wildfires', in Rice, Ronald E., & Paisley, William, eds, *Public Communication Campaigns*, Sage, Beverly Hills, California.

McQuail, Denis (1983), 'Processes of Media Effects', in Boyd-Barrett, Oliver, & Braham, Peter, eds (1987), *Media, Knowledge and Power*, Croom Helm, London.

Marshall, Bethan (1994), 'Books on the box', in The *Guardian*, 19 July 1994, section 2, p. 21.

Martin, G.S.; Serpelloni, G.; Galvan, U.; Rizzetto, A.; Gomma, M.; Morgante, S., & Rezza, G. (1990), 'Behavioural change in injecting drug users: evaluation of an HIV/AIDS education programme', in *AIDS Care*, vol. 2, no. 3, pp. 275–279.

Medved, Michael (1992), *Hollywood vs. America: Popular Culture and the War on Traditional Values*, HarperCollins, London.

Mendelsohn, Harold (1973), 'Some Reasons Why Information Campaigns Can Succeed', in *Public Opinion Quarterly*, vol. 37, no. 1, pp. 50–61.

Mendelsohn, H. (1986), 'Lessons From a National Media Prevention Campaign', in Leathar, D.S.; Hastings, G.B.; O'Reilly, K., & Davies, J.K., eds, *Health Education and the Media II*, Pergamon Press, Oxford.

Messner, Steven F. (1986), 'Television Violence and Violent Crime: An Aggregate Analysis', in *Social Problems*, vol. 33, no. 3, pp. 218–235.

Mielke, Keith W., & Chen, Milton (1983), 'Formative Research for "3–2–1 Contact": Methods and Insights', in Howe, Michael J.A., ed., *Learning from Television: Psychological and Educational Research*, Academic Press, London.

Milavsky, J. Ronald; Pekowsky, Berton, & Stipp, Horst (1975), 'TV Drug Advertising and Proprietary and Illicit Drug Use Among Teenage Boys', in *Public Opinion Quarterly*, vol. 39, pp. 457–481.

Milavsky, J. Ronald; Kessler, Ronald C.; Stipp, Horst H., & Rubens, William S. (1982a), *Television and Aggression: A Panel Study*, Academic Press, New York.

Milavsky, J. Ronald; Kessler, Ronald; Stipp, Horst, & Rubens, William S. (1982b), 'Television and Aggression: Results of a Panel Study', in Pearl, David; Bouthilet, Lorraine, & Lazar, Joyce, eds, *Television and Behavior: Ten Years of Scientific Progress and Implications for the Eighties, Volume 2: Technical Reviews*, National Institute of Mental Health, Maryland.

Milavsky, J. Ronald (1988), 'Television and Aggression Once Again', in Oskamp, Stuart ed., *Television as a Social Issue*, Applied Social Psychology Annual no. 8, Sage, Newbury Park, California.

Miller, T.E.; Booraem, C.; Flowers, J.V., & Iversen, A.E. (1990), 'Changes in knowledge, attitudes, and behavior as a result of a community-based AIDS prevention program', in *AIDS Education & Prevention*, vol. 2, no. 1, pp. 12–23.

Morgan, Michael, & Signorielli, Nancy (1990), 'Cultivation Analysis: Conceptualization and Methodology', in Signorielli, Nancy, & Morgan, Michael, eds, *Cultivation Analysis: New Directions in Media Effects Research*, Sage, Newbury Park, California.

Morrison, David (1993), 'The Idea of Violence', in Hargrave, Andrea Millwood, ed., *Violence in Factual Television*, John Libbey, London.

Morrison, David, & MacGregor, Brent (1993), 'Detailed Findings from the Editing Groups', in Hargrave, Andrea Millwood, ed., *Violence in Factual Television*, John Libbey, London.

Mulkay, Michael (1985), *The Word and the World: Explorations in the Form of Sociological Analysis*, George Allen & Unwin, London.

Murdock, Graham, & McCron, Robin (1979), 'The Television and Delinquency Debate', in *Screen Education*, no. 30 (Spring 1979), pp. 51–67.

Murdock, Graham (1994), 'Visualizing Violence: Television and the Discourse of Disorder', in Linné, Olga, & Hamelink, Cees J., eds, *Mass Communication Research: On Problems and Policies: The Art of Asking the Right Questions*, Ablex Publishing, Norwood, New Jersey.

Neumann, Susan B. (1991), *Literacy in the Television Age: The Myth of the TV Effect*, Ablex Publishing, Norwood, New Jersey.

Newcomb, Horace M., & Hirsch, Paul M. (1984), 'Television as a Cultural Forum: Implications for Research', in Rowland, Willard D., Jr., & Watkins, Bruce, eds, *Interpreting Television: Current Research Perspectives*, Sage, Beverly Hills, California.

Newson, Elizabeth (1994), *Video Violence and the Protection of Children*, mimeo, Child Development Research Unit, University of Nottingham.

Noble, Grant (1975), *Children in Front of the Small Screen*, Constable, London.

Noble, Grant (1983), 'Social Learning from Everyday Television', in Howe, Michael J.A., ed., *Learning from Television: Psychological and Educational Research*, Academic Press, London.

Noelle-Neumann, Elisabeth (1994), 'Are We Asking the Right Questions? Developing Measurement from Theory: The Influence of the Spiral of Silence on Media Effects Research', in Linné, Olga, & Hamelink, Cees J., eds, *Mass Communication Research: On Problems and Policies: The Art of Asking the Right Questions*, Ablex Publishing, Norwood, New Jersey.

O'Keefe, Garrett J. (1985), '"Taking a Bite out of Crime": The Impact of a Public Information Campaign', in *Communication Research*, vol. 12, no. 2, pp. 147–178.

Orozco-Gomez, Guillermo (1988), 'Research on Cognitive Effects of Non-Educational Television: An Epistemological Discussion', in Drummond, Phillip, & Paterson, Richard, eds, *Television and its Audience: International Research Perspectives*, BFI Publishing, London.

O'Sullivan, Tim (1994), 'Effects / Effects tradition', in O'Sullivan, Tim; Hartley, John; Saunders, Danny; Montgomery, Martin, & Fiske, John, *Key Concepts in Communication and Cultural Studies*, Routledge, London.

Paik, Haejung, & Comstock, George (1994), 'The Effects of Television Violence on Antisocial Behaviour: A Meta-Analysis', in *Communication Research*, vol. 21, no. 4, pp. 516–546.

Palmer, Edward L.; Smith, K. Taylor, & Strawser, Kim S. (1993), 'Rubik's Tube: Developing a Child's Television Worldview', in Berry, Gordon L., & Asamen, Joy Keiko, eds, *Children and Television: Images in a Changing Sociocultural World*, Sage, Newbury Park, California.

Palmer, Patricia (1986), *The Lively Audience: A Study of Children Around the TV Set*, Allen & Unwin, Sydney.

Parke, R.D.; Berkowitz, L.; Leyens, J.P.; West, S., & Sebastian, R.J. (1977), 'Some Effects of Violent and Nonviolent Movies on the Behavior of Juvenile Delinquents', in Berkowitz, L., ed., *Advances in Experimental Social Psychology*, vol. 10, pp. 135–172, Academic Press, New York.

Pearson, Geoffrey (1983), *Hooligan: A History of Respectable Fears*, Macmillan, London.

Pearson, Geoffrey (1984), 'Falling Standards: A Short, Sharp History of Moral Decline', in Barker, Martin, ed., *The Video Nasties: Freedom and Censorship in the Media*, Pluto, London.

Perse, Elizabeth M. (1990), 'Cultivation and Involvement with Local Television News', in Signorielli, Nancy, & Morgan, Michael, eds, *Cultivation Analysis: New Directions in Media Effects Research*, Sage, Newbury Park, California.

Perse, Elizabeth M.; Ferguson, Douglas A., & McLeod, Douglas M. (1994), 'Cultivation in the Newer Media Environment', in *Communication Research*, vol. 21, no. 1, pp. 79–104.

Phillips, David P. (1986), 'The Found Experiment: A New Technique for Assessing the Impact of

Mass Media Violence on Real-World Aggressive Behavior', in Comstock, George, ed., *Public Communication and Behavior*, Volume 1, Academic Press, Orlando.

Philo, Greg (1990), *Seeing and Believing: The Influence of Television*, Routledge, London.

Pierce, John P.; Dwyer, Terry; Frape, Gerald; Chapman, Simon; Chamberlain, Anne, & Burke, Nick (1986), 'Evaluation of the Sydney "Quit. For Life" Anti-Smoking Campaign: Part 1: Achievement of Intermediate Goals', in *Medical Journal of Australia*, vol. 144, no. 7, pp. 341–344.

Puska, Pekka; Koskela, Kaj; McAlister, Alfred; Pallonen, Unto; Vartiainen, Erkki, & Homan, Kaija (1979), 'A Comprehensive Television Smoking Cessation Programme in Finland', in *International Journal of Health Education*, supplement to vol. 22, no. 4.

Puska, Pekka; McAlister, Alfred; Pekkola, Juha, & Koskela, Kaj (1981), 'Television in Health Promotion: Evaluation of a National Programme in Finland', in *International Journal of Health Education*, vol. 24, no. 4, pp. 238–250.

Puska, Pekka; Nissinen, Aulikki; Tuomilehto, Jaakko; Salonen, Jukka T.; Koskela, Kaj; McAlister, Alfred; Kottke, Thomas E.; Maccoby, Nathan, & Farquhar, John W. (1985), 'The Community-Based Strategy to Prevent Coronary Heart Disease: Conclusions from Ten Years of the North Karelia Project', in *Annual Review of Public Health*, vol. 6, pp. 147–193.

Radio Times (1993a), letters page, 20–26 March 1993, pp. 121–122.

Radio Times (1993b), letters page, 10–16 July 1993, p. 105

Rafferty, Frances (1993), 'Video connection not backed up', in *The Times Educational Supplement*, 3 December 1993, p. 4.

Reardon, Kathleen K. (1989), 'The Potential Role of Persuasion in Adolescent AIDS Prevention', in Rice, Ronald E., & Atkin, Charles K., eds, *Public Communication Campaigns: Second Edition*, Sage, Newbury Park, California.

Rhodes, F., & Wolitski, R. (1989), 'Effect of instructional videotapes on AIDS knowledge and attitudes', in *Journal of American College Health,* vol. 37, no. 6, pp. 266–71.

Rice, Ronald E., & Atkin, Charles K. (1989), 'Preface: Trends in Communication Campaign Research', in Rice, Ronald E., & Atkin, Charles K., eds, *Public Communication Campaigns: Second Edition*, Sage, Newbury Park, California.

Robertson, Leon S.; Kelley, Albert B.; O'Neill, Brian; Wixom, Charles W.; Eiswirth, Richard S., & Haddon, William, Jr. (1974), 'A Controlled Study of the Effect of Television Mesages on Safety Belt Use', in *American Journal of Public Health*, vol. 64, no. 11, pp. 1071–1080.

Rosengren, Karl Erik; Wenner, Lawrence A., & Palmgreen, Philip, eds (1985), *Media Gratifications Research: Current Perspectives*, Sage, Beverly Hills, California.

Rossiter, John R., & Robertson, Thomas S. (1980), 'Children's Dispositions Toward Proprietary Drugs and the Role of Television Drug Advertising', in *Public Opinion Quarterly*, vol. 44, no. 3, pp. 316–329.

Rubin, Alan M. (1986), 'Uses, Gratifications, and Media Effects Research', in Bryant, Jennings, & Zillmann, Dolf, eds, *Perspectives on Media Effects*, Lawrence Erlbaum Associates, Hillsdale, New Jersey.

Rushton, J. Philipe (1982), 'Television and pro-social Behavior', in Pearl, David; Bouthilet, Lorraine, & Lazar, Joyce, eds, *Television and Behavior: Ten Years of Scientific Progress and*

Implications for the Eighties, Volume 2: Technical Reviews, National Institute of Mental Health, Maryland.

Sawin, Douglas B. (1990), 'Aggressive Behavior among Children in Small Playgroup Settings with Violent Television' in *Advances in Learning and Behavioral Disabilities*, 1990, 6, pp. 157–177.

Schlesinger, Philip; Dobash, R. Emerson; Dobash, Russell P., & Weaver, C. Kay (1992), *Women Viewing Violence*, British Film Institute Publishing, London.

Scott, F.; Chambers, L.W.; Underwood, J.; Walter, S., & Pickard, L. (1990), 'AIDS seminars for senior grades in secondary schools', in *Canadian Journal of Public Health*, vol. 81, no. 4, pp. 290–294.

Shay, Don, & Duncan, Jody (1991), *The Making of Terminator 2: Judgment Day*, Titan, London.

Sheehan, Peter W. (1986), 'Television Viewing and its Relation to Aggression among Children in Australia', in Huesmann, L. Rowell, & Eron, Leonard D., eds, *Television and the Aggressive Child: A Cross-National Comparison*, Lawrence Erlbaum Associates, Hillsdale, New Jersey.

Shuker, Roy (1986), '"Video Nasties": Censorship and the Politics of Popular Culture', in *New Zealand Sociology*, vol. 1, no. 1, pp. 64–73.

Signorielli, Nancy (1990), 'Television's Mean and Dangerous World: A Continuation of the Cultural Indicators Perspective', in Signorielli, Nancy, & Morgan, Michael, eds, *Cultivation Analysis: New Directions in Media Effects Research*, Sage, Newbury Park, California.

Signorielli, Nancy (1993), 'Television, the Portrayal of Women, and Children's Attitudes', in Berry, Gordon L., & Asamen, Joy Keiko, eds, *Children and Television: Images in a Changing Sociocultural World*, Sage, Newbury Park, California.

Singer, Dorothy G., & Singer, Jerome L. (1983), 'Learning How to be Intelligent Consumers of Television', in Howe, Michael J.A., ed., *Learning from Television: Psychological and Educational Research*, Academic Press, London.

Singhal, Arvind, & Rogers, Everett M. (1989), 'Pro-social Television for Development in India', in Rice, Ronald E., & Atkin, Charles K., eds, *Public Communication Campaigns: Second Edition*, Sage, Newbury Park, California.

Skirrow, Gillian (1987), 'Women/acting/power', in Baehr, Helen, & Dyer, Gillian, eds, *Boxed In: Women and Television*, Pandora, London.

Sprafkin, J.N., & Rubinstein, E.A. (1979), 'Children's Television Viewing Habits and Pro-social Behavior: A Field Correlational Study', in *Journal of Broadcasting*, vol. 23, pp. 265–276.

Star, Shirley A., & Hughes, Helen MacGill (1950), 'Report on an Educational Campaign: The Cincinnati Plan for the United Nations', in *The American Journal of Sociology*, vol. 55, no. 4, pp. 389–400.

Stein, Gerald M., & Bryan, James H. (1972), 'The Effect of a Television Model Upon Rule Adoption Behavior of Children', in *Child Development*, vol. 43, pp. 268–273.

Stein, J.A. (1986), 'The Cancer Information Service: Marketing a Large-scale National Information Program Through the Media', in Leathar, D.S.; Hastings, G.B.; O'Reilly, K., & Davies, J.K., eds, *Health Education and the Media II*, Pergamon Press, Oxford.

Stewart, David W., & Furse, David H. (1986), *Effective Television Advertising: A Study of 1000 Commercials*, Marketing Science Institute & Lexington Books, Lexington, Massachusetts.

135

Stipp, Horst (1993), 'The Challenge to Improve Television for Children: A New Perspective', in Berry, Gordon L., & Asamen, Joy Keiko, eds, *Children and Television: Images in a Changing Sociocultural World*, Sage, Newbury Park, California.

The Sun (25 November 1993), 'This boy and his pal murdered James Bulger ...', p. 1; 'Horror video replay: Chilling links between James murder and tape rented by killer's dad', p. 2–3; 'One sobbed ... the other stared', p. 4–5; 'A grim warning of nightmares to come', p. 9.

The Sunday Times (3 April 1994), 'The Nasty Truth', p. 14.

Taylor, C. Barr; Fortmann, Stephen P.; Flora, June A.; Kayman, Susan; Barrett, Donald C.; Jatulis, Darius, & Farquhar, John W. (1991), 'Effect of Long-Term Community Health Education on Body Mass Index: The Stanford Five-City Project', in *American Journal of Epidemiology*, vol. 134, no. 3, pp. 235–249.

The Times (1 April 1994), 'Experts condemn video nasties as form of child abuse', p. 3.

Tucker, Lauren R., & Shah, Hemant (1992), 'Race and the Transformation of Culture: The Making of the Television Miniseries "Roots"', in *Critical Studies in Mass Communication*, vol. 9, no. 4, pp. 325–336.

Tulloch, John, & Tulloch, Marian (1992), 'Discourses about Violence: Critical theory and the "TV violence" debate', in *Text*, vol. 12, no. 2, pp. 183–231.

Van Evra, Judith (1990), *Television and Child Development*, Lawrence Erlbaum Associates, Hillsdale, New Jersey.

Vilain, C. (1986), '"Un Verre Ca Va, Trois Verres Bonjour Les Degats" ["One drink alright, three drinks hello troubles"]: A National Information Campaign on Excessive Alcohol Drinking in France', in Leathar, D.S.; Hastings, G.B.; O'Reilly, K., & Davies, J.K., eds, *Health Education and the Media II*, Pergamon Press, Oxford.

Wallack, Lawrence (1989), 'Mass Communication and Health Promotion: A Critical Perspective', in Rice, Ronald E., & Atkin, Charles K., eds, *Public Communication Campaigns: Second Edition*, Sage, Newbury Park, California.

Wander, Philip (1977), 'On the Meaning of "Roots"', in *Journal of Communication*, vol. 27, no. 4, pp. 64–69.

Ward, Scott; Reale, Greg, & Levinson, David (1972), 'Children's Perceptions, Explanations, and Judgments of Television Advertising: A Further Exploration', in Rubinstein, Eli A.; Comstock, George A., & Murray, John P., eds, *Television and Social Behaviour: Reports and Papers, Volume IV: Television in Day-to-Day Life: Patterns of Use*, National Institute of Mental Health, Maryland.

Wartella, Ellen (1981), 'Individual Differences in Children's Responses to Television Advertising', in Palmer, Edward L., & Dorr, Aimée, *Children and the Faces of Television: Teaching, Violence, Selling*, Academic Press, New York.

Watkins, Bruce A.; Huston-Stein, Aletha, & Wright, John C. (1981), 'Effects of Planned Television Programming', in Palmer, Edward L., & Dorr, Aimée, *Children and the Faces of Television: Teaching, Violence, Selling*, Academic Press, New York.

Whitehouse, Mary (1993), quote from interview in *Doctor Who: 30 Years in the Tardis*, BBC1, 29 November 1993, 2000–2050 hours.

Wiegman, O.; Kuttschreuter, M., & Baarda, B. (1992), 'A Longitudinal Study of the Effects of

Television Viewing on Aggressive and pro-social Behaviours', in *British Journal of Social Psychology*, vol. 31, pp. 147–164.

Williamson, Judith (1978), *Decoding Advertisements: Ideology and Meaning in Advertising*, Marion Boyars, London.

Wober, J. Mallory (1978), 'Televised Violence and Paranoid Perception: The View from Great Britain', in *Public Opinion Quarterly*, vol. 42, no. 3, pp. 315–321.

Wober, J. Mallory, & Gunter, Barrie (1982), 'Television and Personal Threat: Fact or Artifact?: A British View', in *British Journal of Social Psychology*, vol. 21, pp. 43–51.

Wober, J. Mallory, & Gunter, Barrie (1988), *Television and Social Control*, Avebury, Aldershot.

Wober, J. Mallory (1990), 'Does Television Cultivate the British? Late 80s Evidence', in Signorielli, Nancy, & Morgan, Michael, eds, *Cultivation Analysis: New Directions in Media Effects Research*, Sage, Newbury Park, California.

Wolf, Thomas M., & Cheyne, J. Allan (1972), 'Persistence of Effects of Live Behavioral, Televised Behavioral, and Live Verbal Models on Resistance to Deviation', in *Child Development*, vol. 43, pp. 1429–1436.

Wood, Julian (1993), 'Repeatable Pleasures: Notes on Young People's Use of Video', in Buckingham, David, ed., *Reading Audiences: Young People and the Media*, Manchester University Press, Manchester.

Yorkshire Evening Post (1 April 1994), 'Howard "No" to Video Nasty Ban', p. 1; 'Comment: Seeing the light', p. 16.

Zillmann, Dolf; Bryant, Jennings, & Huston, Aletha C., eds (1994), *Media, Children and the Family: Social Scientific, Psychodynamic and Clinical Perspectives*, Lawrence Erlbaum, Hillsdale, New Jersey.

Zimmerman Umble, Diane (1990), 'Mennonites and Television: Applications of Cultivation Analysis to a Religious Subculture', in Signorielli, Nancy, & Morgan, Michael, eds, *Cultivation Analysis: New Directions in Media Effects Research*, Sage, Newbury Park, California.

II. Selected television programmes and movies

The A-Team (1983–1987), 128 episodes of 60 mins each (inc. ads), created by Stephen J. Cannell & Frank Lupo, various writers, transmitted in USA from 26 January 1983.

Beavis and Butt-Head feature, from *The Late Show* (1993), BBC, 11 mins, transmitted BBC2, 26 October 1993, 2330–2341 hours.

Beavis and Butt-Head feature, from *News at Ten* (25 November 1993), ITN, 2 mins, transmitted ITV, 2206–2208 hours.

The Bill (1984–), Thames, 35 episodes of 60 mins each (inc. ads) then episodes of 30 mins (inc. ads), transmitted ITV, from 16 October 1984 in series of 60-min episodes, from 19 July 1988 in continuous twice weekly format, from 8 January 1993 three times weekly, Tuesday, Wednesdays & Fridays, 2000–2030 hours.

Brookside (1982–), Mersey, episodes of 30 mins each (inc. ads), created by Phil Redmond, various writers, transmitted three times weekly from 2 November 1992, Channel Four, originally Mondays,

Wednesdays & Fridays, 2000–2030 hours, from 3 May 1994 on Tuesdays & Fridays, 2030–2100 hours, and Wednesdays, 2000–2030 hours.

Cagney and Lacey (1982–1988), Mace Neufeld/CBS, 125 episodes of 60 mins each (inc. ads), created by Barney Rosenzweig, Barbara Corday and Barbara Avedon, various writers, originally transmitted in USA from 25 March 1982 to 3 August 1988, in UK on BBC1, 9 July 1982 to 27 August 1988.

Callan (1967–1972), ABC/Thames/ATV, 49 episodes of 60 mins each (inc. ads), created by James Mitchell, various writers, transmitted ITV, 4 February 1967 to 24 May 1972; plus one 90-min special, 2 September 1981.

Captain Planet and the Planeteers (1991–1992), DIC/Turner Program Services, episodes of 20 mins each, created by Ted Turner, Pat Allee, Ben Hurst & Phil Harnage, various writers, transmitted in UK from 1991, ITV, various times, e.g. Sundays, October to December 1993, 0757-0817 hours.

Casualty (1986–), BBC, episodes of 50 mins each, created by Jeremy Brock and Paul Unwin, various writers, transmitted from 6 September 1986, annual seasons of 13 episodes (average) from 1986 to 1991, annual seasons of 24 episodes from 1992, BBC1, varying times, e.g. Saturdays, start times around 2000 hours.

– episode: 'No Cause for Concern', written by Bryan Elsley, transmitted 20 February 1993, 2000–2050 hours.

– episode: 'Boiling Point', written by Peter Bowker, transmitted 27 February 1993, 2130–2220 hours.

– episode: 'Tippers', written by Nick McCarty, transmitted 15 January 1994, 2030–2120 hours.

– episode: 'A Breed Apart', written by David Joss Buckley, transmitted 29 October 1994, 2000–2050 hours.

Chandler and Co (1994–), Skreba for BBC, first season – six episodes of 55 mins each, created & mainly written by Paula Milne, directed by Renny Rye and Richard Marchand, transmitted BBC1, Tuesdays, 12 July to 16 August 1994, 2130–2225 hours.

Charlie's Angels (1976–1981), Spelling-Goldberg/20th Century Fox, created by Ivan Goff and Ben Roberts, 109 episodes of 60 mins (inc. ads), originally transmitted in USA from 22 September 1976 to 24 June 1981, in UK from 3 January 1977 to 8 May 1982.

Clangers (1969–1974), BBC/Smallfilms, 27 episodes of 10 mins each, created and written by Oliver Postgate and Peter Firmin, originally transmitted BBC1, 16 November 1969 to 10 November 1972, plus final episode on 10 October 1974. (Partly available on BBC Video, BBFC certificate Uc.)

Close Up North (1994), BBC North, on 'video nasties', 30 mins, transmitted BBC2 North, 17 February 1994, 1930–2000 hours.

Cracker (1993–), Granada, episodes of 60 mins each (inc. ads), first season – *The Mad Woman in the Attic* (2 episodes); *To Say I Love You* (3 episodes); *One Day a Lemming Will Fly* (2 episodes), transmitted ITV, Mondays, 27 September to 8 November 1993, 2100–2200 hours; second season – *To Be a Somebody* (3 episodes); *The Big Crunch* (3 episodes) by Ted Whitehead; *Men Should Weep* (3 episodes), all written by Jimmy McGovern except where stated, transmitted ITV, Mondays, 10 October to 5 December 1994, 2100–2200 hours. (Some stories available on Video Collection International video, BBFC certificate 18 and 15.)

Doctor Who (1963–1989), BBC, 695 episodes of (generally) 25 mins each, created by Sydney

Newman, David Whitaker, Verity Lambert (and others), various writers, originally transmitted in UK from 23 November 1963 to 6 December 1989, BBC1, and worldwide. (Several stories available on BBC Video, BBFC certificates PG/U.)

Doomwatch (1970–1972), BBC, 37 episodes of 50 mins (plus final episode banned and never broadcast), created by Kit Pedler and Gerry Davis, various writers, transmitted BBC1, Mondays, 9 February 1970 to 14 August 1972.

EastEnders (1985–), BBC, episodes of 30 mins each, created by Julia Smith and Tony Holland, various writers, transmitted twice weekly from 19 February 1985, three times weekly from 11 April 1994, BBC1, Mondays, 2000–2030 hours, Tuesdays & Thursdays, 1930–2000 hours.

Edge of Darkness (1985), BBC, six episodes of 50 mins each, written by Troy Kennedy Martin, directed by Martin Campbell, first transmitted BBC2, Mondays, 4 November to 9 December 1985 (repeated on BBC1, early 1986, and in 1992 on BBC2, Sunday 10 May 1992, 2205–2350, then Wednesdays, 13 May to 3 June 1992, 2125–2220 hours). (Also available on BBC Video, BBFC certificate 15.)

The Equalizer (1985–1989), Universal, 88 episodes of 60 mins each (inc. ads), created by Michael Sloan and Richard Lindheim, various writers, transmitted in USA from 11 September 1985 to 24 August 1989, in UK on ITV from 29 October 1986.

Grange Hill (1978–), BBC, 340 episodes [at end of 1995 series] of 25 mins each, created by Phil Redmond, various writers, transmitted from 8 February 1978, BBC1, annual seasons of around 20 episodes; 1995 season on Tuesdays and Fridays from 3 January 1995, 1710–1735 hours.

Inspector Morse (1987–1993), Zenith/Central, 28 episodes of 120 mins each (inc. ads), created by Colin Dexter, various writers, originally transmitted ITV, 6 January 1987 to 20 January 1993. (Also available on Video Collection International video, BBFC certificates PG/15.)

– episode: 'Promised Land', written by Julian Mitchell, first transmitted in UK on 27 March 1992, 2000–2200 hours.

Lipstick on Your Collar (1993), Whistling Gypsy for Channel Four, six episodes of 70 mins each (inc. ads), written by Dennis Potter, directed by Renny Rye, originally transmitted Channel Four, Sundays, 21 February to 28 March 1993, 2100–2210 hours (repeated Channel Four, Tuesdays, 16 August to 20 September 1994, 2200–2315 hours). (Also available on Polygram Video, BBFC certificate 15.)

Lois and Clark: The New Adventures of Superman [UK: *The New Adventures of Superman*] (1993–), December 3rd Productions/Warner Bros., first season – pilot episode of 75 mins, and 20 episodes of 45 mins, originally transmitted in USA from 12 September 1993, in UK from 8 January 1994, BBC1, Saturdays, various start times between 1800–1900 hours.

– episode: 'Man of Steel Bars', written by Paris Qualles, first transmitted in USA on 21 November 1993, in UK on 5 March 1994, 1800–1845 hours.

Longtime Companion (1990), American Playhouse, written by Craig Lucas, directed by Norman Rene, 96 mins.

Look North (1994), BBC North, report on 'video nasties', 5 mins, transmitted BBC1 North, 17 February 1994, 1830–1835 hours.

Medics (1990–), Granada, episodes of 60 mins each (inc. ads), first season of six episodes transmitted from 17 October 1990, annual seasons of six episodes from 31 March 1992, annual seasons of ten episodes from 12 July 1994, ITV, varying times, e.g. Tuesdays, 2100–2200 hours.

139

– episode: 'Going West', written by Sam Snape, transmitted 13 September 1994, 2100–2200 hours.

Natural Born Killers (1994), Warner Bros., written and directed by Oliver Stone [based on a script by Quentin Tarantino], 119 mins, scheduled for release in UK on 18 November 1994, but withheld by the BBFC; finally released on 24 February 1995.

Natural Lies (1992), BBC, three episodes of 55 mins each, written by David Pirie, directed by Ben Bolt, transmitted BBC1, Sundays, 31 May to 14 June 1992, 2110–2205 hours.

News at Ten (25 November 1993), ITN, report after James Bulger murder trial, 6 mins, transmitted ITV, 2200–2206 hours.

Newsnight (17 December 1993), BBC, report on TV/video violence effects, 25 mins, transmitted BBC2, 17 December 1993, 2230–2255 hours.

NYPD Blue (1993–), Steven Bochco/20th Century Fox, episodes of 60 mins each (inc. ads), created by Steven Bochco and David Milch, various writers, transmitted in USA from 1993, in UK from 15 January 1994, Channel Four, Saturdays, 2100–2200 hours.

– first episode, written by David Milch and Steven Bochco, transmitted in UK on 15 January 1994, 2100–2200 hours.

Philadelphia (1993), TriStar, written by Ron Nyswaner, directed by Jonathan Demme, 125 mins, released in UK on 25 February 1994.

Quantum Leap (1989–1993), Bellisarius/Universal, 95 episodes of 45 mins each, created by Donald P. Bellisario, various writers, originally transmitted in USA from 26 March 1989 to 5 May 1993, in UK from 4 November 1991 to 21 June 1994, BBC2, varying times, e.g. Tuesdays, 2100–2145 hours. (Several stories available on CIC Video, BBFC certificates PG/U.)

– episode: 'Nowhere To Run', written by Tommy Thompson, first transmitted in USA on 6 October 1992, in UK on 11 January 1994, 2100–2145 hours.

Regarding Henry (1991), Paramount, written by Jeffrey Abrams, directed by Mike Nichols, 107 mins.

Reservoir Dogs (1992), Live America/Dog Eat Dog, written & directed by Quentin Tarantino, 99 mins, released in UK on 8 January 1993.

Right to Reply Special: Violence (1993), Channel Four, 80 mins (90 mins inc. ads); transmitted Channel Four, 26 June 1993, 1830–2000 hours.

Right to Reply (9 April 1994), Channel Four, views on violence, cuts and censorship, 6 mins, transmitted Channel Four, 9 April 1994, 1837–1843 hours.

Roots: The Next Generation (1978), David L. Wolper/Warner Bros., seven episodes of 94 mins each, based on the book 'Roots' by Alex Haley, transmitted in UK on BBC1, Sundays, 30 September to 11 November 1979, 1915–2050 hours. (Also available on WHSmith Video, BBFC certificate PG.)

Sesame Street (1969–), Children's Television Workshop, programmes of 60 mins each (inc. ads), transmitted in USA from 10 November 1969, in UK on ITV and Channel Four, various times.

'Short Change' (1994), Children's BBC, report on BBFC classifications, 8 mins, transmitted BBC1, 20 February 1994, 1119–1127 hours.

Speed (1994), 20th Century Fox, written by Graham Yost, directed by Jan de Bont, 116 mins, released in UK on 30 September 1994.

Star Trek: The Next Generation (1987–1994), Paramount, developed by Gene Roddenberry, Rick Berman, Michael Piller and Jeri Taylor, 178 episodes of (generally) 44 mins each, originally transmitted in USA from 28 September 1987 to 28 May 1994, in UK from 26 September 1990, BBC2, Wednesdays, 1800–1845 hours. (Also available on Sky One [satellite channel], and on CIC Video, BBFC certificates PG/U.)

– episode: 'Family', written by Ronald D. Moore, first transmitted in USA on 1 October 1990, in UK on 13 April 1994.

– episode: 'The Loss', written by Hilary J. Bader, Alan J. Adler and Vanessa Greene, first transmitted in USA on 21 December 1990, in UK on 8 June 1994.

– episode: 'The Outcast', written by Jeri Taylor, first transmitted in USA on 16 March 1992.

– episode: 'Force of Nature', written by Naren Shankar, first transmitted in USA on 20 November 1993.

Stark (1993), BBC, three episodes of 55 mins each, written by Ben Elton, directed by Nadia Tass, first transmitted BBC2, Wednesdays, 8 to 22 December 1993, 2125–2220 hours. (Also available on BBC Video, BBFC certificate 15.)

The Sweeney (1975–1978), Thames/Euston, 53 episodes of 50 mins each, created by Ian Kennedy Martin, various writers, originally transmitted ITV, 2 January 1975 to 28 December 1978.

Terminator 2: Judgment Day (1991), Carolco/Pacific Western, written & directed by James Cameron, 136 mins, released in UK on 16 August 1991, transmitted on BBC1, 3 September 1994, 2120–2325 hours (slightly edited), and on Sky Movies [satellite subscription channel], various dates, e.g. 25 December 1993, 2200-0010 hours. (Also available on Guild Home Video (1992), BBFC certificate 15.)

True Lies (1994), Lightstorm/20th Century Fox, written & directed by James Cameron, 140 mins, released in UK on 11 August 1994.

The X-Files (1993–), Ten Thirteen/20th Century Fox, created by Chris Carter, various writers, first season – 24 episodes of 46 mins each, transmitted in USA from 10 September 1993, in UK from 19 September 1994, BBC2, Mondays, 2130–2215 hours, then Thursdays, 2100–2145 hours.

Index

Media titles available from John Libbey

Acamedia Research Monographs

Taxation and Representation: Media, Political Communication and the Poll Tax
David Deacon and Peter Golding
Hardback ISBN 0 86196 390 3

Satellite Television in Western Europe (revised edition 1992)
Richard Collins
Hardback ISBN 0 86196 203 6

Beyond the Berne Convention
Copyright, Broadcasting and the Single European Market
Vincent Porter
Hardback ISBN 0 86196 267 2

Nuclear Reactions: A Study in Public Issue Television
John Corner, Kay Richardson and Natalie Fenton
Hardback ISBN 0 86196 251 6

Transnationalization of Television in Western Europe
Preben Sepstrup
Hardback ISBN 0 86196 280 X

The People's Voice: Local Radio and Television in Europe
Nick Jankowski, Ole Prehn and James Stappers
Hardback ISBN 0 86196 322 9

Television and the Gulf War
David E. Morrison
Hardback ISBN 0 86196 341 5

Contra-Flow in Global News
Oliver Boyd Barrett and Daya Kishan Thussu
Hardback ISBN 0 86196 344 X

CNN World Report: Ted Turner's International News Coup
Don M. Flournoy
Hardback ISBN 0 86196 359 8

Small Nations: Big Neighbour
Roger de la Garde, William Gilsdorf and Ilja Wechselmann
Hardback ISBN 0 86196 343 1

European Media Research Series

The New Television in Europe
Edited by Alessandro Silj
Hardback ISBN 0 86196 361 X

Media Industry in Europe
Edited by Antonio Pilati
Paperback ISBN 0 86196 398 9

European Institute for the Media

Television and the Viewer Interest: Explorations in the responsiveness of European Broadcasters
Jeremy Mitchell and Jay G Blumler (eds)
Paperback ISBN 0 86196 440 3

Media titles available from John Libbey

Broadcasting and Audio-visual Policy in the European Single Market
Richard Collins
Hardback ISBN 0 86196 405 5

Aid for Cinematographic and Audio-visual Production In Europe
(published for the Council of Europe)
Jean-Noël Dibie
Hardback ISBN 0 86196 397 0

BBC World Service

Global Audiences: Research for Worldwide Broadcasting 1993
Edited by Graham Mytton
Paperback ISBN 0 86196 400 4

Broadcasting Standards Council Publications

A Measure of Uncertainty: The Effects of the Mass Media
Guy Cumberbatch and Dennis Howitt
Hardback ISBN 0 86196 231 1

Violence in Television Fiction: Public Opinion and Broadcasting Standards
David Docherty
Paperback ISBN 0 86196 284 2

Survivors and the Media
Ann Shearer
Paperback ISBN 0 86196 332 6

Taste and Decency in Broadcasting
Andrea Millwood Hargrave
Paperback ISBN 0 86196 331 8

A Matter of Manners? – The Limits of Broadcast Language
Edited by Andrea Millwood Hargrave
Paperback ISBN 0 86196 337 7

Sex and Sexuality in Broadcasting
Andrea Millwood Hargrave
Paperback ISBN 0 86196 393 8

Violence in Factual Television
Andrea Millwood Hargrave
Paperback ISBN 0 86196 441 1

Radio and Audience Attitudes
Andrea Millwood Hargrave
PAperback ISBN 0 86196 481 0

International Institute of Communications

Vision and Hindsight: The First 25 Years of the Internatuional Institute of Communications
Rex Winsbury and Shehina Fazal (eds)
Hardback ISBN 0 86196 449 7
Paperback ISBN 0 86196 467 5

Acamedia Textbook

Political Mar'.eting and Communication
Philippe J. Maarek
Paperback ISBN 0 86196 377 6

Media titles available from John Libbey

UNESCO Publications

A Richer Vision: The development of ethnic minority media in Western democracies
Charles Husband (ed)
Paperback ISBN 0 86196 450 0

Video World-Wide: An International Study
Manuel Alvarado (ed)
Paperback ISBN 0 86196 143 9

University of Manchester Broadcasting Symposium

And Now for the BBC ...
Nod Miller and Rod Allen (eds)
Paperback ISBN 0 86196 318 0

It's Live – But Is It Real?
Nod Miller and Rod Allen (eds)
Paperback ISBN 0 86196 370 9

Broadcasting Enters the Marketplace
Nod Miller and Rod Allen (eds)
Paperback ISBN 0 86196 434 9

ITC Television Research Monographs

Television in Schools
Robin Moss, Christopher Jones and Barrie Gunter
Hardback ISBN 0 86196 314 8

Television: The Public's View
Barrie Gunter and Carmel McLaughlin
Hardback ISBN 0 86196 348 2

The Reactive Viewer
Barrie Gunter and Mallory Wober
Hardback ISBN 0 86196 358 X

Television: The Public's View 1992
Barrie Gunter and Paul Winstone
Hardback ISBN 0 86196 399 7

Seeing is Believing: Religion and Television in the 1990s
Barrie Gunter and Rachel Viney
Hardback ISBN 0 86196 442 X

Published in association with The Arts Council

Picture This: Media Representations of Visual Art and Artists
Philip Hayward (ed)
Paperback ISBN 0 86196 126 9

Culture, Technology and Creativity
Philip Hayward (ed)
Paperback ISBN 0 86196 266 4

Parallel Lines: Media Representations of Dance
Stephanie Jordan & Dave Allen (eds)
Paperback ISBN 0 86196 371 7

Arts TV: A History of British Arts Television
John A Walker
Paperback ISBN 0 86196 435 7

Media titles available from John Libbey

A Night in at the Opera: Media Representation of Opera
Jeremy Tambling (ed)
ISBN 0 86196 466 7

IBA Television Research Monographs

Teachers and Television:
A History of the IBA's Educational Fellowship Scheme
Josephine Langham
Hardback ISBN 0 86196 264 8

Godwatching: Viewers, Religion and Television
Michael Svennevig, Ian Haldane, Sharon Spiers and Barrie Gunter
Hardback ISBN 0 86196 198 6
Paperback ISBN 0 86196 199 4

Violence on Television: What the Viewers Think
Barrie Gunter and Mallory Wober
Hardback ISBN 0 86196 171 4
Paperback ISBN 0 86196 172 2

Home Video and the Changing Nature of Television Audience
Mark Levy and Barrie Gunter
Hardback ISBN 0 86196 175 7
Paperback ISBN 0 86196 188 9

Patterns of Teletext Use in the UK
Bradley S. Greenberg and Carolyn A. Lin
Hardback ISBN 0 86196 174 9
Paperback ISBN 0 86196 187 0

Attitudes to Broadcasting Over the Years
Barrie Gunter and Michael Svennevig
Hardback ISBN 0 86196 173 0
Paperback ISBN 0 86196 184 6

Television and Sex Role Stereotyping
Barrie Gunter
Hardback ISBN 0 86196 095 5
Paperback ISBN 0 86196 098 X

Television and the Fear of Crime
Barrie Gunter
Hardback ISBN 0 86196 118 8
Paperback ISBN 0 86196 119 6

Behind and in Front of the Screen – Television's Involvement with Family Life
Barrie Gunter and Michael Svennevig
Hardback ISBN 0 86196 123 4
Paperback ISBN 0 86196 124 2

Institute of Local Television

Citizen Television: A Local Dimension to Public Service Broadcasting
Dave Rushton (ed)
Hardback ISBN 0 86196 433 0

Reporters Sans Frontières

1995 Report
Freedom of the Press Throughout the World
Paperback ISBN 0 86196 523 X